The Suburban Squeeze

*California Series
in Urban Development*

EDITED BY PETER HALL AND PETER MARRIS

*California Series in Real Estate
Economics and Finance*

EDITED BY KENNETH T. ROSEN

The Suburban Squeeze

Land Conversion and Regulation in the San Francisco Bay Area

David E. Dowall

UNIVERSITY OF CALIFORNIA PRESS
Berkeley · Los Angeles · London

University of California Press
Berkeley and Los Angeles, California

University of California Press, Ltd.
London, England

©1984 by David E. Dowall
The Regents of the University of California

Printed in the United States of America

1 2 3 4 5 6 7 8 9

Library of Congress Cataloging in Publication Data

Dowall, David E.
    The suburban squeeze.

    (California series in urban development)
    Includes bibliographical references and index.
    1. Land use—California—San Francisco Bay Area.
2. Urbanization—California—San Francisco Bay Area.
3. Suburbs—California—San Francisco Bay Area.   4. Land
use—Law and legislation—California—San Francisco Bay
Area.   5. Building permits—California—San Francisco
Bay Area.   6. Housing policy—California—San Francisco
Bay Area.   7. Zoning—California—San Francisco Bay Area.
I. Title.   II. Series.
HD266.C22S23   1984   333.77'15'097946   83-17945

ISBN 0-520-04968-3

To Diane

Contents

Tables, Figures, and Maps

FIGURES

MAPS

Acknowledgments

This book originated out of a research project commissioned in 1979 by the California Air Resources Board to assess the potential for employing land use controls to improve air quality. That project provided me with the opportunity to closely examine various sets of local land use regulations and to gauge their effectiveness. Since then I have also received funds from other sources that indirectly supported research used to prepare this book: the U.S. Department of Housing and Urban Development, the Solar Energy Research Institute, the Construction Industry Advancement Fund, the Institute of Urban and Regional Development, and the Center for Real Estate and Urban Economics.

Many people helped me to carry out my research, including Noreen Ambrose, John Landis, Jesse Mingliton, and Pamela Westing. Landis deserves special mention: he conducted much of the field work and assisted in preparation of earlier drafts of the case studies. Melvin M. Webber, Director of the Institute of Urban and Regional Development, provided seed money to help me get started on the research for the book and also provided ample typing support over the years as the manuscript took form. Kenneth Rosen, Director of the Center for Real Estate and Urban Economics, provided both financial and intellectual support. Several people read the entire manuscript and provided useful substantive and editorial advice: Marion Clawson, Peter Hall, John Quigley, and Melvin Webber. Brigitte Stelling did a wonderful job preparing the manuscript for submission to UC Press.

Finally, I want to thank my wife Diane for putting up with me while I finished the manuscript, especially when we were in Negril, Jamaica.

CHAPTER ONE

The Local Land Use Planning Dilemma

Land use planners across America are facing hard choices. Should they exert strict control over development, as environmentalists and neighborhood groups demand? Or should they aim for more housing at affordable prices, as employers, housing advocates, and tenants urge? Since the early 1970s, the arguments of well-organized environmentalist and homeowner associations have prevailed in many of the nation's communities. Buttressed by federal and state regulations such as the Environmental Protection Act of 1970, local planners have controlled the use of land far more rigorously than ever before.

The virtues of this policy have been evident. The quality of the environment *has* improved, and people appreciate it. But now the costs of this policy are also becoming clear: wherever stringent land-use controls have come up against burgeoning demand for housing, land and home prices have skyrocketed.

Ever since 1975, when the first twinges of a housing and land "squeeze" were felt, pro-housing groups have argued that most land use controls are too restrictive, and that such controls are stifling suburban growth. They have predicted dire social and economic consequences if nothing is done to dismantle the apparatus of growth management. A number of prestigious and influential studies have also warned of the seriousness of the "suburban squeeze."

Indeed, much evidence linking restrictive land use regulations to higher housing prices has surfaced over the past ten years. Two major federal studies, one by the U.S. General Accounting Office and another by the U.S. Department of Housing and Urban Development, concluded that local

1

land use regulations, building and subdivision codes, and permit-granting processes are frequently excessive and inefficient.[1] Both recommended that development controls be reformed, with the HUD report calling for especially strong medicine—federal limits on local land use controls.

While these studies attracted a good deal of attention from the media, they were hardly novel. In fact, numerous studies since the 1950s have illustrated the inflationary effects of local development controls. The performance of the housing industry in the San Francisco Bay Area was analyzed by Colean and Grebler in 1950, and by Maisel in 1963. They concluded that *housing* production could be more efficient if regulations were relaxed.[2] The 1960s spawned the Douglas and Kaiser Commissions. Both examined the inflationary effects of local land use controls on housing costs and availability, and the Douglas Commission proposed a variety of reforms to local land use and zoning controls.[3] More recently, several "public interest" research groups, most notably the Suburban Action Institute and the Potomac Institute, have assessed the exclusionary effects of local development policies and lobbied for sanctions against communities with restrictive development policies.[4]

Will the latest studies be met by as much indifference as the former ones? I think not, because it is no longer only the poor who are hurt by overly restrictive and exclusionary land use controls, but the majority of first-time home buyers. There is a growing constituency for relaxed land use controls and more affordable housing.

In this book I propose, first, to add my own voice to that chorus. I believe that the highly restrictive controls on growth *do* harm communities, businesses, and individual citizens. Second, I wish to demonstrate the reasons for this conviction, using new data from a region where the inflationary effects of land use regulations have been especially severe: the San Francisco Bay Area. Third, I want to give practical help to local land use planners and communities struggling to preserve environmental quality while also providing reasonably priced homes. Until now, it has been impossible to know just what "too restrictive" means. We have not known how specific land use controls translate into land and housing prices. By pairing communities that have similar geographic and demographic profiles but contrasting land use policies, I have carried out—as far as is possible in the real world—a controlled experiment in urban planning. Finally, I want to speak out for new land use policies at the regional and national level, for the problem is one all of America must reckon with. Legislation and judicial decisions at the state and federal level directly influence the choices open to local planners. And, although housing prices vary markedly from town to town, from region to region, the areas that endure the greatest inflationary increases have a disproportionate effect—both psychologically and statistically—on the nation's economy. Land use planners and housing developers are apt to look nostalgically upon the halcyon days of simple zoning ordinances. From 1926, when the Supreme Court upheld the use of municipal zoning as police power, to 1970, when the National Environmental Protection Act was passed, communities relied chiefly on zoning, in conjunction with a general plan, to guide development. By indicating the type and density of land use—one unit per 10,000 square feet, or thirty units per acre, for example—zoning ordinances succinctly told developers what projects would be acceptable. Developers could easily get permission for projects conforming to the zoning regulations. The process for challenging a particular zoning designation was time-consuming, but reasonably straightforward. Once they learned how to gauge their chances of winning zoning approvals, developers did not mind going through the procedures.

For all its simplicity and straightforwardness, though, zoning had real flaws. It was too insensitive and crude a method of regulating development. It reinforced patterns of economic and racial segregation. It set aside land for uses no one honestly expected to occur. It did not control the timing of development and it prevented multiple uses of land, even if those uses were compatible. Above all, zoning was indifferent to environmental issues, with unhappy results that were all too plain.

Reacting to citizen pressure in the late 1960s, planners began seeking new ways to regulate development and suburban growth. The most important of these was the requirement, imposed by the National Environmental Protection Act, that environmental impact statements be prepared for "major federal actions significantly affecting the quality of the human environment."[5] The California Supreme Court (in Friends of Mammoth vs. Mono County, 1972) expanded the requirement to include all large development projects, private as well as public. To the EIRs demanded by the federal government, the states and local communities added their own layers of rules and regulations.

The eagerness with which communities adopted their own controls on growth was impressive. In 1972, a nationwide survey conducted by the American Society of Planning Officials identified about a dozen communities using growth controls.[6] Two years later, another study found that over two hundred municipalities and counties, from California to Pennsylvania and Florida, were controlling population growth.[7] During the 1970s, growth control efforts became commonplace, especially in California. According to a recent survey of land use planning activity, over 50 percent of communities in the San Francisco Bay Area are actively limiting population growth.[8] Current controversies over neighborhood preservation, farmland preservation, and industrial park development suggest that these trends will continue. Moreover, as citizens resist the imposition of new taxes to pay for the services and infrastructure new development requires, the fiscal arguments for limiting growth become as persuasive as the environmental ones. Many communities now require assessment and mitigation of a proposed project's fiscal impact before granting permission to build.

The whole process of land development has been altered radically by the proliferation of environmental regulations. And while all types of projects have been affected, residential development has been hardest hit. Residential construction is not only the most prevalent form of community development, but also tends to be the most closely regulated. For example, growth rationing systems, such as those used in Petaluma and Davis, California, and Boulder, Colorado, generally limit only residential building permits, not those for commercial or industrial projects.

The increasing reliance on permits and assessment programs to regulate development has also taken a toll on housing construction. The so-called "permit explosion" prolongs the time needed for obtaining development approval and increases both the uncertainty of project approval and the cost of compliance. And, like zoning, permit processes restrict the supply of residential lots granted development permission. Like those in Petaluma, Davis, and Boulder, growth control programs limit the number of lots that can be developed per year.

It would be irresponsible and inaccurate to say that these changes in local land use control are entirely pernicious. On the contrary, land use controls sensitive to the environment are an advance over the blunt instrument of zoning, and on the whole they have fulfilled their original intent. But it is the very success of these new methods that makes it so difficult to respond to concerns with overregulation and to inflationary land and housing prices.

Ironically, it was just as restrictive land use and environmental regulations became more common that demographic forces came more into play. The housing market was overwhelmed as those born during the postwar baby boom began growing up and seeking homes of their own. The consequence, as became evident by early 1975, was an alarming surge in the cost of shelter. Rapid price increases were first seen in the metropolitan areas of California, but the phenomenon soon spread to other parts of the country.[9]

Between 1975 and 1977, U.S. home prices rose at an annual rate ranging from 10.3 to 12.8 percent for new houses, 10.8 and 11.5 percent for existing units (table 1). These increases were far swifter than those experienced in the late 1960s and early 1970s. For example, the rate of annual increase between 1968 and 1970 was only 5.6 to 7.5 percent for new units, and 7.4 to 8.3 percent for existing units. Since 1975, the rise in new and existing home prices has outpaced both the general inflation rate and gains in disposable income (table 2).

However, the rate of housing inflation has varied considerably across the country (table 3). And since 1972, it has consistently been highest in the West, the statistics for which are dominated by California. The differences among regions can also be seen in the average housing prices for various metropolitan areas (table 4). With the recent surge in housing prices, many households—particularly first-time buyers—have been

TABLE 1

ANNUAL RATES OF HOUSE PRICE INCREASES,
UNITED STATES, 1968–77
(COMPOUND RATES)

| | New Houses | | | | | Existing Houses | |
| | *Commerce Department* | | | | | | |
Periods	Current Houses	1967 House	*FHLBB*[a]	*FHA*[b]	*NAR*[c]	*FHLBB*	*FHA*
1968–70	0.0%[d]	5.6%	7.5%	8.5%	7.4%	8.3%	6.0%
1970–72	7.1	5.6	2.5	3.3	8.2	5.5	3.7
1972–74	12.9	9.9	3.7[e]	5.8	9.1	1.9[e]	5.1
1974–76	11.1	10.0	9.9	13.0	8.6	9.1	11.5
1975–77	12.8	11.2	10.3	6.4	10.8	11.5	5.0
1968–77	8.2	8.3	6.5	7.2	8.9	7.1	6.6
1970–77	10.7	9.0	6.3	6.8	9.3	6.8	6.8

SOURCE: Leo Grebler and Frank H. Mittelbach, *The Inflation of Housing Prices* (Lexington, Mass.: Lexington Books, 1979).

[a]Federal Home Loan Bank Board.

[b]Federal Housing Authority.

[c]National Association of Realtors.

[d]The rate was zero, with prices averaging $26,600 both in 1968 and in 1970. The 1969 figure was $27,900. The statistical fluke of identical prices in 1968 and 1970 is discussed in the text.

[e]Influenced by revision of the series in 1973.

TABLE 2

HOUSE PRICE INCREASES COMPARED WITH OTHER PRICE
AND INCOME INCREASES, UNITED STATES, 1968–77
(COMPOUND ANNUAL RATES)

Item	1968 –77	1968 –70	1970 –72	1972 –74	1974 –76	1975 –77
New houses (1967 kind)	8.3%	5.6%	5.6%	9.9%	10.0%	11.1%
Existing houses (NAR)	8.9	7.4	8.2	9.1	8.6	10.8
Weighted average for above two items[a]	8.7	6.9	7.6	9.3	8.9	10.9
CPI[b]	6.4	5.6	3.8	8.6	7.4	6.1
GNP deflator[c]	6.2	5.2	4.6	7.9	7.2	5.4
Housing component of CPI[d]	6.9	6.8	4.2	8.0	8.5	
Rent	4.6	3.7	4.1	4.7	5.3	5.7
Homeowner expenses	7.6	10.3	4.4	7.9	8.4	6.2
Disposable personal income	9.2	8.1	8.5	10.7	9.4	9.9
Disposable personal income, per capita	8.3	6.9	7.1	10.0	8.9	9.0

SOURCE: Grebler and Mittelbach.

[a] Rates of price increases for new and existing houses were averaged for each type derived from the directly reported dollar volume of existing home sales and the computed dollar volume of new home sales (number of homes multiplied by the average sales price). The weights for existing houses are 78 for 1968–77, 75 for 1968–70, 76 for 1970–72, 78 for 1972–74, 81 for 1974–76, and 80 for 1975–77. The weights for new homes are the reciprocals of these numbers.

[b] All items, including the housing component, shown separately under "Housing component of CPI." The weight of the housing component in the total CPI has increased in recent years. Computed from "old" CPI.

[c] The GNP deflator is a broader measure of price changes than the CPI. It reflects price movements for investment goods, export and import goods and services, and government purchases of goods and services, as well as those for consumption.

[d] Total housing component including rent, homeownership expenses, fuel and utilities, and household furnishings and operation.

excluded from the housing market. This problem has not gone unnoticed by employers. In areas with relatively high home prices, recruitment of employees has become increasingly difficult. Concern is running particularly high in the San Francisco Bay Area, which has the highest median housing prices in the nation. In response, business leaders there have created a multidisciplinary task force to study housing costs and their implications for employee recruitment, labor costs, and continued expansion of the regional economy. In Santa Clara County, the home of Silicon Valley, the booming electronics industry is having trouble attracting employees. The Santa Clara County Manufacturing Group has been studying the land use and housing policies of the fifteen cities in the county, as well as surveying

TABLE 3

ANNUAL RATES OF HOUSE PRICE INCREASES, 1968–76
(COMPOUND RATES)

Four Major Census Regions

Period	Northeast	North Central	South	West	United States
New homes[a]					
1968–70	7.1%	4.8%	5.9%	5.4%	5.6%
1970–72	7.6	4.4	6.0	4.5	5.6
1972–74	8.0	9.0	8.5	12.0	9.9
1974–76	7.5	10.1	7.9	13.5	10.0
1975–77	5.7	10.1	8.8	16.3	11.2
1968–77	7.4	7.5	7.3	10.0	8.3
1970–77	7.4	8.3	7.6	11.3	9.0
Existing homes					
1968–70	8.3%	6.6%	7.2%	4.3%	7.4%
1970–72	8.8	6.6	9.1	8.6	8.2
1972–74	8.7	9.1	9.7	9.9	9.1
1974–76	7.5	8.3	6.3	13.6	8.6
1975–77	6.1	10.2	7.7	19.7	10.8
1968–77	8.1	8.1	8.3	10.8	8.9
1970–77	8.1	8.6	8.6	12.7	9.3

SOURCE: Grebler and Mittelbach.
[a]Constant quality house, 1967.

its members to determine their plans for expansion. The group's aim is to reshape local land use and development policies so that industry can be assured of an adequate supply of land and housing to meet future expansion needs. While Santa Clara County is an example of economic hyper-development, untypical even of regions with high housing prices, its experience does suggest the private sector might come to play a greater role in land use and environmental planning.

What are the long-term consequences of very expensive housing? One, mentioned above, is difficulty in attracting employees. If California's housing prices remain well above national levels, firms will either have to pay a premium for new talent or rely upon the local labor pool. In the first instance, labor costs will increase immediately; in the second, it will become commonplace for firms to pirate workers from other firms. But in either case, the long-term impact of high housing costs is the same: higher costs of doing business. Ultimately, those firms able to relocate to lower-cost areas will do so. Those that cannot will have to absorb higher operat-

TABLE 4

AVERAGE PURCHASE PRICES FOR CONVENTIONALLY
FINANCED NEW AND EXISTING UNITS, 1977, AND
PERCENTAGE CHANGE, 1976–77

Metropolitan Area	New	% Difference 1976–77	Existing	% Difference 1976–77
West				
Denver	$61,100	22.0	$53,000	14.0
Los Angeles	72,500	10.0	70,800	18.0
San Francisco	75,200	16.2	71,000	18.1
Seattle	52,100	4.4	46,400	14.6
South				
Atlanta	56,300	4.1	52,200	4.2
Dallas	56,700	5.8	48,800	−1.8
Houston	57,400	7.3	55,800	6.3
Miami	43,300	−15.6	50,800	3.2
North Central				
Chicago	61,400	19.9	57,200	14.2
Cleveland	61,100	14.6	46,100	6.2
Detroit	53,300	7.9	42,600	6.2
Minneapolis	56,000	—	52,900	6.2
East				
Baltimore	56,500	0.0	50,500	14.0
Boston	—	—	50,300	3.7
New York	69,700	26.5	61,000	10.3
Philadelphia	51,500	3.4	44,100	7.0
Washington, D.C.	66,700	13.0	68,900	11.5

SOURCE: Grebler and Mittelbach.

ing costs and lower profits, or else try to offset these costs by increasing productivity.

Then there are those enterprises, such as local governments or educational institutions, that can neither relocate nor merely pass on higher labor costs. These may find themselves suffering a "brain drain" as bright young talent is wooed to areas where the cost of living is lower, or to professions in which the salaries are higher.

If housing costs continue to spiral upward, and rental rates follow suit, the impact on wage scales will ultimately push up the costs of all manner of goods and services. An entire economy can be sapped by the lack of a single basic necessity—housing—while only those who own a piece of the scarce resource benefit. In this context, the high price of housing, whether rental or owner-occupied, is actually a pure economic rent—a return to owners of a scarce, fixed supply of land and housing.

The vision of an enormous economic rent being levied on regions with a scarce supply of housing and residential land is a frightening, but not unimaginable prospect. In some areas of California, lot costs today represent 40 percent of a home's total purchase price. Far higher than what people would pay in more competitive and well-supplied markets, these excessive payments for land and housing impose enormous costs on society. Resources are funneled into exorbitant rents and mortgage payments, and away from other areas of the economy, such as retailing, recreation and entertainment, and savings and investment. Under these conditions, raising capital for reindustrialization becomes a particularly difficult task. Some critics have suggested that Americans are "overconsuming" housing, but it would seem that in many housing markets across the country, there is all too little choice.

For many families, astronomical housing costs are shattering what can best be described as the American dream. When young households find housing prices increasing faster than their incomes, the hope of earning enough to buy a home evaporates, and with it a large element in their motivation to work and succeed.

A final grave, if long-run, outcome of our present housing trend is that it pits the "haves" against the "have-nots." Those who own their homes stand to gain from limits on new housing and are more likely to support land use and environmental actions that protect the environment at the expense of housing production. Those who would benefit from increased housing production most often have little power or standing in the community, either because they do not live there (they can't afford to) or because they are perceived as transient, second-class citizens likely to be "here today, gone tomorrow." But it is important to note that the division between "haves" and "have-nots" is not a purely economic one. The latter group cuts across a broad range of income brackets to include young professionals who haven't accumulated enough capital for the big down payments that are typically required today. While their older brothers and sisters were able to get into the housing market, they've missed the boat. Ironically, it is not unusual to attend public hearings where middle-class households oppose a proposed housing development as "tacky," even though they themselves could not afford to buy the homes.

In light of the current high costs of mortgage capital, generally high interest rates, and a weak economy, many might think that this period of housing price inflation is over. Far from it. While it is true that housing prices have "softened," this is only temporary. For once interest rates drop, housing prices will again be propelled upward by the enormous pent-up demand for housing—and that demand is growing every day. Clearly, we are now in a holding pattern. But without some relief in the form of an increased housing supply, the floodgates of unfulfilled demand will open as soon as more money is available.

Despite the threat of the suburban squeeze and growing pressures for reform, the prospects for sweeping change are slim. As a practical matter, land use regulations can only be altered at the local level, and it is doubtful that either the federal government or the states will impose and enforce standards for land use controls. There will be no quiet land use revolution in the 1980s. Instead, loud skirmishes will be in community after community, all across the country. And while corporations may enter the fray, they will face homeowners, ratepayers, and environmentalists fiercely defending their turf.

Until the direct costs of land use and environmental controls are recognized and explicitly weighed against the benefits of land use and environmental planning, pressures for regulatory reform will escalate. The danger is that legitimate environmental and land use management programs could eventually be overturned in the process. How planners respond to the land use housing controversy will determine whether they are able to head off a major backlash against environmental controls.

The choices are essentially two. The first, rigid opposition to reform, probably won't work because of the intensifying pressures in favor of reform, especially in California. The second and more promising course of action is to seek ways of integrating housing and economic development objectives with environmental and neighborhood-quality objectives, and identifying acceptable compromises when conflicts exist. But unfortunately there is little documented experience that planners, local officials, developers, and citizens can use to develop new, more balanced approaches to local planning. Most existing studies merely attempt to document the general effects of land use and environmental controls on housing prices, or chronicle the inefficiency of environmental regulations.

The aim of this study is to provide some new insights into the process of local land use and environmental control, explaining how suburban communities are affected by rapid urban development, why they have aggressively adopted restrictive land use controls, and how these local actions affect regional land and housing markets. It is hoped that this research will aid planners, public officials, developers, and citizens concerned with land use regulation.

It should be pointed out that this study is not a balanced assessment of the benefits and costs of land use and environmental regulation. I have not attempted to measure the benefits of local land use controls, but have concentrated on a comprehensive evaluation of costs.

In recent years much attention has centered on the effects of local land use regulations. While the effects of such regulations are both beneficial and costly, most literature has examined the costs of environmental regulations. For a review of this cost-oriented literature, see Dowall, Frieden, and Hack.[10]

Environmentalists, planners, and local government officials are quick to point out that this literature fails to consider the corresponding benefits of local land use and environmental controls. For example, restrictions on hillside development, stringent grading and subdivision controls, and broad prohibitions on the development of environmentally sensitive lands have greatly reduced soil erosion and flooding problems.[11] Open-space and farmland protection has saved much land from inappropriate urban development in rapidly growing metropolitan areas. The protection of these lands has provided valuable recreation opportunities and preserved important metropolitan watersheds and farms.[12]

Growth management programs that limit the rate of population or housing growth have helped communities cope with extreme development pressures.[13] By slowing growth, communities can minimize traffic congestion and avoid overburdening public services such as schools. Growth management also helps to keep down local taxes.[14]

Subdivision and building controls protect the housing consumer from shoddy construction and unsafe development practices. For example, road widths and turning radius standards are set to ensure quick fire truck access to subdivisions.[15] Restrictions on building on land with excessively steep slopes also protects the consumer. As the numerous mudslides in California perennially attest, gravity and nature work together to pull poorly sited houses off their foundations.

Zoning and subdivisions play an important role in protecting the housing consumer from unwittingly purchasing or renting homes in unsafe environments. The same benefits apply to commercial and industrial users as well.

Another important benefit of land use regulation is that it helps to ensure the proper balance of land use activities. Too intense levels of development can generate traffic that overwhelms transportation systems. Houston, the nation's largest city without zoning, is nearly paralyzed during commuting hours. Houston's scale of office development is clearly out of step with its transportation system.[16]

Zoning also protects residential neighborhoods from encroachment by inappropriate commercial and industrial uses. Steel mills, auto body shops, and movie theaters would threaten residential tranquility if located in residential areas. Zoning, by blocking these activities, works to protect neighborhoods.[17]

Environmental impact assessment requirements, permits, and review procedures also help to protect people from environmental degradation. The EIR process safeguards the community from development that would generate an adverse environmental impact. The process requires the systematic identification of the likely consequences and the determination of how it can be mitigated. The EIR process is widely used and has been crucial in stopping projects likely to significantly deteriorate the environment.[18]

A final, well-researched area of how environmental regulations benefit society is air pollution control. Through the U.S. Environmental Protection Agency, state and regional air quality control boards regulate polluters, both stationary sources such as factories, and mobile ones such as cars. Air pollution control efforts have paid off and the nation's air has gotten cleaner in many areas. Improvements to air quality yield dramatic benefits: higher crop yields, reduced morbidity, and lower cleaning bills and property damage.[19]

A review of the literature on the beneficial effects of land use and environmental regulations reveals that benefits are many, and frequently significant. The quality of urban development has been uplifted in many communities, and environments have been protected or in some cases even improved.[20] While in this book I emphasize the cost effects of environmental regulation, I do not call for the unilateral abolition or rollback of land development controls. Instead, I urge planners to consider how controls can be made more effective—that is, to better aim the controls toward precise environmental concerns and reduce the costly side effects so often created by blunt regulations.

It should also be emphasized that this is a study of local land use control in the San Francisco Bay Area, and I do not claim that the Bay Area is representative of other metropolitan regions. However, I do believe the trends and conditions described have widespread implications for the nation as a whole, for reasons other than representation. First, in no other area of the country has there been such widespread and longstanding use of sophisticated land use and growth management controls. The Bay Area could be called the cradle of growth control; there is also justification for labeling it the nation's worst case of suburban squeeze. These factors make the Bay Area an excellent laboratory for study of restrictive land use controls and their broader impact. Second, the Association of Bay Area Governments (ABAG), the regional council of governments in the nine-county area, has collected the most detailed land use data of any metropolitan area nationwide, and the availability of such data was essential to the research presented here. Finally, California, and the Bay Area in particular, has traditionally been a trend setter. In fact, the genesis of the growth management movement was in Petaluma, north of San Francisco. The Bay Area experience could well be a portent of what is in store for other metropolitan areas beginning to feel their own signs of the suburban squeeze.

CHAPTER TWO

San Francisco's Suburban Slowdown

While the tension between housing demand and land use control is being felt in areas all across the United States, the problems posed by local land use controls and state environmental regulations are most acute in California. In all the state's major metropolitan areas—San Francisco, Los Angeles, Orange County, and San Diego—local land use regulation is extremely well developed and sophisticated. Nowhere else in the nation do communities so aggressively restrict development.

But it seems the California experience may be a harbinger of things to come in other metropolitan areas, such as Denver, Tucson, Seattle, Portland, and Washington, D.C. As suburban communities in these expanding metropolitan areas develop heightening concerns about environmental quality, a pattern of increasingly complex and restrictive land use controls can be expected.

This study focuses on the effects of land use and environmental regulations of San Francisco Bay Area communities, providing insights to the dynamics of land use regulation in a highly regulated market. The San Francisco Bay Area is an ideal laboratory for assessing the effects of land use controls on land and housing markets. Given the high level of restrictions on the region's land markets, together with the pressures of continuing population growth, the inflationary effects of land use controls come into sharp relief. Thus, the results of this study should provide planners with a better understanding of the potential effects of land use controls in areas with a high level of housing demand.

THE BAY AREA'S SUBURBAN LAND SQUEEZE

Since World War II, the nine-county San Francisco Bay Area has experienced all the elements that add up to a suburban land squeeze: extensive land development, increasing use of growth management controls, more restrictive land use and environmental regulations, and a "go-slow" development posture exacerbated by the passage of Propositions 4 and 13. Although the region contains an enormous supply of vacant land, much of it cannot be developed. In 1975, a detailed land inventory conducted by the Association of Bay Area Governments found that only 350,000 of the region's 4.5 million acres were vacant and "developable."[1] (Map 1 delineates the Bay Area and shows the location of principal cities.)

It is true that much of the Bay Area's vacant land cannot be developed due to its rugged topography or sensitive environmental character. But in the final analysis, the Bay Area's suburban land squeeze results less from natural constraints than from the restrictive land use and development regulations imposed by the region's more than one hundred local governments. Severe limits have been placed on where, when, and how the region can develop. For example, over 15 percent of the region's total land supply is in permanent open space controlled by local governments, the East Bay Regional Park District, and the National Park Service. Previously, development occurred with little controversy, following transportation corridors and filling valleys that lay outside the control of open-space and park administrations. A brief historical review of the region's growth is useful at this point.

HISTORICAL GROWTH PATTERNS

Prior to 1950, development was primarily concentrated in the central Bay Area. The two central cities of Oakland and San Francisco accounted for more than 50 percent of all population in the nine-county region. The older urban centers that line the East Bay from Oakland to Richmond had reached, or were approaching, peak population. Agriculture was still the prevailing land use to the north and south of San Francisco, and to the east of Oakland. The only major cities in the now populous South Bay were San Jose and San Mateo.

But shortly after World War II, the Bay Area entered a period of rapid change. The 1950 census revealed some new patterns of development, sparked by such factors as returning veterans who took full advantage of the Veterans' Administration home loan program. The demand they created was accommodated by developers who availed themselves of the low-cost land on what was then the urban fringe. In 1950, for instance, nearly one-half of all new units in Alameda County were built in unincorporated areas. San Mateo County, once a haven for the wealthy, doubled its population in a decade, while Santa Clara County experienced a two-thirds increase.

MAP 2-1
SAN FRANCISCO BAY REGION

```
0      10      20 MILES
|---|---|
0      16      32KM
```

MAP 1.
SAN FRANCISCO BAY REGION.

Between 1950 and 1960, the Bay Area's population increased by nearly one million, with much of this growth concentrated in southern Alameda, San Mateo, and Santa Clara counties. Along San Francisco Bay south of Oakland, the cities of San Leandro and Hayward grew by 140 and 400 percent respectively. In San Mateo County, along Highway 101, five cities more than doubled their populations. In Santa Clara County, agricultural land was quickly converted to residential use; and San Jose alone accounted for 10 percent of the total population increase in the nine-county Bay Area. Palo Alto, Santa Clara, and Sunnyvale developed into major urban centers with over 50,000 inhabitants each.

Growth was by no means limited to these areas of greatest expansion. Along the thirty-five-mile stretch of bay from Richmond to Antioch in Contra Costa County, an influx of industry was accompanied by a substantial population increase, though the county's central portion remained largely undeveloped. While the counties to the north and northeast of San Francisco were not to experience significant development until the next decade, a number of regional centers began to emerge.

Land development in the 1950s set the pattern for the years to come. Growth spread outward along all major transportation corridors; small towns within commuting range of employment centers became major cities in a few short years. It was common for communities to boast about their growth rates, which in some cases were above 400 percent, and there was keen competition for both industrial and residential development. A list of cities experiencing significant growth during the 1950s is presented in table 5.

During the ten-year period from 1960 to 1970, the region's population again grew by nearly one million, with few cities untouched by the increase. Several notable trends in development emerged. In Alameda County growth spread south into the Fremont/Newark/Union City area, and east along the Interstate 580 corridor into the Livermore Valley area. The widening of Highway 24 in Contra Costa County opened thousands of acres to development, and cities along the freeway (Concord, Lafayette, Pleasant Hill, and Walnut Creek) experienced substantial gains in population. Concord gained nearly 50,000 new residents in ten years, making it the largest city in the county.

Though there was only minimal industrial development to the north of San Francisco, towns along Highway 101 gained significant commuter populations. For example, San Rafael and Novato grew by 90 and 73 percent respectively in the course of the decade. While Sonoma and Napa counties retained their agricultural character, the cities of Santa Rosa and

TABLE 5

BAY AREA CITIES WITH SIGNIFICANT POPULATION
INCREASES, 1950 TO 1960

County and City	Population 1950	Population 1960	% Change
Alameda County			
Hayward	14,272	72,700	409
San Leandro	27,542	65,962	140
Contra Costa County			
Concord	6,953	36,208	420
San Mateo County			
Daly City	15,191	44,791	195
Menlo Park	13,587	26,957	98
Redwood City	25,544	46,990	84
San Bruno	12,478	29,063	133
South San Francisco	19,351	39,418	104
Santa Clara County			
Mountain View	6,563	30,889	370
Palo Alto	25,475	52,287	105
San Jose	95,280	204,196	114
Santa Clara	11,702	58,880	403
Sunnyvale	9,829	52,898	438
Solano County			
Vallejo	26,038	60,870	134

SOURCE: U.S. Bureau of the Census, 1950 and 1960.

Napa developed into regional centers of substantial size. Further east, along Interstate 80, Fairfield and Vacaville joined Vallejo as major urban centers in Solano County.

As in the previous decade, development in the South Bay occurred at an extraordinary pace, propelled by fast-growing high-technology firms. In 1970, Santa Clara County, with 23 percent of the region's population, overtook San Francisco to become the region's second largest county. Table 6 presents the distribution of the region's population by county for 1950, 1960, and 1970.

By 1975 development had consumed nearly 50 percent of all the land

TABLE 6

REGION'S POPULATION DISTRIBUTION BY COUNTY, 1950, 1960, AND 1970

County	% of Population 1950	% of Population 1960	% of Population 1970
Alameda	27.6	24.9	23.1
Contra Costa	11.1	11.2	12.0
Marin	3.2	4.0	4.5
Napa	1.7	1.8	1.7
San Francisco	28.9	20.3	15.5
San Mateo	8.7	12.2	12.0
Santa Clara	10.8	17.6	23.0
Solano	3.9	3.7	3.7
Sonoma	3.8	4.0	4.4
Total	100.0	100.0	100.0

SOURCE: U.S. Bureau of the Census, 1950, 1960, and 1970.

in the Bay Area designated for development. Whereas population had once been concentrated in the central portion of the region, it had now shifted to the south and east, with many cities in those areas solidly built out to their boundaries. Since the North Bay counties of Marin, Napa, Sonoma, and Solano contained only 15 percent of the region's population in 1975, they began experiencing dramatically increased pressures to develop, a shift these traditionally agricultural counties viewed with mixed emotion.

The process of urbanization has worked to shape local land use policies. The historical pattern of centrifugal development introduced an entire new set of rural communities to growth pressures, as development spread eastward into Alameda and Contra Costa counties, north to Marin, and south to Santa Clara and San Mateo counties. The number of towns affected by rapid urban development increased from a handful to several dozen. And as communities began to feel substantial postwar growth—traffic congestion, air pollution, and dwindling open space— they were led to consider a variety of planning issues, as well as more sophisticated development regulations. Pressured by postwar growth, many communities took action to revamp their general plans and zoning ordinances.

LOCAL POLICIES ARE THE CULPRIT

Suburban land conversion is no longer so easy. Most of the easily developable land has been urbanized, and a new mood has emerged in the suburbs. There is growing awareness of the environmental impact of development. Continued suburban land conversion is now viewed as being undesirable. Efforts to limit residential growth are well organized and increasingly effective. And in a climate of mounting financial strain, most communities view new housing as a financial liability. The result is a radically altered climate for suburban development in the San Francisco Bay Region, as documented by several alarming trends.

Residential Densities Are Falling

If future development were to occur at current density levels, and land use policies in effect in 1975 were to remain unchanged, the region could accommodate a population of over nine million. But in reality, densities for new residential construction are substantially lower than historical levels, and recent evidence suggests that density will continue to decline. In 1975, based on existing local development policies, the Association of Bay Area Governments estimated that because residential densities are falling, residential development would not be sufficient to meet projected housing demand beyond 1990.[2] In effect, the region's growth would be capped at its projected 1990 population of just under six million.

The Rise of Local Growth Controls

Local development policies have shifted dramatically since 1975, as the pro-growth attitude that prevailed in most Bay Area communities has been replaced by a slow-growth posture. Cities that once relished their status as regional growth centers now view new development skeptically. This is due not only to environmental concerns, but also the new fiscal calculus of Proposition 13, by which single-family development usually generates public-sector costs that are higher than revenues.

Jobs, But No Housing

Proposition 13 has also motivated communities to alter their approach to land use planning and zoning. Caught in a fiscal squeeze, many towns have stepped up efforts to increase their tax base by attracting more commercial, office, and light industrial development. Unfortunately, most communities have not concurrently adjusted their residential zoning. The result is a serious imbalance between residentially developable land and employment-generating land, and, ultimately, extreme difficulties for those who seek affordable housing near job centers, especially new employees migrating to the region.

Looking Out for Number One: Cities Against Cities and Counties

Bay Area local governments have a strong tradition of independence, "home rule," and pursuit of their own individual interests. The competition between jurisdictions has lately escalated to full-bore battle, but the nature of the conflict has changed: cities no longer engage in a tug-of-war to see who can attract the most development. More and more of them are playing a different game: pushing growth off onto other communities. And the greater the fiscal and environmental costs of development, the harder they push. The long-term implications for the region are enormous. In the past, only a few communities tried to shunt growth off onto their neighbors. The impact on the region was minimal, since other jurisdictions could absorb development without much difficulty. Today, there are few communities that do not try to export undesirable growth.

Falling residential densities, growth controls, the creation of jobs at the expense of housing, combat among local communities—all of these contributed to a severe shortage of residentially developable land. If present trends continue, the inevitable outcome is considerable land price inflation, escalating development costs, and rising home prices.

Ultimately, this inflationary spiral will slow the region's rate of economic growth and skew its economic structure. Wage rates will rise as workers are forced to pay higher housing costs. Higher land costs will also translate directly into higher rents and building costs, reducing the Bay Area's attractiveness to business and industry and dampening its prospects for economic growth. Firms will bypass the region in favor of lower-cost areas, while firms already operating in the Bay Area will tend to choose other locations for expansion or even move altogether.

THE ADVERSITY OF SUPPLY RESTRICTIONS

Firms such as Del Monte and Blue Cross/Blue Shield have already relocated outside the region, causing much hardship for employees who must choose either forced relocation or loss of their jobs. In Silicon Valley, high-technology firms are showing a growing inclination to develop production facilities elsewhere.

If a significant number of firms leave the region, the employment gap may not be easy to fill—particularly if job losses are concentrated in the clerical and blue-collar areas. The region's distribution of jobs could conceivably shift from a relatively balanced mix of professional, blue-collar, clerical, and service workers to a concentration of high-wage, high-productivity executive types. What has happened in San Francisco could happen throughout the Bay Area; the entire region could become a "gilded regional ghetto." Imagine the Bay Area as an homogeneous enclave of white-collar professionals, serviced by poorer workers who commute from Stockton or Tracy. Social equity becomes a hollow goal in an environment where lower-skilled workers find it increasingly difficult to survive.

Those just entering the Bay Area job market will also suffer if the rate of economic expansion continues to slow due to higher land and development costs. The region's younger population will find new job opportunities increasingly scarce, particularly since the region's indigenous population is increasing, and people aren't retiring fast enough to compensate (at least not for the next ten years). We may soon face the prospect of exporting our job-seeking residents to other areas.

But finally, a slackening of growth will hit all workers, whose chances for job promotions, salary increases, and upward mobility will be limited unless they are willing to move elsewhere. In a steady-state economy, the size of a firm will remain constant; promotions will be possible only if someone retires, quits, or dies. Under these conditions, the prospects for economic advancement are very slim indeed.

THE PROBLEMS OF CONTINUED URBAN SPRAWL

All of these manifestations of economic strangulation could occur if we let cost pressures dictate the region's development. But this is not to suggest that the San Francisco Bay Area should permit unfettered sprawl. The prospect of paving over the region's exceedingly fine landscape is every bit as alarming as the effects of land inflation.

Fears that the Bay Area will turn into another Los Angeles have been voiced since the late 1950s; many planners in particular were afraid that the region would become completely urbanized. In 1963 a series of Lane monographs contained several papers that expressed concern over the land use and environmental implications of the region's population growth. For example, two highly regarded demographers, Kingsley Davis and Eleanor Langlois, projected a rapid rise in the region's population between 1960 and 2000, along with a continuing decrease in population

TABLE 7

PROJECTED POPULATION, DENSITY, AND URBANIZED LAND
AREA, SAN FRANCISCO BAY AREA

Year	Population (millions)	Density Population (sq. miles)	Urbanized Area (sq. miles)
1970	4.1	1,689	2,428
1980	5.7	1,389	4,104
1990	7.6	1,263	6,017
2000	10.3	1,344	7,663

SOURCE: Kingsley Davis and Eleanor Langlois, *Future Demographic Growth of the San Francisco Bay Area* (Berkeley: Institute of Governmental Studies, 1963).

density. They concluded that urbanization would claim a steadily growing portion of the region.[3] (Table 7 presents Davis and Langlois's projections of Bay Area population, density, and urbanized land area.)

Davis and Langlois anticipated a regional population of between 7.3 and 13.2 million people by the year 2000, an average population density of between 953 to 1,723 persons per square mile, and an urbanized land area of 7,663 square miles. The environmental impact of development at this scale is substantial:

In 1920, when the urbanized area included only 157 square miles, it was not hard to get out of the city. When the sprawling metropolis of the year 2000 covers 7,663 square miles, the distance from the center to the periphery will be approximately fifty miles. Even after one has traversed the fifty miles, there will be no necessary release from urban congestion, for the traveler may simply find himself in the Sacramento or Stockton urban complex.[4]

It is enlightening to compare the projections of Davis and Langlois with actual growth patterns, as well as with the projection of the Association of Bay Area Governments (ABAG). In 1970, the region's total population was 4,635,987—almost identical to the authors' high estimate. According to ABAG's Series Two projection model, the amount of urbanized land in 1970 was an estimated 711 square miles, while population density was 6,519 persons per square mile. (It should be noted that the ABAG method of estimating urbanized land is fundamentally different from that used by Davis and Langlois, since they include all municipal land and ABAG records only developed land.)

ABAG estimated the region's 1980 population at 5,128,310, a figure that falls approximately 1.5 million short of Davis and Langlois's high estimate but is fairly close to their lower-range projection. ABAG does not estimate the total urbanized area of the region for 1980, but does give a projection for the year 2000: a total urbanized land area of 1,069 square miles. The associated population projection for 2000 is 6,205,018, well below the estimates prepared by Davis and Langlois. While the projections prepared by ABAG differ from those prepared by Davis and Langlois, both support the conclusion that the density of the region will continue to fall. ABAG's projection of population density for 2000 is 5,805 persons per square mile, a decline of 11 percent from present levels.

There are two reasons why the Davis and Langlois projections diverge from ABAG's. First, the rate of population growth in the state and even the nation has fallen off greatly since the mid 1960s. Second, the days of aggressive freeway expansion have ended, along with the era of land grabbing by annexing cities.

So the problem is no longer whether the region will be paved over, but whether there is enough developable land to accommodate development. If Catherine Bauer Wurster were alive today, she would not be stumping for a stop to mindless urban sprawl, even though she was correct in arguing that population densities would continue to fall. She would acknowledge that she had overestimated that drop and would be speaking out instead for an increase in housing development opportunities.[5]

PRESSING REGIONAL PROBLEMS

For many planners, fears that the San Francisco Bay Area will become completely urbanized have been replaced by concerns that local land conversion and development controls are putting a stranglehold on the region. The future of the entire Bay Area is being determined by the individual land use decisions of over one hundred local governments. In the past, the staunch independence of the region's localities has been regarded as desirable, guaranteeing diversity in living environments and public services. There were efforts to make local governments more responsive to the needs of the region's low-income households, as when State Assemblyman John Knox introduced in the 1960s a bill to establish a regional government. But the creation of a Bay Area regional government with broad controls over land use and development has never been a serious possibility. Attitudes toward local governments' traditional independence are changing, however, as the collective effects of their actions become clear:

- The region's housing supply is being restricted, and its growth is not keeping pace with housing demand.

- Land and housing prices are escalating sharply.

- As workers scramble to find affordable housing, there is a growing disjunction between job and housing locations.

- The jobs/housing imbalance is crowding the region's transportation system. Particularly in the southern portion of the Bay Area, freeways are becoming progressively more congested as growing numbers of workers are forced to live in lower-cost housing areas in southern Santa Clara County and southwestern Alameda County, while commuting to jobs in northern Santa Clara County.

- Communities are encouraging sprawl, as they restrict residential development or continue to reduce permitted densities. As a result, development leapfrogs out to more hospitable areas, or continues consuming land at very low densities.

Since 1970 the production of housing in the region has failed to keep pace with demand. In a study prepared for the Bay Area Council's Housing Task Force, Theresa Hughes and Associates estimated that substantial production shortfalls occurred in 1970, 1977, and 1978. Table 8 presents these housing demand and supply estimates. Since 1976, building permits have not met ABAG's housing construction goals. In 1976, the total number of building permits issued was 37,663. By the following year, the number had increased to 46,235, but fell back to 38,472 in 1978 and 33,763 in 1979. Given the current mortgage credit squeeze, the region can expect a continuing decline in housing construction.

TABLE 8

HOUSING SUPPLY/DEMAND ESTIMATES FOR THE
BAY AREA, 1970–79
(IN THOUSANDS OF UNITS)

	1970	1976	1977	1978	1979
Households	1552.8	1781.8	1832.6	1875.4	1913.4
Demand	1633.7	1875.6	1929.0	1974.1	2014.1
Supply	1622.8	1889.5	1926.7	1969.1	2003.6
Surplus (+)/Deficit (−)	−10.9	+13.9	−2.3	−5.0	−10.5

SOURCE: Theresa Hughes and Associates, Albany, California, April 1980.

A SURVEY OF LOCAL PLANNING DEPARTMENTS

In an effort to assess the regional implications of local land use policies, I conducted a telephone survey of Bay Area planning departments in
the spring of 1979. I received excellent cooperation; ninety-one of the
region's ninety-four community departments agreed to be interviewed.
Interviews lasted approximately forty-five minutes and included questions about local land use issues, present land policies, and future land
policy directions. The survey results provide a good, up-to-date picture of
local land use policies, and lead to several important conclusions about
the regional impact of restricting development opportunities in suburban
communities. (For a complete description of the telephone survey, see
Appendix A.)

When considered from a regional perspective, the survey results are
startling. The future of land conversion in the Bay Area is not bright.
Opportunities for continued residential development appear to be
limited, and there are already signs that a severe housing shortage is
beginning to hamper expansion of the electronics industry in Santa
Clara County.

The survey also revealed that Bay Area communities are being highly
cautious in assessing future development possibilities. For instance, many
cities once characterized as land grabbers are now wary of service expansions to outlying unincorporated areas and no longer court annexation
proposals. While some cities limit annexation to adjacent parcels, others
simply refuse to annex unless forced to by the Local Agency Formation
Commission (LAFCO). In most instances, no annexation means no new
development. It is still possible to get county approval for development in
unincorporated areas, but counties too are facing fiscal constraints. In
Alameda County, for example, a proposal was recently put before the
board of supervisors to further reduce rural development densities. Impetus for the proposal was concern that groups of new residents living in
close proximity would band together to demand costly upgrades in fire
and police protection.

Fiscal considerations also play an important role in shaping the development of incorporated areas. Many planners indicated great interest in
the possible use of the fiscal cost-revenue impact models to assess the tax
and expenditure implications of land development proposals. Such findings are often used to oppose projects unlikely to be a fiscal asset.

This survey also confirmed that continued development is gaining prominence as a public issue. Thirty-four of ninety-one respondents, representing over one-third of the communities surveyed, indicated that growth is a major local issue. Of these thirty-four communities, nine had implemented growth management ordinances, and seven others had proposals pending for either adoption or consideration. While these ordinances differ in design, their effect is the same—to restrict the pace and extent of development. In fact, because of the way they are administered, many of these programs delay *all* development, in some cases up to a year. For instance, cities using a competitive allocation system accept proposals throughout the year, but meet only once or twice annually to decide which projects can proceed.

The increasing use of development controls to protect environmentally sensitive areas was also documented by the survey. Nearly one-half of the region's cities have, or are currently developing, slope-density ordinances to regulate hillside development. With slope grade used as the determining factor, residential areas may be downzoned from minimum lot sizes of 10,000 to 20,000 square feet to one- to ten-acre minimums. The widespread use of this technique suggests that development, having consumed much of the land on the valley floor, is now encroaching on the hillsides.

Downzoning is by no means limited to environmentally sensitive areas, the survey showed. Over one-third of the planning agency informants indicated that density and preservation of a community's "single-family" character were significant concerns. This again supports the conclusion that citizen expectations can have as great an impact on land use as the inherent characteristics of the land itself.

For instance, one Bay Area developer designed a mixed project combining both high- and low-density residential units, but made the unfortunate mistake of constructing the single-family units first. When he later tried to phase in the multifamily units, he met with considerable opposition from the newly settled residents in the single-family homes. My research found such concerns about density to be increasingly evident as the motivation for recent zoning changes. Some thirty-nine communities reported downzoning of residential densities over a significant portion of the community, further reducing development potential in the region.

Another indication of local governments' qualms about development is the frequent use of moratoriums to halt growth while cities study their options. The results of the telephone survey revealed that since the mid-1970s over forty-five communities have used this technique to defer development, while devising new plans or policies to deal with the environmental effects, service-capacity constraints, or other growth-related issues.

While these actions are understandable when viewed at the community level, they have a cumulative regional impact that must not be ignored. It is apparent that the long-term economic and social well-being of the San Francisco Bay Area depends in large part on the availability of land suitable for residential, commercial, and industrial use. Communities may be furthering their own short-run interests by questioning the benefits of continued development, but they are adopting policies that, when seen collectively, are likely to have dire consequences for the region.

WHY LOCAL LAND USE POLICIES HAVE CHANGED

A community's pattern of land conversion and development control results from a variety of historical, cultural, political, fiscal, and environmental factors. Land development policy is not static, but shifts with the winds of political change. Communities have not been capricious in revising land development policies in recent years. Rather, they have reflected a new mood surrounding land development issues—a mood that shows little sign of changing and has already begun to restrict the level of development in many areas.

Critics of those who advocate the "go-slow" posture are quick to paint them as elitist newcomers trying desperately to preserve what they came to enjoy—sometimes referred to as the "gangplank syndrome." But this characterization is incorrect and overly simplistic, ignoring the other factors at work, such as intergovernmental finance, environmental degradation, and what Toeffler calls "future shock"—namely, a general inability of people to cope with rapid social and cultural change.[6] While one can hardly determine how each of these isolated factors affects local decision making, it is possible to consider how they operate in combination to shape the form and content of local land use policy.

Until recently many Bay Area communities have been passive in the face of substantial ongoing residential and commercial development. Most accepted growth as inevitable, and a few actively pursued new expansion. To guide development, towns and counties relied on zoning and general plan guidelines that were, at least in the beginning, very unsophisticated. For example, most community zoning ordinances failed to consider the environmental characteristics and development implications of the region's hillside areas. In fact, until the early 1960s many hillside areas were zoned at the same level of intensity as flatlands. Up until that time, it usually didn't matter since there was ample room for development in the level areas.

Growth Pressures Created the New Mood

Over time the rapid rate of land conversion in the region's rural areas began to attract considerable attention. The conversion of fruit orchards in Santa Clara County and encroachment on the vineyards of Napa and Sonoma Counties dramatized the adverse effects of urban development on the region's landscape. By the late 1960s the environmental movement had shifted into high gear, and in 1972 environmental regulation in the Bay Area reached a high water mark when a new phenomena emerged in Sonoma County. The city of Petaluma adopted a growth management plan that limited new building permits to five hundred per year. The subject of both regional and national controversy, the Petaluma case had a decisive influence on the course of land use and environmental regulation in the region.

It was in the 1960s that the widening of Highway 101 placed the city of Petaluma within San Francisco's sphere of influence. Residential construction boomed as the city attracted commuters in search of inexpensive housing, large residential lots, and good schools. At the same time, growth put a substantial strain on city services, forcing costly extensions. There was increasing congestion on the city streets, and long-time residents vilified newcomers for destroying Petaluma's small-town character.

In response to these concerns, a series of goals were adopted. Growth was to be limited to approximately 500 new housing units annually from 1973–1977. The city's small-town character and surrounding open space were to be preserved by controlling the rate and distribution of growth. Development was tied to school and utility capacity and balanced between eastern and western sections. With the cooperation of Sonoma County, all urban and suburban development near the city would be approved by and acceptable for annexation to the city. A permanent greenbelt of open hills and marshland and open space for recreation would be provided. Environmental design plans, planned community districts, and planned unit developments would be required to gain the best design possible. Multifamily units would be encouraged and a variety of densities and building types ensured. The central business district was to be rehabilitated as the principal commercial center of southern Sonoma County.[7]

The Petaluma Plan, as it has come to be referred to, marked a radical departure from traditional community planning. Particularly during the postwar period, local planning in the United States had been characterized by an almost universal effort to accommodate new growth in an orderly fashion. Prior to Petaluma's growth management plan, most communities had made no overt attempts to limit or restrain development. Given widespread attention, the Petaluma plan had an impact on local planning that went beyond the lively discussions that had become ritual at annual meetings of the American Institute of Planners and the American Society of Planning Officials. After Petaluma's unprecedented step, many other communities confronting similar growth pressures began to experiment with growth management. By the mid-1970s, a growing trend toward the use of growth management devices was evident in both California and U.S. planning surveys. In response to an International City Managers Association Survey, over 220 cities and counties indicated that they were using planning controls to regulate the rate of urban development.[8] In California, a 1975 survey conducted by the State Office of Planning and Research found that over 300 of the state's 445 local planning agencies were using both growth management and more traditional techniques to control the rate of land development.[9] Nearly fifty communities were attempting to control the pace of development in the Bay Area alone. But the shock waves of growth management have by no means reached full force. As more and more towns adopt growth management programs, the effects on housing and land markets will become even more pronounced.

Current events do suggest that growth controls will continue to proliferate in California communities, since they are a means to avoid increased public costs, minimize the rate of land conversion, and preserve environmental and overall community quality. The fiscal squeeze created by Proposition 13 has made communities exceedingly cautious about new development. Because tax revenues from new development are limited to only 1 percent of the full market value, many projects will not generate enough tax revenues to support the public services that they need. As a consequence, many communities routinely disapprove fiscally questionable projects, while others use sophisticated cost-revenue estimation models to determine which projects will generate an acceptable level of net tax revenue. Proposition 13 has provided slow-growth advocates a potent argument for limiting urban development.

At the same time, concern for environmental and neighborhood quality has been intensifying. Local citizen groups, whether small neighborhood associations or more broadly based environmental coalitions, have become much more influential in local decision making. As citizens have become more sophisticated about environmental issues, they have claimed a greater role in shaping land use policy. Rising incomes and increased leisure time have also contributed to demands for a high level of environmental quality. Rejecting the notion that planners or elected officials know what is best for them, citizens today play an active and vocal role in local planning. Like their planners, they no longer assume that they must passively accommodate new development.

As a result of these trends, communities are more aggressively pursuing their own objectives, and placing less and less importance on regional development needs or the regional implications of their actions. While it would be foolish to suggest that local communities have not always pursued their own self-interests, it seems clear that the motivation behind local development decisions has changed in some fundamental ways. In the early postwar years, communities were passive in accepting development or aggressive in pursuing it. The regional impact of their actions was rarely troubling, since the competition among jurisdictions guaranteed that regional growth would occur—perhaps not always in the "right" place, but at least somewhere. Today there is a much different style of competition among communities. They are still interested in high-quality development, especially research and development centers, the proverbial "dream industry," but they are also interested in exporting or blocking out undesirable growth. Communities will accept a new revenue-generating research and development center, but at the same time curtail housing production, even if it is targeted to the new research and development workers.

Of course, efforts to block all but the most desirable types of development are nothing new. Land use and zoning history chronicles numerous cases where local communities exert draconian control over the type of residential development permitted within their borders. In fact, zoning in the United States is founded on the principle that it should be used to protect and preserve property values.[10] So it is hardly surprising that towns try to skim off only the cream of development; but the difference today is that the practice of limiting growth has become so widespread. The days of uncritical progrowth boosterism are over, seemingly forever.

As each community attempts to carefully control the rate and type of development, the regional impact of these restrictions becomes much more pronounced. But there is no indication that local governments will begin to incorporate regional needs into their decision making in the near future. The fragmented nature of local land use and environmental planning is well documented. More than ten years ago, the *California Law Review* published an article deriding the selfish and shortsighted nature of local government development policies.[11] Despite frequent attempts to pass legislation countering the mercantilist stance of local governments, reform is no more likely now than it ever was.

Perhaps the most intensive discussion of the regional problems engendered by local actions has taken place in Santa Clara County. Concerned by the rapid growth of the electronics industry in Silicon Valley, the county commissioned a task force to study the growing problem of limited housing. Communities in the northern portion of the county have aggressively sought new manufacturing activity and employment expansion, but nearly all have also limited the construction of new housing. Although the price of housing has been spiraling upward, and the county's rate of economic development has begun to slow in reaction, no community appears willing to alter its land development policies. The need for more housing is one of the key points in the task force report, *Living Within Our Limits*.[12] The validity of this conclusion has been widely acknowledged and recognized, but little action attempting to solve the problem has resulted.

The main source of concern with the county's housing problems has not been traditional prohousing advocates, but the private sector. The Santa Clara County Manufacturing Group has been monitoring the trends and has taken a high-profile stance in calling for more residential construction. The Bay Area Council, the region's most influential private-sector organization, has also studied the area's housing markets and has established an action task force to carry out strategies designed to increase housing opportunities.

These organizations acknowledge that the impetus for change will not come from local planners or elected officials, who must reflect the interests of their constituents or risk losing their jobs. When there is strong and vocal opposition to a residential project at planning commission or city council hearings, local officials see little choice but to deny a permit, even though additional housing is desperately needed.

The fundamental contradiction between local and regional interests is painfully apparent in the housing arena. In fact, the problem is an excellent example of the so-called "prisoner's dilemma." If one of the Silicon Valley communities, for example, were to announce plans to accommodate more housing, the other cities in the area would lose no time in exporting residential development to that well-intentioned community, while welcoming only fiscally desirable economic development themselves.

Examples of mercantilist action in Santa Clara County are abundant. The city of San Jose, once the fastest growing community in the nation, recently altered its policy on residential development. Citing fiscal pressures and the longstanding predominance of residential development within its borders, the city has now taken steps to limit the location and type of residential development, while attempting to attract more industrial and commercial development. In effect, this policy shift changes San Jose's position from a provider of housing to a competitor for economic development opportunities. Another example is that of the city of Santa Clara, which has also taken steps to limit residential development and attract additional light industrial construction. The zoning and general plan of the city greatly curtail residential projects, and the vast majority of vacant land in the city is zoned industrial. The city has taken no steps to balance this economic development potential with the level of housing necessary to meet the needs of additional workers.

Needless to say, the regional implications of such actions are adverse, especially as other communities follow suit. Unfortunately, recent surveys of local development policy show that this is in fact happening. If this trend continues, the housing market will become extremely tight, and eventually high housing prices will exert severe economic pressures on all sectors of the region's economy.

CONCLUSION

Over the years, land use regulation in the Bay Area has become highly sophisticated and, with increasing awareness of development's environmental impact, progressively restrictive. This trend has been accelerated by the passage of Proposition 13. The cumulative effects of the widespread use of restrictive land use controls are potentially enormous. Limited land availability, constrained housing production, and an imbalance between job and housing locations will adversely affect the region's environmental quality, as well as its economy.

Why have so many communities adopted strict land use control policies? What kinds of growth pressures have they had to confront? How do they regulate land conversion? It is to these questions that we turn in the next two chapters. To better understand the dynamics of suburban land conversion and the pressures that it places on communities, we shift the scene from the regional scale to a closer look at six Bay Area cities.

CHAPTER THREE

Profile of Growth and Land Conversion in Six Bay Area Cities

This chapter looks at the process of land conversion and urbanization in the postwar period, and assesses how six communities responded to these growth pressures. How quickly did they grow? How did growth affect them? Has growth forced them to reconsider their basic land use and environmental programs?

Since my research effort was concerned with how communities developed their particular land use and environmental regulations, and how these regulations have affected land and housing markets, I controlled all factors that influenced the price and costs of housing units but were not associated with land use regulation. The control strategy was based on a two-step procedure. First, communities were grouped, as much as possible, into homogeneous clusters. Second, based on its land use and environmental controls, each community was paired with a community using an opposite approach. The land use policy interviews described in the previous chapter were used to help make these judgments. This somewhat experimental research design provided me with a way of pairing communities with similar social, economic, physical, and environmental factors, but with divergent land use and environmental policies. (Appendix B contains a detailed discussion of how the six cities were chosen.)

Map 2 shows the location of the six towns: Concord, Fremont, Napa, Santa Rosa, Novato, and San Rafael. This group is fairly representative of the region geographically, but no communities from the Peninsula or from Santa Clara County are present. It was difficult to create good pairs from these areas, because the communities had land use policies that were almost identical. But aside from geographic distribution, the six towns are quite representative of the region's developing areas.

Table 9 presents information on the basic character of these six communities. While there are some differences in background variables of paired communities, they are not significant. The Concord-Fremont pair has the largest population, about 100,000 each, as well as the slowest population growth over the 1970–75 period, reflecting the position of

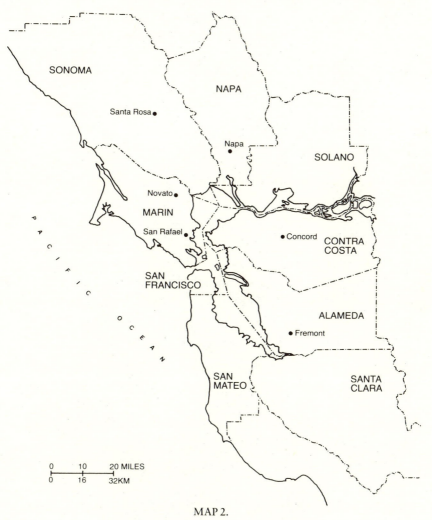

MAP 2.
LOCATION OF SIX CASE STUDY CITIES.

TABLE 9

PAIR-WISE COMPARISON OF SELECTED ATTRIBUTES FOR CASE
STUDY COMMUNITIES

	Population	% Change Population 1970–75	% of Families w/$15,000 income	Mean House Value 1975	% Homeowners	% Change Houses 1970–75	Non-White School Enrollment	Basic Employment	Local Serving Employment
Concord	93,750	10.1	51.1	58,700	64.8	31.5	—	9,580	17,960
Fremont	115,461	14.5	29.3	59,200	66.8	26.6	11.8	11,430	15,660
Napa	46,857	29.8	26.6	59,500	64.6	28.3	6.8	6,380	13,740
Santa Rosa	65,611	31.2	21.2	51,900	43.6	31.2	—	12,570	28,600
Novato	31,066	—	37.0	74,000	67.8	21.4	7.8	10,500	3,190
San Rafael	45,611	17.0	33.7	95,000	54.8	24.8	N.A.	7,680	16,820

these communities as older suburban centers. Both are solidly middle-class and suburban in character. Napa and Santa Rosa, on the other hand, are more exurban than suburban. Both are county seats, with a sizable employment base relative to their population. Incomes are lower than in Concord and Fremont, while their growth rate is much higher than that of the other pairs. Both Napa and Santa Rosa have experienced tremendous growth pressure. Novato and San Rafael are the smallest in population. Novato is the more suburban of the two; San Rafael is more mature and more upper-income.

FREMONT AND CONCORD: GROWTH CENTERS COME OF AGE

Fremont and Concord played major roles in the development of the San Francisco Bay Area during the 1950s. By converting large areas of inexpensive raw land to new single-family housing tracts, they provided homeownership opportunities to thousands of new Bay Area households. Between 1950 and 1980, the two cities together added approximately 210,000 residents to their populations—an increase accounting for 10 percent of the region's growth during that period. Table 10 documents the rapid transformation of Fremont and Concord from small rural towns to suburban centers. Among Bay Area cities with 1970 populations in excess of 50,000, Fremont and Concord were the region's fastest and second fastest growing cities between 1960 and 1970.

The factors responsible for this phenomenal rate of growth were the same for both cities: expansion of the freeway system brought large areas of inexpensive agricultural land into commuting reach of San Francisco and Oakland job centers. The upgrading of Highway 24 in Contra Costa County cut travel time between Concord and Oakland to thirty minutes, and the construction of Interstate 680, linking Central Contra Costa County with San Jose, opened the Diablo Valley to residential development. Interstate 680 was also a contributing factor to Fremont's rapid growth during the 1960s, as was improvement of the Nimitz Freeway (Highway 17). These two arteries provided Fremont commuters with access to both the Oakland and the San Jose employment centers.

Fremont—Building a Planned City

As late as 1960, much of Fremont's acreage was still in agricultural use. The city itself was only four years old, having been forged in 1956 through the union of five previously unincorporated villages.* From the

---

*Niles, Centerville, Irvington, Mission San Jose, and Warm Springs.

TABLE 10

POPULATION AND HOUSING GROWTH IN CONCORD AND
FREMONT, 1950–80

| | Concord | | Fremont | |
	Population	% of Contra Costa County	Population	% of Alameda County
1950	6,953	– 2.3	10,040	1.4
1960	36,208	8.9	45,950	5.1
1970	85,164	15.3	101,930	9.5
1975	95,500	16.4	115,400	10.6
1980	100,000	—	130,450	—
Percentage change				
1960–70	+135.2%		+121.8%	
1970–80	+17.4%		+27.9%	
Annualized growth rate				
1960–70	8.9%		8.3%	
1970–80	1.6%		2.5%	

| | | Concord | | | Fremont | |
| | | Single-Family Units | Multi-Family Units | | Single-Family Units | Multi-Family Units |
	Total			Total		
1970	25,779	19,201	5,252	27,303	23,450	3,740
1975	33,392	21,504	10,518	37,506	28,061	8,840
Percentage change						
1970–75	29.5%	12.0%	100.3%	37.3%	19.7%	136.3%

SOURCES: U.S. Census of Population, 1950, 1960, 1970; State of California Department of Finance Special Census and Estimates, 1975, 1980.

beginning, Fremont was conceived as a "planned city," where commercial development and multifamily housing would line the wide, recently up-graded boulevards linking Fremont's original five districts. Housing construction would be orderly and neat; residential streets would be straight or gently curving, lot lines would run perpendicular to streets, and cul-de-sacs would be encouraged. To screen out the noise of Fremont's freeways and major thoroughfares, acoustical walls would be required on the edges of residential subdivisions. Much of Fremont's housing construction during this period took the form of subdivision and tract developments. Tract construction became popular in the 1950s, as builders discovered the economies of scale attainable by constructing many similar or identical homes each on a single parcel. Further savings were possible by making all required subdivision improvements (e.g., road construction, grading, and utility installation) at one time. Early subdivisions featured row after row of identical homes on lots determined by a uniform and rectilinear road system, but by the early 1960s tract developments had become more sophisticated. Four or more different housing styles might be constructed. The cul-de-sac had replaced the rectangular block, and lot configurations became more varied.

Tract-type construction was well suited to the large, undivided parcels of vacant agricultural land readily available in Fremont and Concord during the 1950s. Pioneering in this more "enlightened" form of residential construction, the city of Fremont also insisted that builders construct the streets and utility lines linking their projects with the existing infrastructure. This constraint encouraged fairly orderly development and discouraged leapfrogging to take advantage of lower land costs. A review of Fremont's recent history reveals that postwar development occurred in what is essentially a radial pattern. The city's older housing is clustered around Fremont's five original centers, now referred to as districts. During the 1950s, all of these centers expanded radially, with the greatest growth occurring in the Centreville and Irvington Districts, which are closest to the Nimitz Freeway. Eventually the two districts were linked by what now appears to be an unending sea of subdivisions, tract housing, and acoustical walls.

By the late 1960s, few vacant parcels remained that were zoned for low- and moderate-density housing, and these were located close to the Nimitz Freeway and Fremont's developing commercial center. Developers in search of buildable, inexpensive land pushed north toward Union City, east up the hillsides, south through Warm Springs toward Milpitas, and finally west over the Nimitz Freeway into the previously undeveloped Northern Plain. Throughout this period, residential expansion was in the form of the detached single-family home. Because lot sizes were modest, averaging less than 7,000 square feet, new homes remained relatively inexpensive.

Fremont's rapid growth during the 1960s was not limited to single-family housing. Shops and services began lining the city's main boulevards, where they catered to a highly mobile, increasingly auto-oriented population. Attempts to cluster shopping opportunities in a central business district (CBD) met with only partial success. Only with the introduction of BART service in 1972 did new commercial construction begin to occur outside the pattern of auto-oriented strip development. Industrial development proceeded at a slower pace. Not until the 1963 opening of the six-thousand-worker General Motors Assembly Plant was Fremont viewed as a regional employment center. As in most commuter suburbs, multifamily housing construction lagged far behind single-family starts. As long as vacant land and financing were available, builders continued to supply what consumers wanted: the single-family home.

Concord's Development

In many ways Concord is Fremont's mirror image, transposed to central Contra Costa County. The residential construction that pushed Concord's population from 36,208 in 1960 to over 95,000 in 1970 consisted primarily of single-family homes. As in Fremont, Concord's residential growth occurred in a radial fashion, moving outward from the existing village center—what is now "downtown" Concord. During the 1950s, close-in parcels to the north, east, and south were gradually subdivided and developed as single-family home tracts. Faced with expansion constraints to the north (Naval Ordinance Testing Center) and west (Pacheco), developers opened up agricultural parcels to the east (along Clay-

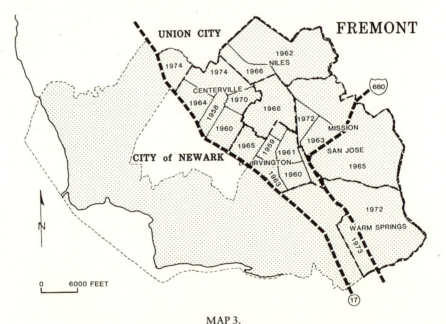

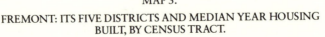

MAP 3.
FREMONT: ITS FIVE DISTRICTS AND MEDIAN YEAR HOUSING
BUILT, BY CENSUS TRACT.

ton Valley Road) and south. This conversion of land continued well into
the late 1960s, when builders were constrained by the borders of Clayton
and Walnut Creek, and turned to the southeast. (Map 4 illustrates the
radial pattern of Concord's development.) Multifamily rental housing
starts kept pace during the late 1960s and early 1970s, but have been
depressed since 1974. Still, multifamily housing remains a significant part
of Concord's housing stock (30.5 percent in 1980). Not surprisingly, most
existing multifamily units are located in close-in neighborhoods with
good transit service.

The Boom Years

The addition of over 175,000 new residents to Fremont and Concord
between 1950 and 1970 totally changed the character of the two cities.

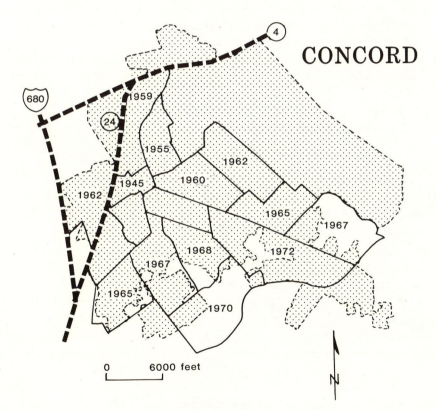

MAP 4.
CONCORD: MEDIAN YEAR HOUSING BUILT,
BY CENSUS TRACT.

Sleepy village centers before World War II, they had by 1970 grown into modern suburban cities where housing tract developments, shopping areas, and sprawling traffic arteries were rapidly consuming the remaining supply of vacant land. In both cities the majority of the new residents were homeowners.

During the 1960s and early 1970s, Fremont's housing was very affordable. In 1970, 72 percent of the city's owner-occupied housing had value-to-income ratios below 2.5, the cutoff point then used by lenders in granting mortgages, and 58 percent of Fremont's renters paid gross rents (including utilities) representing less than 25 percent of their incomes.

Many of these same trends were visible in Concord during the 1960s. Homeownership in 1975 stood at 65.4 percent, down from a high of 72.4 percent in 1970, due to the large amount of multifamily rental construction that had taken place. Housing prices were stable. For example, in 1964 the average price of a single-family home in Concord was roughly $25,000; by 1970 that average had only increased to $27,000. Turnover rates in Concord were also high, since the area attracted first-time home buyers who were soon able to trade up into larger and more expensive homes.

Taxes remained low, because both cities offered fewer public and social services than older, more urbanized communities. Infrastructure was to a large extent provided by builders, and subsidized by an expanding business and residential base. Subdivision regulations assured that new construction would be neat, orderly, and if not beautiful, at least not displeasing. The fact that most subdivision homes were similar in design was often viewed as a small penalty for reasonable prices, particularly among first-time home buyers. Most important, buildable land was readily available and inexpensive, making it possible for both cities to grow outward as growth pressures increased. This meant the cities were able to accommodate growth without increasing residential density or sacrificing the orderly, suburban character of which many Concord and Fremont residents were proud. Problems of congestion could be minimized, neighborhoods could be preserved, and new residents need not encroach on current homeowners.

Reaching Maturity

If the 1960s and early 1970s were "boom years" for Fremont and Concord, the middle and late 1970s must be seen as a period of transition and reassessment. A series of circumstances and events—some common to the two communities, some different—combined to slow the pace of development and cast doubt on the desirability of continued growth.

The local scene was changing, but there was also another element: two macroeconomic events that produced shock waves nationwide. The first was the so-called "Arab Oil Embargo" during the last quarter of 1973 and the first quarter of 1974. Accompanied by long gas lines and seemingly steep price hikes for gasoline, the embargo led many potential Fremont and Concord residents to rethink the economic benefits of a home in the suburbs. Although BART might eliminate the need to use a car for the work trip, most households still required at least one auto for shopping and other trips. Moreover, in 1973 BART service was still in the fledgling stages and was generally viewed as unreliable. Coming on the heels of the "gas crunch" was the second event, a nationwide recession that left the housing industry very hard-hit, and many planned subdivisions unbuilt.

Growth rates dropped sharply in both Concord and Fremont. Whereas Fremont had been attracting four thousand to six thousand new residents each year, by 1974 in-migration had virtually ground to a halt. Similarly, Concord's expansion slowed from a pre-recession growth rate of 4 percent annually (averaged over the previous five-year period) to a rate of well below 1 percent per year. And as figure 1 shows, low levels of population growth were accompanied by a big drop in the number of housing starts in both cities.

Fortunately, the recession was brief, and by 1975 new residents again began moving to Concord and Fremont—albeit not at the pace of the early 1970s. Many of these new residents were young, two-income families seeking moderately priced housing. They spurred a quick recovery in single-family housing starts, though multifamily starts remained depressed in both cities. The cities' growth slowdown was explained by the "gas crisis" and recession. Yet Concord and Fremont began to mature and face an entirely new set of problems.

The first and most obvious problem was a decline in the supply of land available for development. By 1975, Concord had been almost completely developed to its western, southern, and eastern borders. Of the city's twenty-seven square miles, only 1,523 acres remained available to residential builders as of 1978. About 400 acres of this total were in the form of large parcels (50 acres or more) suitable for tract construction, with an additional 750–900 acres consisting of "infill parcels" (averaging 10 acres or less). Much of this latter acreage included so-called "under-utilized parcels" that could not be developed without aggregating parcels under varied ownership and removing existing structures. Aside from these infill parcels, there is little developable land in Concord to this day, since the area on the city's western, southern, and eastern borders has been almost completely developed. Concord's "sphere of influence," as determined by the Local Agency Formation Commission, includes thou-

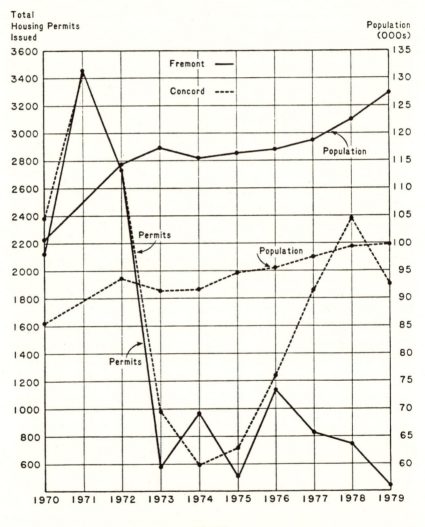

FIGURE 1.

POPULATION AND HOUSING GROWTH TRENDS IN
CONCORD AND FREMONT, 1970–79.
SOURCE: Concord and Fremont Building Departments, State
Department of Finance

sands of acres to the north, but because of high service costs the city has no current plans to annex or service this area. Concord's impending land shortage did not go unnoticed by Contra Costa builders. Believing a shift in residential construction in eastern Contra Costa County to be inevitable, many of the latter have moved their operations to Brentwood, Antioch, and Pittsburg.

In Fremont, the absolute decline in vacant land supply has been neither as serious nor as obvious. According to land availability surveys conducted by the Association of Bay Area Governments in 1975, over five thousand acres of "prime developable land" remained in Fremont—more vacant land than in any other Bay Area city except San Jose. But Fremont's raw land supply is not of uniform quality. Except for the Northern Plains area, few large buildable parcels remain north of the Mission San Jose District. As a result, builders are increasingly petitioning to develop hillside acreage or, as is the case with the Northern Plain, areas considered to be environmentally sensitive.

Prior to the passage of Proposition 13, rising property taxes were of major concern to Fremont homeowners. In 1970, Fremont's city budget totaled $8,440,000, or roughly $82.80 per capita. By 1978, the city budget stood at $27,225,000, an increase of almost 225 percent. Although more than half of this increase could be attributed to inflation, most of the real increase went to finance an expansion in local public services, and by 1978 per capita expenditures were $225.15.* The average Fremont homeowner paid approximately $1,750 in local property taxes in 1975; by 1977 the yearly payment had risen to $2,500. Financial analysts correctly point out that the reason for this steep increase was an equally rapid rise in housing prices, not an increase in property tax rates. Nevertheless, few communities responded to this windfall by lowering property tax rates. Much the same dynamic was occurring in Concord, where the city's budget rose from roughly $15,296,000 in fiscal year 1974–75 to $24,622,000 in 1977–78—a 60 percent increase in three years.

Yet despite these rather dramatic increases in municipal spending in the 1970s, voters were not willing to let this escalate further. As a result, Proposition 13 passed with a solid majority in both Concord and Fremont, and since then the growth of their budgets has halted or even been reversed. For example, in current dollars, Fremont's 1979–80 budget was some $2.5 million below 1978–79 levels. In Concord, the 1979–80 city

---

*In 1978, the year of Proposition 13's passage, more than 44 percent of Fremont's expenditures financed community safety (police and fire services), 21.5 percent went to local transportation, and 16 percent was earmarked for local government administration.

budget was roughly $650,000 more than in 1978–79—a substantial cut (in constant, uninflated dollars). Both cities have managed to avoid police, fire, and public works layoffs, cutting back administrative and capital expenditures instead. But Proposition 13 had another effect: it forced new residential development to pay its own way more than in the past. Both cities raised planning and building fees to cover the costs of review services. Fremont raised the construction tax it had recently instituted and added a "school impact fee." Finally, local utility districts were encouraged to assess developers and, by extension, new home buyers for the full costs of additional infrastructure.

Concern with development's adverse environmental effects was less evident in Fremont and Concord during the early 1970s than it was in many other Bay Area communities. Few of Concord's environmentally sensitive areas were available to residential developers, and hillside areas were either protected as permanent open space or owned by the U.S. Naval Weapons Testing Station. In Fremont, hillside areas were protected by Williamson contracts,[1] hillside zoning, or permanent open-space designations. Until 1974, there was little pressure for baylands development, and local decision makers were less oriented toward land conservation than those in other Bay Area cities.

But it was in 1974 that Fremont's environmental complacency was shattered by pressures to develop the Northern Plains, a large baylands area west of the Nimitz Freeway that had been vacant or in agricultural use. The Fremont City Council swiftly proposed amending the Fremont General Plan to keep major portions of the Northern Plains in agricultural use until 1985. Singer Housing (now Citation Homes), the largest of the prospective developers, responded by suing the city to prevent the contemplated plan revisions. In an out-of-court settlement on February 15, 1977, Fremont agreed to let Citation develop 317 acres of the Northern Plains. To forestall similar litigation, the city quickly mounted a series of major studies to outline development options for the Northern Plains, and identify an acceptable trade-off between residential construction and baylands preservation. In light of the Northern Plains experience, Fremont officials are now increasingly concerned that residential development will also begin creeping further into the city's foothill areas.

Growth also tends to breed congestion, a serious problem in both Fremont and Concord. Because of Concord's radial street pattern, its downtown becomes highly congested during commuting hours. According to one Concord planner, traffic congestion has become the city's number one growth-related problem. Traffic problems are less serious in Fremont, where arterial streets are arranged in a grid pattern and there is no single major employment center.

With their expanding populations and increasing densities, these two communities face increasing pressures to limit their future growth. Fremont planners report rising attendance at public meetings where residential projects are discussed, and new homeowner and citizen groups continue to spring up. Still, both Fremont and Concord city planners remained "progrowth" during the 1970s, convinced that existing laws and land use policies were adequate to ensure the development of high-quality neighborhoods. In Concord, where the supply of vacant land decreased steadily, city officials understood that explicit controls were unnecessary because the private land market would itself ration growth. In Fremont, where speculative construction was an everyday occurrence, a small growth-management constituency appeared in 1976 to advocate the passage of a timed development system that would restrict residential development to a set number of new units per year. Although there was some staff support for the concept, the TDS never made it past the Fremont Planning Commission.

NAPA AND SANTA ROSA: DIFFERING RESPONSES TO GROWTH AT THE URBAN FRINGE

Of all the communities studied, Napa and Santa Rosa offer the most striking contrasts. Both communities are the economic and political centers of their counties, and their expansion between the close of World War II and the mid-1960s was at roughly the same rate. Both are satellite cities that experienced accelerating economic and residential development pressures as the Bay Area spread outward in the 1960s.

But despite these similarities, Santa Rosa and Napa have responded to regional growth in vastly different ways. Napa residents and elected officials came to believe that their city was expanding too quickly, and saw the large tract subdivisions built in the early 1970s as threatening Napa's rural lifestyle. This perception was reinforced by the realization that Napa's growth had been primarily residential in nature, turning it into another bedroom suburb of San Francisco. In Santa Rosa, on the other hand, growth has been more balanced. Led by Hewlett-Packard in 1969, several large manufacturing firms migrated to Santa Rosa during the early 1970s. Although the city is not yet the "Silicon Valley of the North," as some real estate analysts confidently predicted several years ago, economic development has been substantial. One indication of the recent economic boom is job growth. Santa Rosa now boasts fifty thousand jobs, compared to thirty-six thousand in 1972. A steadily expanding economy and tax base have encouraged Santa Rosa to view growth as a benign or even beneficial force. Santa Rosa has been one of the few cities able to reconcile environmental quality, a comfortable suburban lifestyle, and continued economic and residential development. (See table 11 for both cities' population growth.) Although these divergent attitudes toward the desirability of growth became evident in the mid-1970s, they had their beginnings twenty years earlier. They are best symbolized, perhaps, by an unlikely pair of products: wine and electronics.

TABLE 11

POPULATION AND HOUSING GROWTH IN NAPA AND
SANTA ROSA, 1950–80

	Napa		Santa Rosa	
	Population	*% of* *Napa County*	*Population*	*% of* *Sonoma County*
1950	13,575	29.1	17,903	17.3
1960	22,170	33.6	31,027	21.0
1970	35,978	45.5	50,000	24.4
1975	46,867	52.5	65,611	26.9
Percentage change				
1960–70	62.2%		61.1%	
1970–75	30.3%		31.1%	
Annualized growth rate				
1960–70	5.0%		4.9%	
1970–75	6.1%		6.2%	

	Napa			Santa Rosa		
	Total	*Single-* *Family* *Units*	*Multi-* *Family* *Units*	*Total*	*Single-* *Family* *Units*	*Multi-* *Family* *Units*
1970	12,718	9,471	2,709	19,132	13,866	4,751
1975	17,861	12,177	4,724	27,856	16,613	8,706
Percentage change						
1970–75	40.4%	28.5%	74.4%	45.6%	19.8%	83.2%

SOURCES: U.S. Census of Population, 1950, 1960, 1970; California Department of Finance Special Census and Estimates, 1975, 1980.

Growth Threatens Napa's Agricultural Base

In 1969, per capita wine consumption in the United States stood at 1.01 gallons annually, but by 1980 it reached 2.1 gallons per year. As the wine market grew, so did the acreage required for wine production and the number of operating vineyards. Leading this explosion, at least in the western United States, were the wines produced in the Napa Valley. In 1965, there were only 35 winemaking operations in the Napa Valley. According to the Napa Valley Grape Growers Association, there were more than 150 separate wineries operating in 1980. Wine production was naturally accompanied by wine tasting, and so tourism quickly became an important source of revenue for the little Napa Valley cities of Calistoga, Yountville, and St. Helena. Little wine is produced within the borders of the city itself, but as the economic, social, and political center of the Napa Valley, Napa is affected by wine production as much as any of its smaller sister cities.

By the mid-1970s, demand for housing was already threatening the grape-growing lands surrounding the city of Napa. Spurred by the expansion of government services, including health and education, the city's population more than doubled between 1960 and 1975. What had been a small rural city was transformed into a subregional retailing and distribution center. Highway connections between Napa and other Bay Area centers were improving, and a small but growing number of Napa's new residents were daily commuters to San Francisco or the East Bay. For many of these incoming households, Napa combined the advantages of a rural setting and lower housing prices with the amenities of a metropolitan area. Though hardly malicious in their intent to "close the door behind them," new residents were determined to avoid the urban congestion from which they had fled.

Like many small inland cities largely unencumbered by topological constraints, Napa had a radial pattern of residential growth (see map 5). Prior to World War II, the city's downtown (located where Napa Creek joins the Napa River) defined Napa's outer boundary. Today that area contains a mixture of apartments, two-family homes, and older, single-family detached houses. In the 1950s and early 1960s Napa grew in all directions, and a middle ring of moderately sized tract-style homes and larger semicustom homes developed along Napa's eastern hillsides and directly to the north and south of the expanding downtown. To accommodate the residential growth of the late 1960s, agricultural areas to the west and northwest were opened up, almost all of them to tracts of fairly large and expensive single-family homes. One outlying area in particular,

Browns Valley, has been the focal point of much of Napa's recent residential construction. Until the imposition of a construction moratorium in
August 1978, Browns Valley was the site of almost half of the city's new
housing starts.

Through the late 1960s, nearly four of every five new units constructed
were single-family homes. But by the early 1970s the supply of vacant,
serviceable land began to dwindle, and single-family housing starts lev-

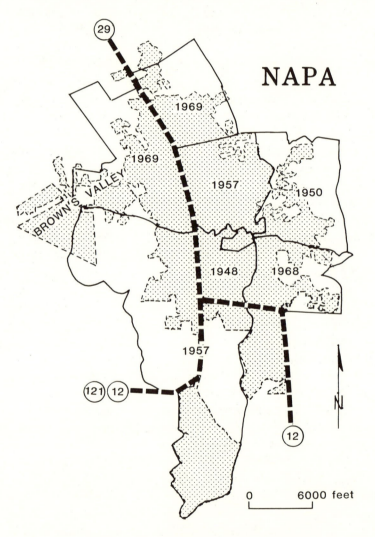

MAP 5.
NAPA: MEDIAN YEAR HOUSING BUILT, BY CENSUS TRACT.

eled off to 250–350 units per year—a range surprisingly constant from 1970 through 1978, except for the boom and bust years of 1972 and 1974 (figure 2). In contrast, multifamily starts have varied widely since the late 1960s. Favorable demographics, smaller household sizes, and tax incentives produced a brief boom in multifamily construction during 1970 and 1971. Since then, multifamily starts have varied inversely with single-family starts—the higher the number of single-family units, the lower the level of multifamily construction.

FIGURE 2.

NAPA AND SANTA ROSA HOUSING UNIT ADDITIONS.
Source: Napa Building Department, Santa Rosa
Building Department

The 1974 Napa County General Plan and the 1975 City of Napa General Plan were the first official documents to address the rising tension between the forces of urban development and those who hoped to preserve the Napa Valley as an agricultural center. The County General Plan recommended stabilizing county growth rates at 1 percent per year. The Plan's goals were simple and straightforward: "To plan for agriculture and related activities as the primary land uses in Napa County and concentrate urban uses in the county's existing cities and urban areas."[2] City governments were encouraged to adopt urban limit lines, if they had not already done so, and all other valley lands were classified as "agricultural resource" areas; hillside areas were to remain as open space. To implement these policies the county board of supervisors, through the Napa Planning Department, began a comprehensive effort to downzone county lands—in many cases to a minimum of one dwelling unit per forty acres. It was hoped that the combination of urban limit lines and downzoning would confine intense residential and commercial uses to existing urban areas. Where urban development had once threatened to spill over city boundaries and consume county lands, it would not be redirected inward.

As the focal point of county development pressures, the city of Napa was also trying to confront the growth issue. During the mid-1970s, the city council and the Planning Commission believed that the designation of a Rural-Urban Limit Line (RUL) and the judicious use of zoning would be sufficient to keep the year 2000 population below 75,000—a population limit the community supported through two plebiscites. Yet in early 1978, the planning staff notified the city council that residential growth had continued unabated, and some allocation system would be necessary. In August 1978, the city council on a three-to-two vote elected to suspend additional residential development for six months pending the consideration and adoption of an effective growth-management system. At first glance the moratorium seemed highly restrictive, but construction interests had anticipated some development limitation, and the immediate impact was lessened by a large backlog of previously approved developments.

Napa's construction industry is relatively small and unorganized, and the larger, unified business and construction interests failed to mobilize in opposition to the no-growth action. Moreover, the real estate lobby was too fragmented to mount any effective protest. Thus neither the residential development moratorium nor the subsequent Residential Development Management Plan (adopted by the Napa City Council in February 1979) has been the target of large-scale challenges by the building industry.*

_____

*One exception to this is the two legal suits being brought against Napa by the Raja Development Company.

The goals of the Residential Development Management Plan (RDMP) were clear from the start. Besides limiting yearly housing construction to less than 350 units, the RDMP was designed to encourage infill development and otherwise minimize single-family home construction at the urban fringe, where services were less accessible and more expensive. During the development of the RDMP, the point system used to evaluate competing projects became a key subject of debate. The Napa Planning Department favored a point system evenly split between locational and design criteria, while in an effort to keep local expenditures low, the city council pushed for a point system based primarily on locational and accessibility criteria. The yearly housing allocation was less of an issue. The community had supported an ultimate population of 75,000, and a formula was adopted that would allow the city to reach that level gradually. As it happens, Napa is now growing at a slower rate than first anticipated, and the formula may have to be modified downward in order to prevent large increases in the yearly permit allocation.

Santa Rosa: Growing and Growing

The 1970s were a period of impressive population growth and economic development in Santa Rosa. Between 1970 and 1979 the city added population at a rate of roughly 3,000 new residents per year. It is even more remarkable that almost 14,000 new housing units were added during that period, a growth rate of nearly 70 percent.

In those years Santa Rosa's growth pattern closely matched the standard process of suburbanization—an outlaying, previously independent city was gradually enveloped by an expanding, land-hungry metropolitan area. Highway 101 brought a variety of expansionary forces to southern Sonoma County. In the late 1960s many new and existing Bay Area firms, particularly those involved in "high technology" (electronics, instrumentation) and finance, were searching for growth opportunities. They sought an agreeable climate, pleasant environment, inexpensive land, a skilled but non-unionized labor force, and good access to regional and local markets. Hewlett-Packard was the first of many such firms to settle in Santa Rosa. The labor force followed, spurring population growth in the city of Santa Rosa and throughout Sonoma County.* At the same time, there was a shrinking supply of developable land in suburban Alameda and Contra Costa Counties, and particularly in Marin and San Mateo Counties. As a result, the search for developable parcels moved in

---

*In fact, too much labor followed, and despite its enviable record of job creation, Santa Rosa continues to suffer chronically high unemployment.

ever-widening circles, focused primarily along major highway corridors. In the North Bay, Marin County's high land prices, high construction costs, and restrictive land use policies pushed residential development across the border into Petaluma, leading to that city's now famous building permit rationing system. Stymied by Petaluma's growth management system, home builders flooded into Cotati, Santa Rosa, and Rohnert Park, which watched its population triple between 1970 and 1979.

Although some of southern Sonoma County's new householders remained tied to livelihoods in San Francisco, still others were Marin County employees who couldn't afford to live near their jobs. An ongoing rise in the number of commuters moving to Sonoma County has alarmed some who fear that their county might ultimately become a moderate-income bedroom suburb of San Francisco and Marin. Data show, however, that this trend is not significant; less than 8 percent of Santa Rosa's employed residents commute to Marin or San Francisco.

On the whole, the economy of Santa Rosa is extremely well balanced. About 25 percent of Santa Rosa's workers are employed in retail and wholesale trade. Manufacturing, transportation, and utilities add another 20 percent, while services, finance, and real estate contribute 25 percent of the city's employment. Santa Rosa's 1975 basic employment per capita, an indicator of economic vitality, is 20 percent higher than Napa's.

As in Napa, Santa Rosa's growth has occurred radially. The current and historical downtown area, located at the junction of Highways 101 and 12, is ringed by older single-family and multi-family neighborhoods developed during the 1940s and 1950s (see map 6). It was during the late 1950s and 1960s that residential construction began to extend outward along the flat corridors surrounding Highways 101 and 12, and then gradually moved up the hillside areas in the northeast. As late as 1970, most Santa Rosa homes lay within a 1.5 mile radius of the city's downtown area. To accommodate the massive in-migration of households during the early 1970s, the city annexed land in all directions, constrained only by the borders of Rohnert Park and Cotati in the south and the steep hillsides of the Sonoma Mountains to the northeast. In one of its last major acquisitions, Santa Rosa annexed the Oakmont corridor and extended city services and infrastructure more than seven miles out from the CBD to provide for an ambitious 1,500-unit planned development.

Annual housing starts dipped below the 1,000 mark only once during the 1970s—in 1975, the year of the nationwide housing recession. With land plentiful and relatively inexpensive, single-family homes have long been the predominant form of housing in Santa Rosa, and in 1970 three

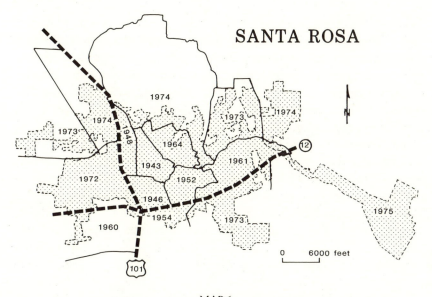

MAP 6.

SANTA ROSA: MEDIAN YEAR HOUSING BUILT,
BY CENSUS TRACT.

out of every four dwelling units in the city were single-family homes. As a result of an influx of smaller households, multifamily starts grew dramatically during the early 1970s, averaging almost 800 new units per year between 1970 and 1974. But as in so many other cities, multifamily construction failed to recover from the housing crash of 1974–75, and since 1975 has hovered between 200 and 350 new starts annually. Santa Rosa's low housing prices have contributed to an annual housing construction rate of 7 percent. Due both to the area's lower land costs and the economies of scale achievable in tract construction, as late as 1978 a family could purchase a 1,500-square-foot home for less than $70,000. Along with Napa, Santa Rosa is one of the two most affordable middle-sized cities in the Bay Area.

SAN RAFAEL AND NOVATO: MAINTAINING THE GOOD LIFE

Among advocates of open-space preservation, Marin County is highly regarded as one of the most successful practitioners of open-space and environmental-protection programs. Yet critics of such programs argue that environmental quality has been secured only at the sacrifice of affordable housing. While some residents point to the county's quality housing and expanses of parkland, others note that less than 10 percent of Marin County residents are members of minority groups. Whatever viewpoint one might hold, there is a tendency to see Marin County as a whole—a tendency that often obscures important local distinctions. Because of the county's comparative wealth, many see it as having escaped urban problems, sprawl, and the fiscal difficulties posed by Proposition 13. But upon closer inspection a rather different picture emerges.

The recent histories of Novato and San Rafael, the last of Marin's cities to be developed, are best understood in the broader context of North Bay growth. Throughout the last twenty-five years, residential and economic development has been pushing outward from the traditional centers of San Francisco and Oakland. Early residential construction in Marin County took place during the 1920s and 1930s on the flat, coastal corridor between San Rafael and Sausalito. Included in this developing plain were the cities of Larkspur, San Anselmo, and Fairfax. Lot sizes were generous, there was no shortage of developable land, and homes were large, reflecting the wealth of their owners. The completion of the Golden Gate Bridge in 1938 made southern Marin County accessible to the Bay Area's rapidly growing population. By the close of World War II, Sausalito, Belvedere, and Tiburon were being intensively developed, though steep hillsides and the large-lot zoning instituted by earlier residents made these latter areas more costly to develop, and later construction occurred at a relatively slow pace. The 1950s brought population growth throughout the Bay Area. Those Marin cities bordering Highway 101 south of San Rafael shared in the region's population surge of the 1950s and were largely built out by the early 1960s. But even though its population had doubled since 1950, Marin County in the 1960s was still regarded, as it is today, as a highly desirable place to live. Improvements to Highway 101 soon brought northern San Rafael and Novato into commuting range of San Francisco, and except for valley acreage in its northwest corner, San Rafael was also almost entirely developed by 1975.

Although San Rafael and Novato are neighbors, they remain quite different communities. As Marin County's oldest city, San Rafael is the county's employment and government center. It also boasts the county's most diverse population. Novato is the youngest city in Marin County. It developed primarily as a residential suburb and, despite the increasing growth pressures of the early 1970s, has successfully maintained its suburban and, in places, rural character. The numerous differences between the two cities exist for four historical reasons:

1. Downtown San Rafael stands at the intersection of Highway 101 and 17, Marin County's two gateways to the rest of the Bay Area. Because of the advantages of its location, San Rafael has long been the county's commercial and industrial center. With the construction of the Marin Civic Center, the last building designed by Frank Lloyd Wright, San Rafael became the focal point of Marin County's government and cultural activities.

2. San Rafael's residential development peaked in the 1950s and early 1960s, before the heyday of large-scale, single-family tract developers. The city's housing stock includes a mixture of multifamily dwellings, older and smaller single-family homes constructed in the ten-year period after World War II, and larger, more modern single-family homes, located primarily in the Terra Linda District.

3. Running out of developable land, the city of San Rafael annexed the village of Terra Linda and an unincorporated area between old San Rafael and Novato (map 7). In the process, San Rafael gained roughly 7,000 acres of

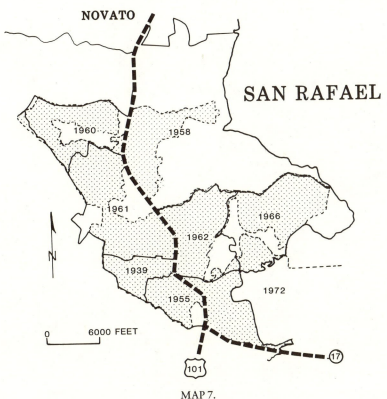

MAP 7.
SAN RAFAEL: MEDIAN YEAR HOUSING BUILT,
BY CENSUS TRACT.

land in which to expand. Parcels adjoining Highway 101 were reserved for commercial and industrial activity, and inland parcels were zoned for single-family homes or left unzoned as an unofficial way to reserve open space. Even today, some twenty years after the Terra Linda annexation, there are visible differences in character between older San Rafael, with its traditional downtown, and the newer residential and commercial areas in the Terra Linda District.

4. Topographical constraints prevented Novato from expanding radially as the demand for housing grew, so instead the city inched outward along three valley corridors. At first, new residential development was confined to the mile-wide Indian Valley corridor surrounding Highway 101. New housing construction next extended into the San Marin Valley, an east-west valley in northern Novato. Developed during the last decade has been the Ignacio Valley, a narrow east-west corridor in southern Novato (map 8).

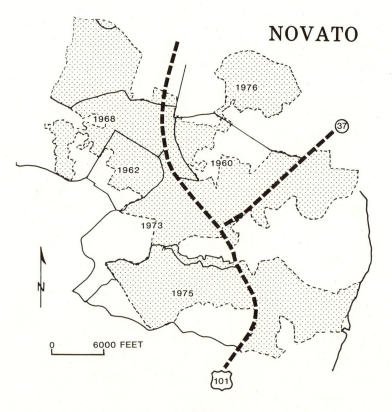

MAP 8.

NOVATO: MEDIAN YEAR HOUSING BUILT, BY CENSUS TRACT.

The County Connection

The recent history of land use policy in Novato and San Rafael is also the story of Marin County's efforts to grapple with the problem of excessive and unmanageable growth. More than any other Bay Area county, Marin has taken the lead in framing and coordinating local land use policy. As we shall see, Marin County was not always so aggressive.

The county's concern over residential development stemmed from more than the influx of new residents; it also reflected the solid consensus that development would destroy Marin's unique physical environment. Hence, when antigrowth land use policies were adopted in the early 1970s, they stressed open-space preservation and low-density, clustered development.

In 1960, the population of Marin County stood at 146,820. San Rafael, its largest city, had 20,500 inhabitants; Novato was a small town of 17,880. Ten years later, the number of Marin County residents had swelled to 208,000, San Rafael had grown to a population of 39,000 (table 12), and little Novato suddenly found itself a city of 31,000 people and the focal point of the county's growth. In just ten years the Marin urban corridor had grown from a series of separate towns into a twenty-mile continuum of urban and residential development.

Prior to the early 1970s, neither the Marin County Board of Supervisors nor the County Planning Department had coordinated population and growth data. Consequently, the level of growth that had occurred in the Marin urban corridor wasn't fully appreciated until the release of the 1970 Federal Census.

There were several additional factors contributing to the lack of "growth awareness" during the 1960s. First, Marin's eleven cities had experienced differing rates of residential expansion. Although San Rafael and Novato had seen their populations almost double during the 1960s, other older and more established cities such as Mill Valley, Sausalito, San Anselmo, and Fairfax grew by an average of only 1,500 residents. Second, growth was not perceived as a systematic problem simply because of the form it took. In the older and more established valley communities such as San Anselmo and Fairfax, new residential construction occurred not in the form of tract developments, but as small-scale additions to existing hill and valley neighborhoods. Because growth was occurring incrementally, there was little perception of degradation in environmental or community quality. Third, in the 1960s Marin County enjoyed greater access to accessible open space and parkland than any other Bay Area county.

TABLE 12

POPULATION AND HOUSING GROWTH IN NOVATO AND
SAN RAFAEL, 1950–80

	Novato		San Rafael	
	Population	*% of Marin County*	*Population*	*% of Marin County*
1950	—	—	13,850	16.2
1960	17,880	12.2	20,500	14.0
1970	31,006	15.0	39,000	18.9
1975	37,250	17.3	45,325	21.0
1980	42,550	18.4	44,300	19.2
Percentage change				
1960–70	73.4%		90.2%	
1970–80	37.2%		13.6%	
Annualized growth rate				
1960–70	5.7%		6.6%	
1970–80	3.2%		1.2%	

	Novato			San Rafael		
	Total	*Single-Family Units*	*Multi-Family Units*	*Total*	*Single-Family Units*	*Multi-Family Units*
1970	8,500	6,690	1,703	13,900	8,165	5,720
1975	12,745	—	—	18,412	—	—
Percentage change						
1970–75	49.9%	—	—	32.5%	—	—

SOURCES: U.S. Census of Population, 1950, 1960, 1970; California Department of Finance Special Census and Estimates, 1975 and 1980.

And since Marin's housing prices were higher than average, newcomers were overwhelmingly similar to existing residents in terms of income level, job choice, and lifestyle. Accordingly, the demand for public services remained low, and existing residents did not find their community's quality threatened by an influx of "outsiders." Finally, growth during the 1960s was generally regarded as desirable, even in Marin County. New households encouraged the expansion of local economies, and the entry of additional taxpayers kept property tax bills down, as new schools were constructed and cultural activities expanded. In short, growth was accompanied by a perceived improvement in the quality of the community. It is interesting to note that when Highway 101's peak-hour congestion reached an intolerable level, the roadway was widened to six lanes throughout most of Marin County.

Pulling In the Reins

During the 1960s, few Marin cities adopted policies intended to stem the tide of new residents. Land use controls consisted primarily of zoning and subdivision regulations, and in contrast to the wealthy suburbs of the northeast, large-lot zoning was not a widespread means of exclusion. Utility capacity was adequate to serve the expanding population, and to most people the term "open space" was synonymous with neighborhood parks. Although San Rafael and Novato were experiencing tremendous growth pressures during the 1960s, it was generally assumed that these communities had enough vacant land to handle the demand. In addition, both cities actually fueled residential growth pressures by zoning inexpensive outlying land for single-family homes.

But in 1968, there began a series of trends and events that would ultimately lead to a complete reversal of previous policies, culminating in the production of the 1973 Marin Countywide Plan. For the first time, there would be a concerted effort to slow—or even stop—the growth juggernaut.

The first of these trends was a growing awareness of the fragility of the physical environment. This awareness was marked at the federal level by the introduction of legislation that would ultimately become the National Environmental Policy Act (NEPA).[3] Throughout the United States, "ecology" and "the environment" were the newest rallying cry for popular protest. By 1970, concern over the destruction of the environment had become so widespread that "Earth Day" was being celebrated as a national holiday. The environmental movement found a natural constituency in Marin County. Many recently entering households had located in Marin precisely because of the county's rural flavor. Open space was plentiful and easily accessible, narrow wooded valleys had been maintained between the imposing ridgelands of the coastal range, deer roamed freely throughout the county, and the significant number of working farms and ranches proved that agriculture didn't have to be incompatible with suburban development. There was also widespread agreement that Marin's combination of baylands, rugged mountain areas, ridgelines, wooded valleys, coastal wetlands, and beaches was unmatched in the United States. In Marin County, "environmentalism" had become synonymous with "preservation"—a code word for blocking the in-migration of outsiders.

The county's growth trends first received widespread attention with the release of Phase One of the Marin County Balanced Transportation Plan in 1970. In the wake of strong local opposition to new highway construction during the mid-1960s, the Marin County Board of Supervisors had established the Balanced Transportation Program to coordinate transportation and land use planning in Marin County. The Phase One report estimated that left unchecked, Marin's population would reach 800,000 by 2020 (from the 1970 estimate of 208,000), and that a massive roadbuilding program would be needed to serve projected commuter demand. Citizens and elected officials greeted these estimates with nothing less than horror. It was this vehement reaction that led to the decision to undertake the Marin Countywide Plan. In the process of developing the Countywide Plan, local planners revised the previous population forecast of 800,000 residents by 2020 downward to 365,000 residents by 1990—still a frightening rate of growth to most county residents. These estimates were based on what now seems an incomplete understanding of regional and land economics. Forecasts were generated by extrapolating recent growth rates, and little attention was paid to the historical development patterns of the larger Bay Area.

Another antidevelopment factor was the belated realization that ten of the eleven urban corridor communities had exhausted, or would shortly exhaust, their supplies of easily developed land; only Novato had any significant land reserves. Even San Rafael, which had accommodated 20,000 new residents in ten years, was running out of vacant residential land. Several large-scale tract developers had recently entered the Novato housing market, and it was feared that Marin County's hillsides and ridgelines would soon be layered with acres of single-family housing tracts.

The Countywide Plan crystallized these and other growth-related concerns. Unlike other county governments in the Bay Area, the Marin County Board of Supervisors and Planning Department took the lead role in determining the land use, housing, economic, and environmental issues facing Marin cities and villages. But this had not always been the case. County legislators and agencies had previously limited land use decisions to regulating use of the 250,000 Marin County acres under county jurisdiction. But with the frightening growth projections published by the Balanced Transportation Program, it seemed imperative that any major study be conducted on a countywide level and that the county coordinate any policies to slow growth.

Preparation of Marin Countywide Plan was the responsibility of the Marin County Planning Commission and the City-County Planning Council. In addition, various special-assessment districts and service agencies were involved in drafting the Plan's growth estimates. The plan preparation process consumed more than three years and involved fifteen separate studies, surveys, and preliminary reports. The Plan is regarded as a landmark example of a well-conceived, well-written, and comprehensive county general plan. Its opening sentences accurately convey some of the sentiments of Marin residents:

We want to retain the open spaces surrounding our communities, but development continues to encroach upon the hillsides before they can be secured in open space. Market projections show population increasing at an average of about 7,700 per year until 1990, compared with about 6,300 per year over the past decade. The Countywide Plan would result in an average annual increase of about 4,500 persons over the next eighteen years. . . . We would like to live and raise our families in diverse communities with many kinds of people, but rising housing costs are making it difficult for any but the rich and childless to live in Marin. . . . Many Marin residents would prefer working close to home, but are forced into the daily commuting routine because of the lack of job opportunities here. . . . Many of us would be willing to leave our cars at home and take transit, but adequate service for trips within the county is still not available. . . . Present individually adopted plans for local communities if carried out, would not reverse these trends, but in many cases would make Marin's problems worse. Many of these plans accommodate growth trends rather than changing them, and they would produce an ultimate population of about 800,000 in Marin, with little open space remaining. These individually adopted plans have generally been prepared by different jurisdictions at different times, without regard for their relation to plans for other communities or for their cumulative effect on the county as a whole.[4]

The goal of the Countywide Plan is, in its simplest form, to reduce the county's anticipated 1990 population from the "free market" estimate of 365,000 to a more manageable 300,000. This reduction meant that some 23,000 fewer dwelling units would be built, 5,500 acres of open space would be saved, and 61,000 additional acres of open space would be permanently preserved. Gross residential densities would rise from the 1970 estimate of 3.0 units per acre to 3.5 units per acre (versus 3.6 units per acre under the "market scenario"); total civilian employment would rise by 35,000. Despite what some critics have alleged to be a "no-growth" attitude, the Countywide Plan's vision of the future encompassed substantial residential, economic, and population expansion.

The county's major strategies for slowing development included preempting vacant land through open-space acquisition or zoning, and making it more difficult for private developers to gain project approvals. Tightly defined urban limit lines assured that these measures would be implemented on county lands. But if these growth-limiting strategies were to succeed, it was crucial that they be adopted by Marin's cities, particularly Novato and San Rafael—the two cities expected to bear the brunt of development pressures.

Both Novato and San Rafael were receptive to the county's suggestion. San Rafael's recent policies had begun to focus on environmental protection. For example, in September 1972, fully twelve months before the adoption of the Marin Countywide Plan, the San Rafael City Council placed before the electorate a $2,250,000 bond issue for the purpose of purchasing vacant or agricultural land. The bond issue passed with a 75 percent majority. In a subsequent countywide election, San Rafael citizens approved a ten-cent (per $100 of assessed valuation) property tax increase, also for the purpose of acquiring open space. In Novato, as part of a city General Plan update, the Planning Commission heard neighborhood and community groups express overwhelming concern over unmanaged growth. The Novato City Council revised the Plan to include strict density guidelines intended to reduce Novato's residential growth potential, as well as a statement suggesting that new dwelling units be limited to five hundred per year.

Land Use Policy in the Slow-Growth Era

Marin County's battle against unconstrained residential development will be much easier in the 1980s. The Association of Bay Area Governments now predicts a 1990 county population of 250,000, rather than 300,000 as estimated in the Marin Countywide Plan. (As of January 1980, the population of Marin County stood at 225,200.) Since the adoption of the Countywide Plan in October 1973, ten of Marin's eleven incorporated cities have either lost population or added fewer than 300 new residents; only Novato has had a population expansion of more than 1,000.

Why did this reversal occur, and what role have county-initiated housing and land use policies played in reducing Marin County's growth rate? We now realize that the projections included in the Marin Countywide Plan (as well as the earlier Balanced Transportation Study) greatly overestimated the county's growth potential. In essence, the two sets of projections assumed that the rate of population growth would continue to accelerate, though by 1970 it was already beginning to slow. In addition, the projections failed to take into account the very real development constraints that a diminishing vacant land supply were beginning to impose. The dwindling supply of land appears to have been a key factor in slowing growth.

According to the Marin Countywide Plan, the urban corridor in 1970 contained roughly 9,000 acres of vacant, residentially developable land. Of this land, 25 percent was located in the Richardson Bay communities of Belvedere, Mill Valley, Sausalito, and Tiburon; 10 percent in Larkspur and Corte Madera; and another 5 percent in the inland communities of

Fairfax, San Anselmo, and Ross. The remaining 5,400 vacant acres were distributed almost evenly between San Rafael and Novato. The Plan estimated that these 5,400 acres, developed at gross residential densities varying between 3.5 and 4.2 units per acre, could accommodate an additional 20,000 dwelling units by 1990. But how much of this land was genuinely developable? In projecting land totals the county planning staff had drawn on local government inventories, including all parcels either zoned or unzoned but anticipated for residential construction. The holding capacities of particular parcels had not been investigated.

The Association of Bay Area Governments tried to remedy this shortcoming in its 1975 inventory of local land use policy. All vacant land—not just residentially zoned land—was divided into one of two categories: "prime developable land," meaning parcels zoned or committed for development for which services and infrastructure could economically be provided, and "secondary developable land," which included all other vacant parcels.[5] ABAG's findings were substantially different from the county's. Specifically, ABAG found that far less economically developable land existed in Marin County than had been estimated five years earlier. Although all eleven incorporated cities had maintained large reserves of vacant (secondary developable) land, most was on ridgelines, in unstable soil areas, or too far from existing services. Thus, the majority of vacant land parcels were not directly in the path of development. Only San Rafael and Novato had large holdings of vacant land remaining; and in the case of San Rafael, much of that land consisted of infill parcels or unzoned acreage reserved for open space. The Countywide Plan had greatly overestimated the urban corridor's development potential.

The land supply story has another dimension to it: price. Urban areas typically expand outward from the existing fringe where land (and hence construction) is comparatively inexpensive. Even in the 1960s, when vacant land was available in southern Marin County, it cost in excess of $50,000 per raw acre. Many builders responded by moving north to Terra Linda and Novato, where land was less expensive and, thanks to improvements in Highway 101, accessible to the San Francisco employment market. Soon afterward, supplies of easily developed vacant land began to dwindle, and Novato land prices began to escalate sharply. By the late 1970s land prices in Novato had reached $50,000 per acre, and affordable housing was more and more difficult to produce.

As a result of market forces and government policies, Marin County housing starts have decreased steadily. According to estimates provided by the California Department of Finance, only 1,336, 1,082, and 858 new housing units were constructed in Marin County in 1976, 1977, and

1978, respectively—an annual housing-start rate ranging from a high of 1.5 percent (1976) to 1.0 percent (1978).

In hindsight, it appears that the policies embraced in the Marin Countywide Plan have been successful beyond even the county's initial expectations. But along the way the motivation behind these various land use policies appears to have changed from managing and reducing growth to excluding new development. In particular, the administration of local ordinances now makes it extremely difficult to construct more than a few dwelling units at a time in Marin County.

There seem to be two reasons for this shift in purpose. First, the reduction in Marin County growth that occurred during the 1970s was basically the result of private market forces. Local land use restrictions made residential construction difficult, but did not stop it. Second, many residents interpreted the adoption of a policy to manage growth as an intention to exclude growth. As development slowed, and preservationist groups were flushed by their apparent success, they began training their sights on any and all new development. What had been conceived as a countywide plan for allocating growth became a neighborhood mechanism for excluding outsiders.

There was one more thing that validated and reinforced the wisdom of slow-growth policies: the drought. Unlike most other Bay Area counties that draw their water supplies from the Sierra snowpack, Marin County depends entirely on local reservoirs fed by ridgeland runoff. As the drought continued into 1978, Marin's water resources were quickly exhausted. What had been a minor inconvenience swiftly became a major problem. Water was strictly rationed, a connecting pipeline to Contra Costra County via the Richmond–San Rafael Bridge was quickly constructed, and several cities adopted temporary moratoriums on new water service hookups. County officials and residents were faced with the reality that their lifestyle *was* directly related to the local ecology, and that the facilities they depended on could, in some circumstances, be inadequate.

CONCLUSION

The six communities examined have been affected by the pressures of suburbanization in slightly different ways. In the cases of Fremont, Concord, and San Rafael, postwar development pressures were similar in terms of time frames and intensity, but each community's unique historical, physical, and economic characteristics have considerably influenced the direction of growth. Ultimately, the impact of urbanization depends on a community's stage of development, its character, and the kinds of pressures it experiences. For example, Concord easily accommodated new development by establishing new residential tracts radially. Little effort was made to shape the form of new development, and the city was gradually built out as development approached the city limits. Now Concord aims planning efforts at preserving its current character and developing parcels that have been passed over. Though it faced growth pressures similar to Concord's, Fremont's development history is quite different. From the very beginning Fremont was interested in planning and consciously worked to weave together the five villages within its boundaries. Perhaps because Fremont has always seen itself as a planned community, new development has been well integrated into the community over the years. Fremont has absorbed about the same amount of development as Concord; it has simply been able to do a better job of it.

Napa and Santa Rosa are extremely different. Neither has experienced the classic pattern of suburbanization. Both developed as county seats with indigenous economies that predate suburban development. Napa and Santa Rosa have accommodated considerable development in the past ten years. In the case of Napa, the environmental pressures generated by suburbanization led to a backlash against growth. Because of substantial agricultural land conversion, the city and county of Napa have been controlling the location and rate of development. Much of the negative reaction to development has been based on the importance of the wine-growing industry in the county, and the perception that more development would greatly damage this important resource. Unlike Napa, Santa Rosa has continued to grow at a rapid rate and is still accommodating additional development. Urban development has been viewed more favorably in Santa Rosa than in Napa, for two reasons. First, Santa Rosa's economic future is less dependent on agriculture, and second, since it is not as fully integrated into the Bay Area economy as Napa, it must accept new development in order to generate its own economic base.

In Marin County, San Rafael is nearing the end of its era of suburbanization, while Novato is still a hotbed of development activity. Since county policy channels development into the urban corridor, growth pressures will intensify even further in Novato, Marin County's last possible outlet for expansion. There was recently an unsuccessful attempt to stop growth in Novato; others will undoubtedly be made in the future.

Each community studied is at a different stage in its growth cycle, and each is experiencing development pressure. The next chapter examines ways in which each city has moved to control and shape its growth.

CHAPTER FOUR

Responding to Growth: Local Land Use Controls in Six Bay Area Cities

Bay Area suburbanization pressures have been strong. Some cities such as Fremont, Fairfield, and Sunnyvale have welcomed growth, regarding it as beneficial and necessary for the development of a healthy economic base. These communities have become the growth centers of the 1980s. Other communities, such as Napa, Petaluma, and Vacaville, view growth as less benevolent, having seen it convert acres of agricultural land and open space to residential subdivisions. This chapter examines these varying responses by looking at the land use policies of the six case study communities.

My analysis has been based not on a few controversial projects proposed, but on the full spectrum of local controls used to shape development in the six communities, in order to provide a more accurate picture of what local land use controls have been implemented, and why.

Two of the six case towns are clearly progrowth: Fremont and Santa Rosa. Both view expansion as a means to develop their economies, and a way to avoid becoming an economically dependent suburban satellite. Concord is a mature community that, rather than attempting to limit development, has decided to build out slowly and gracefully. In terms of attitude, San Rafael comes close to Concord: it too is close to being built out, and development moves at a slow pace. Napa and Novato are the two towns attempting most aggressively to limit population growth. Both have been hard-hit by development in the past ten years, and many newcomers are exerting considerable pressure for the adoption of growth controls. A growth management proposal was recently defeated in Novato, and Napa's program has been shelved. However, when the building industry recovers from the national recession, and growth pressures reassert themselves, growth control proposals are sure to reappear in both towns.

STEADY AS SHE GOES: CONTROLLING DEVELOPMENT IN CONCORD AND FREMONT

By the mid-1970s regional growth trends had widened differences between Fremont and Concord. In 1978, housing production in Concord began for the first time to reflect that city's declining land supply. According to Building Department records, permits for 438 new units were taken out in 1979, a 46 percent drop from the average for the previous two years. Local planners project that Concord will grow by less than 200 households per year between 1980 and 2000.[1]

Concord officials say the city's land development policy for the 1980s will be "steady as she goes," meaning no major shifts in current policies, ordinances, or regulations. City planners acknowledge that the lifting of the sewer moratorium sometime in the early 1980s will briefly accelerate the construction of housing in the moratorium area, but expect that land supply constraints will keep building to a trickle over the long run.[2] At least one Concord planner indicated that the decreasing availability of buildable land may spur the Planning Commission to become more critical of poorly conceived projects and more aggressive in shaping the design process. Like the mature bay plain cities, Concord is finding that its major housing problems have to do with existing housing. In particular, the city has become very concerned about condominium conversion.

Fremont's future is more difficult to forecast. Since 1978, an increasing number of Santa Clara County firms unable to find suitable vacant commercial or industrial land in Palo Alto, Mountain View, Santa Clara, Sunnyvale, and San Jose have been moving east to Fremont and Milpitas. Likewise, an increasing number of households unable to find affordable housing in these same Santa Clara communities have been buying homes in Fremont and Newark. This influx has caused an increase in speculation on Fremont real estate of all kinds: commercial, industrial, and residential. Another effect has been an increase in the city's housing prices, which are bid up by arriving households, many of which boast higher incomes than most current residents.

Neither ABAG nor the city of Fremont expects this trend to be reversed in the near future. Until the current housing start slowdown, Fremont was growing at a consistent rate of 3,000 to 4,000 persons per year. As the nation slowly recovers from the 1980–82 recession, housing starts are expected to pick up rapidly. According to ABAG, the spillover effect will peak by the mid-1980s with a growth rate of 3,000 new residents per year. Afterwards Fremont's yearly population expansion is expected to drop below 2,000, declining to less than 1,000 by 1990.[3] Until recently, the Fremont Department of Economic Development estimated that the city's ultimate population would be in the neighborhood of 150,000. Now, however, local planners admit that these estimates were probably too low, and that the ABAG year 2000 forecast of 163,000 is more realistic. There is clearly enough vacant land in the community to accommodate that level of growth, but development will increasingly occur in the outlying, environmentally sensitive Northern Plains area. Exactly how much land will be consumed depends on the mix of single- and multifamily dwelling units. While neither ABAG, the city of Fremont, nor any large South Bay builders is willing to speculate on future housing mixes, development may become denser as land costs rise. However, as in Concord, an increasing percentage of new units will be semicustom homes on large lots, designed to appeal to upper-income homeowners with existing equity. Discussions with area builders reveal that many are planning to construct homes in the $130,000-and-up range. Of the very large builders, only Citation Homes continues to provide "starter homes."

As the recipient of South Bay growth spillover, Fremont will continue to grow through the 1980s. Although land use regulations may be used to minimize the fiscal and environmental impact of new construction, the city is not expected to limit the supply of housing or the rate of land conversion.

Land Use Regulation

Both Concord and Fremont have aimed their land use and housing policies at regulating the quality of development, not its rate. This emphasis is evident in the general plans of both communities. Concord's General Plan, which was last updated in 1971, is still regarded as current. Its goals convey the nature of the city's concerns with development:

- Orderly growth with balanced land uses.

- Preservation of open space and natural features.

- Protection of residential amenities and the provision of high levels of services to residents.

- Benefits to the community of a broad tax base and efficient use of public funds.

Goals of the 1975 Fremont General Plan are directed more toward continued growth:

- Development of Fremont as a single, unified city.
- Growth of Fremont as a physically, socially, economically, and culturally balanced city.
- Provision of optimum public improvements at the lowest possible cost.
- Retention of natural differences in hills, plain, and bay.
- Development of an adequate employment and tax base.

Recent general plans for many other Bay Area communities reflect the notion that additional growth is inconsistent with environmental quality. These city governments may explicitly limit residential growth by implementing policies such as Napa's Residential Development Management Plan (RDMP), which includes a ceiling on the number of dwelling units constructed per year. In contrast, Fremont and Concord continue to believe that orderly and balanced development need not entail widespread environmental destruction. Their development policies are intended to shape rather than constrain growth. In Fremont and Concord, land use regulations stress the need to produce pleasant suburban neighborhoods, maintain community services, and reduce the municipal tax burden.

Urban Service Boundaries and Annexation

The Concord city limits define the area in which the city provides services such as police and fire protection and sewer systems. Concord is surrounded on three sides by neighboring communities—Walnut Creek to the south, Pleasant Hill to the west, and Clayton to the east. In addition to its incorporated area within the city limits, Concord has a "sphere of influence" including over seven additional square miles of undeveloped land north of the city. Concord's land use powers and municipal services extend into this LAFCO-designated area. However, Concord has no current plans to extend sewer and water lines beyond its incorporated area, and city planners report that pressures to do so have been minimal.

Prior to the mid-1970s, Concord frequently annexed county lands committed for development or already partially developed. But due to the scarcity of such lands, Proposition 13, and pressures to service incorporated areas, annexation virtually ceased in 1977. Because Concord is surrounded on three sides by cities, and because development pressure in the city's northern areas has not materialized, Concord's annexation and urban-service policies have not been major constraints to growth. The situation is much the same in Fremont, where the spatial limits of development are defined by neighboring communities and topographical features—not city policies.

Density Restrictions

While residential density ceilings do not directly limit growth, they often restrain it. But fortunately, this has not turned out to be the case in either Fremont or Concord. The largest density classification is the low-to-medium range in which a maximum of eight to sixteen dwelling units are permitted per acre. Lower-density areas are located along hillsides, higher-density areas in or near the CBD. A second relevant feature of Concord's General Plan is the Land Use Intensity (LUI) system, under which maximum floorspace-to-lot-area ratios are established. Given the current guidelines, the city could ultimately accommodate over 44,000 dwelling units—some 7,500 more than the city's estimated 1979 housing stock. That means that at an average of 2.75 persons per household, Concord's population could grow by 20,625.

The density guidelines in Fremont's General Plan are completely integrated with that city's zoning. Each zoning classification corresponds to a dwelling-unit-per-gross-acre limit as set forth in the General Plan (table 13). Normally a builder is allowed to construct the maximum number of units specified for a given area/zoning classification. For example, in the case of an R-1-6 district (6,000-square-foot minimum lot size)—Fremont's most common residential designation—builders can normally construct up to five units per gross acre. If, however, a builder elects to

TABLE 13

FREMONT'S RESIDENTIAL ZONING CATEGORIES

Classification		Minimum Lot Size
Residential estate	(RE-1)	1 Acre
	(RE-1/2)	1/2 Acre
Single-family residential[a]	(R-1-6)	6,000 sq. ft.
	(R-1-8)	8,000 sq. ft.
	(R-1-10)	10,000 sq. ft.
One- and two-family residential	(R-2-6)	6,000 sq. ft.
	(R-2-8)	8,000 sq. ft.
Multifamily residential	(R-G-25)	2,500 sq. ft.[b]
	(R-G-15)	1,500 sq. ft.[b]
	(R-G-X)	As specified
Planned district		As specified

SOURCE: City of Fremont Zoning Ordinance, 1979.
[a]Lot area per dwelling unit.
[b]Exclusive of step densities.

vary the lot density within a particular project and pays an additional fee, greater densities are permitted. For single-family homes, payment of an additional $1,000 per unit will allow the builder to construct some units at a gross residential density of six units per acre. Thus Fremont's Step Density System provides incentives for builders to construct projects of mixed lot sizes, but generally the incentive is effective only in the case of larger projects.

Zoning

Zoning ordinances are the most well known and widely employed form of local land use regulation. Initially, zoning was used to segregate inconsistent land uses and to specify maximum densities. Over the years zoning ordinances have broadened to cover additional lot characteristics such as minimum length, width, and setback. According to California statutes, a city's zoning map must be in accord with its general plan, a requirement both Concord and Fremont have met.

Both cities rely on the municipal zoning ordinance as the principal basis for local land use control. Fremont's zoning ordinance, last updated in 1972, incorporates twenty-five general districts and specifies use, height, and lot standards for each. The five residential districts are further broken down into subgroups according to minimum lot size. For example, Fremont's most common residential district, R-1-6 (single-family residential), permits a minimum lot size of 6,000 square feet. (See table 13.)

Concord's zoning ordinance also specifies twenty-five zoning districts, of which seventeen are set aside for residential uses (table 14). Eleven separate single-family districts are listed, ranging in minimum lot size from 6,000 to 200,000 square feet. Multifamily districts are classified by lot area per dwelling unit; they range from low-density Duplex Residential Districts (D-3, 3,000-square-foot lot area per dwelling unit) to High Density Apartment Districts (M-I, 1,000-square-foot lot area per dwelling unit). In addition, Concord's zoning ordinance includes two residential classifications, LUI-4R and LUI-5R, which allow a broad variety of residential uses but set maximum densities. LUI District standards are drawn directly from the Concord General Plan. The LUI-4R District permits a maximum of eight units per acre; between eight and sixteen units can be constructed on an acre zoned LUI-4R-5R.

Despite the differences in their zoning classifications, the zoning ordinances of Fremont and Concord are quite similar. Single-family residential uses account for the spatial majority of residential land uses, and both cities allow single-family lot sizes down to 6,000 square feet. Multifamily

TABLE 14

CONCORD'S RESIDENTIAL ZONING CATEGORIES

Classification	Minimum Lot Size
Single-family residential	
R-6	6,000 sq. ft.
R-7	7,000 sq. ft.
R-7.5	7,500 sq. ft.
R-8	8,000 sq. ft.
R-10	10,000 sq. ft.
R-12	12,000 sq. ft.
R-15	15,000 sq. ft.
R-20	20,000 sq. ft.
R-40	40,000 sq. ft.
R-100	100,000 sq. ft.
R-200	200,000 sq. ft.
Multifamily residential	
D-3	3,000 sq. ft.
M-2.5	2,500 sq. ft.
M-1.8	1,800 sq. ft.
M-1	1,000 sq. ft.
APO—apartment/professional office	
Planned district	

SOURCE: City of Concord Zoning Ordinance, 1979.

districts are generally located around existing commercial/service centers and transit corridors. As a result of these shared characteristics, the two communities are also similar in terms of average residential lot sizes and housing styles. Similarities in housing style extend beyond physical dimensions; in both Concord and Fremont newer subdivisions are designed around cul-de-sacs, parks, or schools. This design style has been particularly popular among builders because it combines both high densities and privacy.

Neither city has prepared detailed breakdowns of acreage by zoning classification, although Concord has compiled rough estimates by category (table 15). Existing single-family housing occupies 47 percent of Concord's incorporated area (13.44 square miles); there is 0.5 square miles of multifamily units. Vacant or developable parcels account for 1.46 square miles, of which 90 percent are reserved for single- and 10 percent for multifamily construction. In Fremont, according to summaries of ABAG data for 1975, 7.85 square miles were in residential use. After adding local service uses and street acreage and dividing by the number of

TABLE 15

CONCORD: LAND AREA BY USE, 1979

	Land Area (sq. miles)	% of Total Land Area
Single-family	13.44	46.5
Multifamily	.50	1.7
Commercial	1.31	4.5
Industrial	.63	2.2
Military	8.64	29.9
Open space/parks/schools	2.87	9.9
Vacant	1.46	5.1
Total	28.85	100.0

SOURCE: City of Concord, 1979.

dwelling units, these figures translate to a gross residential density of 3.6 units per residential use acre. Duplicating the same calculation for Concord yields 4.1 units per gross residential use acre. Although these density ranges are comparable, the 0.5 difference in units per acre is related to Concord's larger stock of multifamily housing.

Differences Between Concord and Fremont

There are three important differences between the zoning laws of Concord and Fremont, all of which have had practical implications for local development patterns. The first distinction is in the role of planned districts. In Fremont, the Planned District classification is intended to facilitate the construction of residential neighborhoods with a wide variety of lot sizes and housing styles. Much the same logic underlies Concord's Planned District zoning regulations, with one important exception: whereas Fremont's Planned Districts can be established only upon the request of a builder, Concord's were established by the city during its last comprehensive rezoning in 1971. In fact, most of Concord's larger remaining parcels of vacant land, including the Newhall parcel at the city's eastern edge, are currently zoned Planned District. By eliminating the rezoning step for those builders desiring to take advantage of Planned District design flexibility, the Concord system greatly shortens the plan approval process. This contrasts with Fremont's system, under which builders must apply for rezoning to the Planned District category. It appears that few builders believe the extra design latitude is worth the additional project approval time; only twelve residential Planned Districts were created in Fremont between 1976 and 1978.

The second difference between Fremont and Concord is that Fremont has a Step Density System. Under this system, builders can construct a portion of a project's units on smaller sized lots than specified in the Fremont Zoning Ordinance, provided that the average density of the entire project conforms to General Plan guidelines. This system affords builders one of the primary advantages of a Planned District—flexible lot sizes and designing—without requiring a potentially lengthy Planned District rezoning. The ease and necessity of obtaining a rezoning also differs in the two cities. In Fremont, many of the larger outlying parcels now being funneled into the residential development process are zoned for agricultural use or as agricultural hillside areas. Rezoning to a Planned District or residential district requires the approval of both the Fremont Planning Commission and the Fremont City Council, and can be a time-consuming process. In Concord, where the city processes considerably fewer subdivision and development applications, the rezoning process is quicker.

Finally, Fremont's zoning ordinance is set apart from Concord's by its historical goal of combining five separate districts into a modern suburban city. By initially zoning parcels along Fremont Boulevard for commercial and multifamily uses, and later creating a special Central Business District, Fremont planners hoped to de-emphasize the purely local centers of Irvington, Centreville, Niles, Mission San Jose, and Warm Springs. Similarly, the designation of a single large industrial district in southern Fremont represented an attempt to end the previous fragmentation of industrial areas. Although the older village centers are still evident, Fremont's zoning policies have, by and large, succeeded in integrating the five districts. In Concord, zoning ordinances have been used primarily to enforce existing land use patterns: commercial and industrial activities at the city's historical center, surrounded by residential areas.

Neither in Concord nor in Fremont have zoning ordinances been used to restrict residential growth. On the contrary, each city's zoning ordinances incorporate incentives for development of detached single-family homes. In Concord, these incentives consist of relatively speedy rezonings and the existence of flexible Planned Districts. Fremont's Step Density system allows builders to bypass the lengthy Planned District rezoning procedure and still propose flexible high-density designs. In both cities, residential zoning is heavily biased toward small lots (6,000 or 8,000 square feet), with large-lot and agricultural zoning utilized primarily in outlying areas.

Ensuring Quality Development

Modern zoning ordinances specify not only permissible uses and minimum lot sizes, but also lot length and width, setback limits, and building height. Critics of municipal zoning have charged that these various regulations are exclusionary because they set housing quality standards and minimum production cost. But while this may be true for other Bay Area cities, it is not true for Fremont or Concord. In these two communities, residential land falls under a wide variety of zoning classifications, with the greatest supply in the 6,000- to 8,000-square-foot minimum lot size category. In addition, both cities have set aside substantial acreage for multifamily residential development. Finally, density restrictions can be reduced even further by using such means as Concord's Planned Districts and Fremont's Step Density System. In short, there is little evidence that either Fremont or Concord is using its zoning regulations in an exclusionary manner, or that zoning regulations add greatly to the cost of producing new housing.

However, both cities do use subdivision regulations to ensure development quality. Table 16, which summarizes these subdivision requirements, reveals some important differences between the two communities. In addition to basic subdivision improvements such as streets, curbs, and

TABLE 16

REQUIRED SUBDIVISION IMPROVEMENTS IN CONCORD
AND FREMONT

Improvement	Concord	Fremont
Noise barriers (generally walls)	varies with location	X
Streets and thoroughfares	X	X
Curbs, gutters, and sidewalks	X	X
Utility lines (sewer, water, and electrical)	varies with location	X
Lots in conformance with applicable zoning standards	X	X
Drainage and erosion controls	X	X
Fire hydrants and water delivery system	hydrants only	X
Utility hookups for each lot	X	X
Street lighting	X	X
Street trees and mailboxes	X	X
Telephone hookups for each lot		X
Railroad crossings		X

SOURCE: Concord and Fremont Subdivision Ordinances.

sidewalks, Fremont builders must provide sewer and water utility mains as needed. Concord developers building in the sewer moratorium area must now also provide additional sewer capacity, but water service is still provided by the Contra Costa County Water District.

When Fremont was first incorporated in 1956, city planners recognized that new residential construction would generally be provided by large developers. But in looking to the East, the Midwest, and even the San Francisco Peninsula for models, Fremont planners were often dismayed at what they saw: row upon row of identical houses, poorly constructed, on minuscule lots. To prevent occurrence of a similar pattern, Fremont adopted a number of zoning and subdivision ordinances aimed at ensuring quality development: two-car garages would be required for all single-family houses, lots would be subdivided no smaller than 6,000 square feet, residential streets would be wide, with proper curbs and sidewalks, and careful erosion controls would be implemented.

At the same time, planners also realized that the developing city's tax base was insufficient to subsidize new capital improvements fully, particularly roadways and utility capacity. Fremont's solution was like many other suburban cities: require builders to provide streets, sidewalks, and utility lines. Because land was inexpensive, readily available, and suitable for very large housing tracts, builders could realize substantial economies of scale in production. At the same time, housing would be plentiful, affordable, and of generally high quality, and the fiscal burdens of development on the city would be minimized.

In many respects, the "developer pays" strategy has been a successful one. Even today, more than twenty years after many of these ordinances were first proposed, Fremont subdivisions are recognized as being superior to their counterparts in Union City—a city that imposes fewer requirements for subdivision improvements. The apparent success of Fremont's policy has ensured its continuation. In fact, Fremont has imposed additional requirements on builders in the last twenty years. First, the city moved to require parkland dedication (or a $300-per-unit fee in lieu of land). In 1975, a new dwelling unit construction tax was imposed to provide for the construction of offsite capital improvements. Finally, after the passage of Proposition 13, a one-time school impact fee was imposed. Yet despite these very substantial increases in fee costs, the lure of developable land has continued to draw builders to Fremont.

Unlike Fremont, Concord has not been guided by a single, unified development plan. Although residential development during the late 1940s and early 1950s was generally in a radial pattern centered in Concord's commercial core, it had occurred piecemeal, and large tract developments were uncommon. Accordingly, extensions of sewer and water service were modest in scale, and new capacity was less expensive than in Fremont, where new water mains might be required for each developing tract. Concord's utility capacity was partially subsidized through the rate base, and builders were not required to provide water or sewer trunk lines.

However, Concord's position on subdivision improvements changed substantially with the imposition of a sewer-related moratorium on building permits in June 1977. Now builders can develop in the moratorium area only if they agree to finance construction of a sewer main along Clayton Valley Road. The moratorium was to be lifted in June 1980, but Concord planners now admit that the ban may remain in effect for several months beyond the original termination date.

Charting the Project Approval Process

The process of administering all these individual ordinances and policies varies greatly in complexity, depending on the type and location of the proposed development and the expertise of the builder. At a minimum, the approval process may take two months and involve the granting of a single building permit. More frequently, the project approval process involves a half-dozen steps, several reviewing agencies, and numerous submittals.

In Concord, the project approval process may include up to six separate steps: prezoning, preliminary development plan, rezoning if necessary, granting of a use permit, design review, and building permit approval. Figure 3, obtained from the city of Concord, includes most of the steps involved and the primary municipal actors. Though the process seems highly complex, the time required for project approval averages three to six months, depending upon whether the plan involves a standard residential subdivision or a Planned District.

In Fremont, the project approval process consists of a maximum of five individual steps, including rezoning, Preliminary Development Plan, Precise Development Plan, subdivision approval, and permit approval (figure 4). Although Fremont allows applicants to combine Preliminary with Precise Development Plans, or tentative subdivision maps with rezoning requests, the average duration of the approval process varies from six to eighteen months, depending on the scale and location of the project.

As a comparison of these two regulatory structures demonstrates, the pace and intensity of residential development may depend more on the intricacies of the approval process than upon the formal development policies and ordinances themselves. For instance, because Concord's Planned District and conventional residential approval processes are of comparable length and complexity, many builders take advantage of the design flexibility possible in a Planned District. Conversely, the uncertainty and length of Fremont's Planned District review process pose great

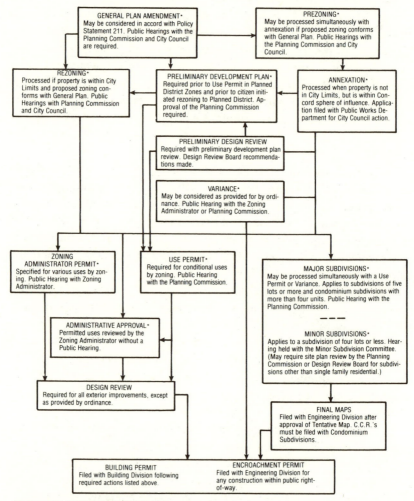

*ENVIRONMENTAL REVIEW UNLESS PREVIOUSLY DONE

GEOLOGIC REPORT/NOISE STUDY/TRAFFIC STUDY AND/OR OTHER RELATED/SIMILAR STUDIES
May be required depending on site location and size or intensity of project.

FIGURE 3.

CONCORD'S PERMIT PROCESSING.

disincentives to Fremont builders, most of whom continue to develop single-family subdivisions. While Fremont and Concord's zoning and subdivision ordinances appear similar on paper, they are quite different as administered. For example:

- In Concord, most development approvals, including Precise Development Plans, Use Permits, and subdivisions, are handled by the Planning Commission. In Fremont, both the Planning Commission and the city council review each application, lengthening the process and increasing uncertainty. For example, the Fremont City Council may stipulate a design change that the Planning Commission, in its previous review, felt unnecessary. The necessity of going through two scheduled hearings also adds time to the approval process.

- Multifamily units in Concord must be approved by the Design Review Board.

- Concord's various reviewing agencies are committed to expediting the approval process, while the Fremont planning staff generally does not help coordinate procedures. That task is left to the applicant.

Delays in receiving approvals (a problem covered in greater detail in chapter 5) are due to more than just time lags in scheduling applications. Even more pertinent is the level of development and reviewing activity.

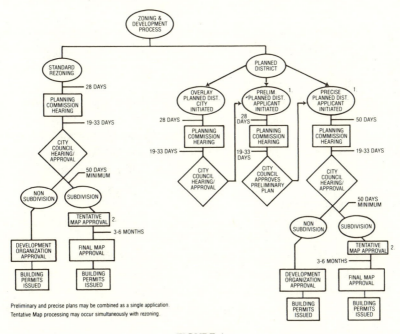

FIGURE 4.

CITY OF FREMONT DEVELOPMENT PROCESS, APRIL 1979.

Although project review times are greatly affected by planning budget and staff levels, in the final analysis these factors must also be seen as reflecting a local government's attitudes toward the review process. In Concord, both the Planning Commission and the city council can be characterized as "progrowth"; they operate on the basis that cooperation between the Planning Department and developers is one key to high-quality construction. In Fremont, where the competition among builders for land and construction approval is more intense, the city council and Planning Commission are basically "progrowth," but tend to place the burden of project planning entirely on the shoulders of developers. Until recently, Fremont officials did not generally perceive that this attitude might lead to increases in the cost of new housing.

STOP-AND-GO: DEVELOPMENT POLICIES
IN NAPA AND SANTA ROSA

Napa and Santa Rosa have responded to strong population growth pressure in completely different ways. Napa's residents and elected officials came to believe that their city was growing too quickly. They also saw that the large new subdivisions added in the early 1970s as signaling the end of Napa's rural lifestyle and the beginning of the suburban sprawl that had engulfed other North Bay communities. This perception was reinforced by the realization that Napa's expansion had been primarily residential, not economic.

Santa Rosa has had the benefit of more balanced growth. Hoping to find relief from the high land and living costs of the exploding Santa Clara region, Hewlett-Packard moved one of its plants to Santa Rosa in the early 1970s. Several other manufacturing companies were close behind. Although Santa Rosa is not yet the "Silicon Valley of the North," it has experienced substantial economic development, leading it to view growth as a more benign force.

The broad objectives and goals enumerated in the general plans of the two cities reflect their divergent attitudes toward population growth. Sensing that their city was falling into the sphere of influence of San Francisco and Oakland, Napa residents took steps to avoid the bedroom-suburb syndrome. Santa Rosa, on the other hand, had maintained economic independence and could afford to pursue a more balanced development policy.

Napa County residents were also concerned about the destabilizing effects of recent growth, particularly in the small vineyard towns of the

Napa Valley. Accordingly, through its 1975 General Plan, the county adopted a year 2000 population limit of 115,000 residents, 75,000 of which were expected to live in the city of Napa. To keep the county's population below this limit, the General Plan established development densities for the entire county. The cities of Napa, Yountville, St. Helena, Calistoga, and parts of American Canyon were declared "urban," while the vineyards surrounding Highway 29 were designated as agricultural preserve. With the exception of some industrial areas in the south, the remainder of the county was designated as agricultural/open space.

The county General Plan relied on two regulatory mechanisms to achieve these uses: the Residential Urban Limit Line (RUL), a boundary beyond which essential public services will not be provided, and a rezoning of county rural lands. Pursued by the county in concert with the city of Napa, these two policies were intended to confine residential and commercial development to existing urbanized areas. Whereas urban development once threatened to break through city boundaries, it would now, the city hoped, be redirected inward.

Designation of a Residential Urban Limit Line works to limit Napa County population growth and also to limit expansion by the city into the county. For example, Napa city planners estimate that at 1975 densities, 7,000 additional housing units could be accommodated within the Napa RUL. At the time the RUL policy was adopted by the city of Napa in 1972, the Napa City Council and Planning Commission believed that this mechanism, together with judicious use of the city's zoning power, would be sufficient to keep the city's year 2000 population below 75,000. Yet early in 1978, the Napa planning staff notified the city council that residential development was continuing unabated, and that some growth allocation system would now be necessary. The city council responded by voting three-to-two to suspend additional residential development for six months, pending consideration and adoption of an effective growth-management system. The result was the Napa Residential Development Management Plan (RDMP), adopted by the council in February 1979. The RDMP placed a yearly ceiling on residential construction (100 units in 1979, 349 units in 1980 and 1981, and a decreasing number thereafter); it also provided a project evaluation scale for ranking competing proposals. Together with traditional zoning and the city's pledge not to expand beyond the RUL, the RDMP is the basis of a system intended to ensure a slow but steady rate of growth in the city of Napa.

Santa Rosa's General Plan is fundamentally different from its Napa counterpart. First and foremost, it recognizes that Santa Rosa's recent growth is likely to continue through the remainder of the century. The year 2000 population of the Santa Rosa Planning Area, which includes unincorporated land surrounding the city-limit line, is projected to total 164,000. This represents a 65 percent increase from the estimated 1975 population of 99,624. The Planning Area's housing stock is expected to grow at the same rate, reaching 67,187 units by the year 2000. Santa Rosa's economic development is also expected to continue, with employment more than doubling from 35,700 jobs in 1972 to over 72,900 jobs in the year 2000.

The land use element of the Santa Rosa General Plan, adopted in 1978, does not attempt to minimize future development but establishes an urban boundary beyond which development is not permitted. Like the Napa RUL, the Santa Rosa urban line separates urban from rural uses. The difference is that Santa Rosa's designated urban area is large enough to accommodate expected new residential development at current densities and household sizes. *Thus, the urban area boundary is not currently envisioned as a means to limit population growth.* On the contrary, the boundary is intended to be flexible, and it can be extended should the need arise in the future.

A variety of infill and density-increasing policies have been proposed to achieve Santa Rosa's General Plan objective of compact growth. These policies are based on the establishment of five residential density groups for all parcels within the urban area, ranging from very low densities suitable primarily for agricultural uses (1–5 acres per unit) to very high densities intended for multifamily development (16 or more units per acre). Also included are guidelines for slope-density zoning in hillside areas, and for selective increases in density.

To regulate the rate and intensity of residential development, Napa employs a development-constraining Residential Urban Limit Line intended to limit the city's population to 75,000. Napa's regulatory system contrasts sharply with Santa Rosa's plan for accommodating expected growth. Although the Santa Rosa regulatory system officially promotes housing infill and densification, to date it has been less concerned with controlling the yearly flow of development than with ensuring the environmental and aesthetic quality of new housing.

Napa's Development Approval Process

By implementing the Residential Development Management Plan, Napa has severed the traditional connection between the land subdivision process and the granting of building permits. The primary interplay between planner and developer has shifted from subdivision approval to the permit allocation process. Nonetheless, developers must still satisfy existing subdivision/plan approval requirements, many of which add to delays and hence increase the costs of providing new housing.

Subdivision approval is a three-step process in both Napa and Santa Rosa (figure 5). A developer must first submit a preliminary subdivision map noting important boundaries, land features, and easements. The preliminary map must also display the location of dwelling units to be built. At the discretion of the Planning Department, an Environmental Impact Report may also be required. Following review of the preliminary map by the Planning Commission and city engineer, it is then approved or disapproved by the city council. The second step involves submission of a tentative subdivision map giving further information on the proposed development, including the locations of streets and land dedications. After the Planning Commission and city engineer comment, the proposal again goes to the city council for approval. In order to reduce approval times and paperwork, the preliminary subdivision map and tentative subdivision map can be combined into one submission. The last step is approval of a final subdivision map by the city council and Planning Com-

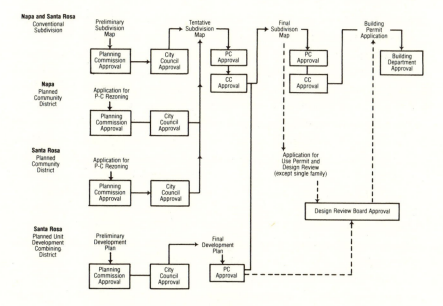

FIGURE 5.

NAPA AND SANTA ROSA RESIDENTIAL DEVELOPMENT
APPROVAL PROCESS.

mission. A developer's offer of land dedication is negotiated prior to this point, as are any other controversial features. Although numerous approval certificates are required and the map must follow a precise format, the council normally approves the final subdivision map, once the tentative subdivision map has been approved.

After the rezoning request is approved by both the Napa Planning Commission and the city council, the developer can move to subdivide his land. If nonresidential development is planned, the builder must also apply for a use permit before a final building permit can be obtained.

Neither Napa planners nor developers have pursued the creation of Planned Community Districts. The remaining vacant land parcels are generally too small to make planned-district development profitable, and density incentives tend to be seen as insufficient to justify the additional time and expense. Implementation of the RDMP is likely to further discourage Planned Community Districts in Napa. In the past, approval of a rezoning request virtually guaranteed obtaining a building permit. This is no longer the case, and the separation of rezoning and building permit approvals poses an unacceptable risk to most developers.

Santa Rosa regulations are more flexible in dealing with planned districts. A developer with a parcel in excess of fifty acres can apply to a Planned Community District (P-C) for rezoning, submitting a policy statement describing all anticipated development and its impact.

Still less restrictive is the Santa Rosa Planned Unit Development Combining District (PD), intended primarily for residential construction. This type of approval occurs in two stages. The first stage involves the submission and approval of a Preliminary Development Plan that describes current and intended uses, anticipated building locations, likely traffic patterns, and soil conditions. Contingent upon Planning Commission and city council approval of the Preliminary Development Plan, the developer can proceed to file a Final Development Plan with the Planning Commission. In most cases, the same document serves as the Final Development Plan, the use permit application, and the design review information. If the plan is approved by the Design Review Board and Planning Commission, the applicant can begin subdivision of the parcel. No matter which of the above paths is chosen, obtaining development approval in either Santa Rosa or Napa can be a complicated process, one in which delays are widespread and approval conditions frequently stipulated.

The Residential Development Management Plan

Napa's city government views the Residential Development Management Plan not as an attempt to shut off residential development, but as a method for bringing order to a previously uncontrolled situation. The ordinance has two complementary provisions: the annual allocation of building permits and the evaluation of competing projects. Under Section 31-3 of the RDMP, new housing construction within the city of Napa is limited to 100 units in 1979, 349 for 1980 and 1981, and then a decreasing allocation based on actual population growth and housing vacancy. Other than its reference to vacancy rates, the allocation formula does not include indicators of housing market performance.

So that it can ameliorate potential shortages, the city council is empowered to increase the allocation by 5 percent for a given year, subtracting the increase from the subsequent year's application. Single units to be constructed on parcels subdivided prior to August 1975 are exempt from allocation, in order that the plan not unfairly burden builders of single houses. Also exempt are subdivisions creating four or fewer lots, and residential projects intended for occupancy by low- and middle-income senior citizens (over sixty years of age).

The project evaluation process begins on April 1 of each calendar year. Prior to March 31, applicants proposing single- or multifamily residential developments must submit a formal project application, along with the necessary fees, environmental documents, detailed project plans, and any other information deemed vital by the Napa Department of Planning and Community Development. After receipt of the completed applications, the planning staff conducts a preliminary evaluation of each project based on the project rating scale. Preliminary ratings are returned to all applicants, published in the local newspaper, and then forwarded to the Project Evaluation Board, which in turn holds public hearings and makes final recommendations to the Napa City Council. Prior to August 1, the city council formally distributes the annual housing allocation among the recommended applicants. The allocation ordinance policy goals for 1980 and 1981 call for a minimum unit mix of 10 percent duplexes and townhouses, 25 percent multifamily units, and 40 percent single-family units.

The project rating scale is divided into two point groups that reflect Napa's explicit policy of encouraging "infill" development, as well as innovative or varied unit designs. At fifty points per category, locational attributes and design features are weighed equally; twenty additional points can also be earned for outstanding features. The locational features valued most highly include fire station access and walks to parks, schools, and shops. Of the design criteria, architectural innovation and site design weigh most heavily.

The rationale for the RDMP was clear from the start: the plan was intended to encourage infill development and minimize single-family home construction at the city's fringe, where services are less accessible and more expensive. Throughout the evolution of the RDMP point system, debate centered on the relative importance of the various design and locational criteria. The Planning Commission pushed for an even split between location and design points, but the cost-conscious city council argued for a system based primarily on locational criteria. According to Planning Director Mike Foley, the resulting compromise was workable in 1979 but may need updating now. The yearly housing allocation proved less of an issue, and a formula was adopted with the intent of permitting an ultimate population of 75,000—the number voted on by the community. (As it happens, the city has grown at a slower rate than first anticipated, due to a decrease in Napa's average household size. Because of the way the allocation formula is structured, it may have to be altered to ensure that the yearly allocation does not exceed 350 dwelling units as originally intended.)

Thus, when the six-month building permit moratorium expired in February 1979, the Napa Residential Development Management Plan was ready. Builders had until July 31, 1979, to compete for 449 building permits covering the years 1979 and 1980.

Summing up their first year of experience with the RDMP, Napa planners complain that the quality of the submittals was somewhat disappointing. They attributed this to the newness of the RDMP and the fact that most of the development plans had been prepared prior to the publication of the project evaluation criteria. Of the thirty initial submittals, seven applicants proposed townhouses/duplexes, seven proposed apartments, and sixteen proposed detached housing. Unit mixes were renegotiated between the initial and final evaluations: the final total was 47 percent townhouses/duplexes, 21 percent apartments, and 32 percent detached houses. Clearly, the RDMP did succeed in promoting the development of more multi-family housing, one of its primary goals. As expected, it was more difficult for detached housing to accumulate both locational and design points than multifamily housing. In particular, few detached houses were awarded points for park access, project and area mix, or recreational facilities. While the architecture of the units themselves was generally regarded as good, site design reviews were mixed.

Santa Rosa: A Steady Course for Two Decades

Santa Rosa passed its first zoning ordinance in 1928, but it wasn't until 1962 that a cooperative effort between Sonoma County and Santa Rosa produced the city's first General Plan. In reviewing the city's land development history, the 1962 Plan noted:

For many years Santa Rosa had a stable land use pattern typical of most agricultural communities and a compact form of urban development with residential areas surrounding the retail and commercial core of the city. Warehousing and heavy commercial uses were oriented toward the railroad in a manner particular to each industry. The relatively small amount of industry located in or near Santa Rosa was basically concerned with serving local needs.[4]

The 1960s were a period of unprecedented change for Santa Rosa. Although the city almost doubled in size, both new and longtime residents seemed to take growth in stride. As farms and wholesaling firms declined in importance, government, services, and retail trade grew to be the city's major employers. Mirroring a national trend, retailers began abandoning traditional downtown areas for large suburban shopping centers, three of which sprang up along Highway 101 between 1955 and 1965.

As Santa Rosa's economy became dependent on agriculture, large quantities of land were freed up for housing, most of it single-family. Santa Rosa became an early territory for tract developers. Between 1960 and 1965, the number of residentially developed acres in the city more than doubled, growing from 3,792 to 7,586.

The 1962 General Plan called attention to problems of "scatteration," and suggested that city officials use the capital-budgeting process to guide development, but produced little action beyond the continued production of small-area plans. Zoning and subdivision improvement ordinances were strictly enforced, ensuring that newly developed residential tracts were well laid out and of consistent quality.

Unfortunately, the factor that facilitated Santa Rosa's rapid growth—the availability of flat, stable, and generally inexpensive land—was also the force behind "scatteration." In 1965, the Santa Rosa Planning Area included roughly 115 square miles, most of it undeveloped. Population studies suggested that this area might ultimately accommodate some 500,000 residents. As part of a 1967 update of the previous General Plan, city officials estimated that 40 percent of the planning area would be developed by 1990, encompassing a resident population of nearly 188,000.

Concern over unplanned growth came from two sources: those concerned that the public service base required by a sprawling city of 200,000 might ultimately bankrupt the city treasury, and those who felt that suburban sprawl was causing the decline of Santa Rosa's downtown. Open-space advocates were notably absent from the coalition arguing for more "rational" land use planning, primarily because the expanding city had taken great care to acquire large parcels for recreational use. The city's planners did, however, acknowledge the need to control sprawl. The

1967 Santa Rosa General Plan offered three proposals: (1) establish urban area land reserves to meet the land and housing needs of the 1990s; (2) extend rapid transit from San Francisco to Santa Rosa; and (3) establish formal guidelines for hillside development and conservation.

To help guide development, the General Plan classified the planning area into four density categories, ranging from less than one unit per acre in rural areas to more than twenty-five units per acre in the Santa Rosa CBD. In addition the Plan designated lands near the city's official boundary as urban reserve—that is, to be developed only after 1990.

The debate over how best to manage Santa Rosa's growth took place in the Office of Community Development. With real estate and business interests fully represented, and with the tax base growing at a sufficient rate to finance public services, the Santa Rosa City Council was reluctant to turn off the growth tap.

But as Santa Rosa entered the 1970s, some cracks began to appear in the previously solid prodevelopment facade. As in Marin County, the environmental movement, emphasizing conservation and slow growth, had introduced doubts about the benefits of continued development. A 1976 survey of Santa Rosa residents revealed that what they liked most about their city was its moderate size, sunny climate, and unique combination of urban shopping/employment opportunities with a semirural atmosphere. Of those surveyed, 50 percent indicated that Santa Rosa had grown too fast for their liking during the late 1960s and early 1970s, and 60 percent favored a stronger city role in managing future growth. One out of every two Santa Rosans advocated development restrictions for hillside areas (a policy recommended in 1962 and 1967 but never implemented) and 70 percent of those surveyed supported city purchases of permanent open space.

Members of the Santa Rosa business community were also becoming concerned. The growth in manufacturing employment that was supposed to follow Hewlett-Packard's move had not fully materialized. Unemployment rates were consistently higher than the regional average, and although it was not yet a serious problem, a series of studies had called attention to the increasing number of Santa Rosans driving south to work. For those who had worked to make Santa Rosa an independent, economically healthy city, the prospect of becoming just another San Francisco bedroom suburb was disappointing. To address these and other growth-related issues, the city council commissioned the Santa Rosa Optimum Growth Study in 1972.

Both the Santa Rosa Optimum Growth Study and ongoing General

Plan update work concluded that Santa Rosa's growth problems were at least partly related to the development limitation programs then being implemented in Marin County and the city of Petaluma. However, the studies noted that a number of local actions had also served to stimulate new residential development. The city's continuing policy of providing water and sewer service to accommodate all new development (against recommendations of the 1962 and 1967 General Plan) had exacerbated the problem of sprawl. New school construction in outlying areas and the extension of wide boulevards into undeveloped countryside also served to stimulate as well as subsidize new residential growth.

All of these findings and concerns were channeled into a 1976 effort to completely revise the Land Use Element of the Santa Rosa General Plan. Although at first glance the 1976 update appears to be merely a slight revision, it is in fact a significant departure from the previous Plan. First and foremost, the revised Land Use Element recognized that without directly limiting growth—a strategy that no one embraced—the city would continue to grow throughout the remainder of the century. It was estimated that the planning area population would grow to approximately 164,000 by the year 2000 (up from 99,000 in 1975) and that the number of dwelling units would reach 67,000. These estimates represented a substantial reduction of previous forecasts and were accompanied by reductions in the number of dwelling units per acre permitted in each of the four General Plan density categories. Downzoning undeveloped lands was not only an attempt to limit growth; it was also a tacit admission that detached single-family homes would continue to be the dominant form of housing in Santa Rosa. In fact, the Land Use Element forecast residential development densities of less than 4.0 units per acre for twelve of the twenty subareas comprising the Santa Rosa Planning Area. In addition, the 1976 Land Use Element formally established slope-density zoning for Santa Rosa hillside areas—a step first advocated fifteen years earlier.

As mentioned above, the 1978 Santa Rosa General Plan specified an urban boundary beyond which city services would not be provided. The adoption of the urban boundary does appear to have had some effect on land prices in the Santa Rosa area. Immediately following the announcement of the policy, the asking prices for large undeveloped parcels inside the urban boundary rose substantially.

While Santa Rosa planners were wrestling with issues of balanced growth, Santa Rosa builders were facing another problem. The advent of the environmental impact assessment process had greatly lengthened approval times for residential projects. The flow of new units onto the market continued at historical levels, but processing delays produced a situation where the average period between first submission and recording the final subdivision map was 530 days. Delays were due to the volume of projects being reviewed (856 separate reviews in 1978), increased use of detailed environmental assessments, and the fact that the Santa Rosa review procedure was two-tiered—that is, all subdivision maps, both tentative and final, had to be approved by both the Planning Commission and the city council. Prodded by Assembly Bill 884, which set a maximum one-year evaluation timetable for most projects, along with the outcries of local homebuilders, the Santa Rosa Department of Community Development revamped its review procedures to reduce the approval period. The result was impressive; approval time for tentative subdivision maps had fallen from an average of 240 days in 1977 to only 80 days in 1978.

One final feature of the Santa Rosa project review process merits mention. All applications for zoning, use, and building permits are subject to approval by the Design Review Board, a five-member panel appointed by Santa Rosa's mayor. Intended primarily to ensure architectural quality of commercial/industrial structures, and consistency among large-scale residential projects, the design review process does not apply to single-family homes that are not part of Planned Districts.

MARIN GROWTH PUSHES NORTH: COPING IN SAN RAFAEL AND NOVATO

The struggle to limit population growth in Marin County was based on more than just the prejudices of a few upper-income residents. Rather, it drew on the conviction that continued residential construction would mean the destruction of the county's prized valleys and ridgelands. Accordingly, the growth policies pursued by San Rafael, Novato, and other cities in Marin County have been aimed first and foremost at the preservation of open space and the establishment of local greenbelts.

San Rafael's General Plans

As a comparison of San Rafael's 1974 General Plan with its 1966 predecessor clearly indicates, the city's residents underwent a radical shift in attitude toward continued growth. The 1966 Plan envisioned an entirely built-out city, and promoted high-density cluster zoning to accommodate an ultimate city population of 125,000. The 1974 Plan was prepared after the publication of the "controlled growth" Countywide Plan, and foresaw an entirely different future for San Rafael. It was actually a blueprint for limiting new residential growth through the acquisition of remaining vacant land as open space, the adoption of an aggressive project review process, and the use of a land capability analysis designed to preclude construction from "environmentally sensitive areas" subject to seismic, geologic, flooding, and fire hazards.

San Rafael's first General Plan was completed in 1966. The four broad objectives of the Plan were to: (1) further San Rafael as the market, administrative, and cultural center of Marin County; (2) enhance San Rafael's position as an attractive residential area; (3) improve the transport system so as to encourage economic development; and (4) conserve hillsides, valleys, and baylands. Although the 1966 General Plan recognized that employment location decisions and commuting preferences would shape San Rafael's future, it put forth no firm position on desired levels of employment or residential growth.

The major tools used to achieve the above goals were to be existing subdivision and zoning ordinances and especially "hillside cluster zoning." The promotion of hillside clustering was based on a theory that assumed that private builders would be attracted to the idea because of potential construction cost savings. At the same time, however, city officials recognized that new and revised zoning ordinances would be necessary to ensure developer compliance. By and large such changes were not forthcoming. Though San Rafael had adopted slope-related density limits for hillside areas in 1965, the ordinance did little to discourage ridgeline development. In 1968 the city council adopted an ordinance establishing Planned Unit Development and combining districts in which builders might propose flexible site designs, but builder response to the change was minimal.

San Rafael's second General Plan was adopted by the city council in October 1974. Fourteen policies for guiding the city's future were set forward. Five of these policies are particularly relevant, and illustrate the change in community attitude that occurred between 1966 and 1974:

1. A policy to discourage disruptive population growth.

2. A policy to create an integrated pattern of open spaces throughout the planning area. These open spaces would serve as greenbelt dividers between urbanized areas and also preserve those lands that are uniquely suitable because of environmental resources or recreation potential.

3. A policy to protect and improve the air, water, noise, and scenic quality of the Planning Area Environment, and to protect ridgelands, tidal marshes, and access to waterways.

4. A policy to rely heavily on soil, geologic, seismic and other environmental information as bases for shaping development policy, and to require that all public and private proposals that are likely to significantly alter the environment show explicit cause why such changes are justified.

5. A policy to ensure that proposals for residential development and housing include a variety of densities, housing types, and housing opportunities.

The prevention of unwanted, environmentally destructive growth was to be accomplished through the implementation of a Residential Review Ordinance and Procedure (RRP). The quarterly RRP was intended to apply to housing developments of more than two units. As of this writing the RRP has not been adopted, nor is it likely to be—a turnabout resulting less from a change in policy than a sharp drop-off in residential development. In place of the RRP, the San Rafael City Council relies on a far less ambitious Design Review Ordinance adopted in 1972. The Environmental and Design Review Ordinance, as the procedure is formally known, is aimed primarily at commercial, industrial, and office buildings. Residential developments that must undergo review include townhouses, condominiums, and single-family projects of more than fifteen units; projects of fifteen units or less are evaluated only when a building permit is applied for, and the evaluation is generally linked to building code compliance.

Confronting Rapid Growth in Novato

While Marin County and San Rafael were dealing with problems of excess growth and environmental degradation in a very general way, Novato was faced with a steadily rising number of subdivision and building permit applications—a tangible and worrisome indicator of growth. The Novato General Plan, approved in 1973, reflects some of these acute concerns.

Conscious of the increasing value and cost of raw land, the city proposed "to assist neighborhood residents in creating neighborhood identity buffers and connecting greenways," thus reducing the municipal role and tax burden. The Plan's land use element also reflected growing public concern over the rate of residential construction by proposing specific land use density guidelines that overlay the city's traditional zoning map. Intended to match the level of residential development with presumed land capability, the Plan's three basic density classifications were designed to keep yearly starts below 500 dwelling units. The 1973 General Plan also contained what amounts to a warning: should yearly housing starts exceed the 500-unit ceiling, the city would implement a growth management program with a yearly limit of 375 dwelling units. In 1979 this threat materialized as the proposed Residential Development Review Ordinance.

Open-Space Preservation

The preservation of open space—a goal of both the San Rafael and Novato city governments—has two explicit and not completely separable purposes. First, open-space acquisition is used to ensure and maintain community environmental quality by preventing the development of ecologically or socially valued hillsides, ridgelines, meadowlands, and bay marsh. Second, open-space acquisition can be used deliberately to limit residential growth by withdrawing specific parcels from the stock of developable land.

In San Rafael, three large open-space preserves and a dozen smaller tracts have been acquired as permanent open space. The three large tracts—Big Rock Ridge (which is outside city limits), San Pablo Marshland, and Point San Pedro Ridge—encompass hillside and ridgeline areas that could not otherwise be intensively developed. Most of the smaller open-space areas, which could potentially be developed for residential use, were acquired for recreational purposes.

Much of the open space in the San Rafael Planning Area is controlled by Marin County. In the Lucas Valley area, along the northern shore of Point San Pedro, and at San Rafael's northern border are large tracts of vacant land that lie within the San Rafael Planning Area and sphere of influence but fall under county jurisdiction. Many of these tracts could accommodate residential development ranging in density from 0.5 dwelling units per acre to more than 10 units per acre, but remain undeveloped, and have been zoned as permanent urban-corridor open space. From Marin County's perspective, this arrangement allows for the preservation of urban open space that, if under the control of San Rafael, might be residentially developed. From San Rafael's perspective, the city is spared both the responsibility of controlling development in these areas and the cost of purchasing these areas as open space. In short, there are strong political, fiscal, and environmental reasons why San Rafael's borders have not been reconciled with the city's actual service area.

One way to preserve open space while avoiding outright purchase is to leave large vacant parcels unzoned. As of 1978, nearly 25 percent of San Rafael's land area was not zoned. These unzoned parcels are evenly divided between those that could economically be developed (those along San Rafael's southern border, for example, and adjoining Highway 101 north of the Marin Civic Center) and undevelopable parcels (those at Point San Pedro). An alternative means of temporarily preserving open space is to zone vacant parcels as Planned Community Districts. Since developers of P-C Districts are required to gain special-use permits, this type of zoning gives San Rafael planners increased discretion over both uses and densities.

Thus, by implementing planned community zoning, leaving particular parcels unzoned, and relying on county control of tracts within the planning area but outside city boundaries, San Rafael has withdrawn substantial acreage from the stock of vacant land available for residential development.

Novato's open-space strategy is somewhat different. Novato uses a combination of land purchase and zoning policy to preserve parcels as open space, but unlike San Rafael, it aims its open-space program at securing a permanent greenbelt at the city's fringe. In particular, Novato has tried to preserve three major ridge areas as green space: Big Rock Ridge (along Novato's southern border), the Mt. Burdell Foothills, and the smaller ridge separating the Ignacio Valley from central Novato. In the first two cases, the city has augmented land purchases with P-C zoning, a classification that precludes intense residential development when combined with Novato General Plan density guidelines.

Novato's General Plan Density Guidelines

The Land Use Element of the Novato General Plan, adopted in June 1973, is essentially a map overlay that divides the city into three use designations: (1) residential, (2) nonresidential, and (3) special uses (agriculture, public open space, and recreational areas). Nonresidential districts tend to be clustered downtown and along Highway 101; special areas are located throughout the city. All residential parcels fall into one of three categories defined according to maximum development density: Low Density (0.1 to 1 dwelling units per gross acre), Medium Density (1 to 5 dwelling units per gross acre), and High Density (5 to 20 dwelling units per gross acre).

A review of Novato's vacant land parcels reveals that most fall under the hillside, equestrian, or water-related designations in which maximum densities are limited to 3 dwelling units per gross acre.

In 1978 the Novato Planning Department conducted a survey of land development potential under the density limits set forth in the Novato General Plan; a summary of their findings is presented as table 17. Of the 4,689 acres identified as developable (including infill parcels, but exclud-

TABLE 17

1978 NOVATO RESIDENTIAL DEVELOPMENT POTENTIAL
BY CENSUS TRACTS

Census Tract	Total Acreage	Developable Acreage	Residentially Developable Acreage	Dwelling Unit Potential
1011	2,325	1,222	936	1,455–1,811
1012	2,127	811	668	319–762
1021	4,874	532	380	281
1022	1,433	337	240	667
1031	984	141	141	142
1032	909	260	255	622–771
1041	1,777	783	752	1,412
1042	3,284	603	590	657–757
1050	(Hamilton Airfield not included)			
Total	17,713	4,689	3,962	5,555–6,603

SOURCE: Novato Planning Department, 1978.

ing Hamilton Airfield), 3,962 were zoned for residential construction.
Based on the Plan's density limits, between 5,500 and 6,600 additional
dwelling units could be constructed on the vacant acreage. At current
household sizes, such a housing increment would add between 15,500
and 18,460 residents to Novato's population. The gross residential densities of the additional dwelling units would range from 1.4 to 1.66 units per
acre; if vacant parcels in Novato's downtown area are subtracted, the
gross density of new residential construction falls to under 1.3 dwelling
units per acre. Under the land use guidelines put forth in Novato's General
Plan, future residential construction will occur at less than half the density of past development.

In defense of the Novato General Plan Guidelines, it should be said
that intense residential construction would be ecologically disastrous to
the city's hillside and bayland areas, and in many instances would lead to
the widespread and permanent destruction of the Novato environment.
To the extent that the guidelines preclude such destruction, they must be
regarded as procedurally and legally valid.

However, such policies do involve tradeoffs. It is virtually impossible
to produce affordable new housing at densities below three units per acre,
and few homebuyers can afford land prices once minimum lot sizes climb

to 8,000 square feet. At the same time, when densities are low, builders are unable to construct housing on the scale necessary to keep unit costs down. As a result, the new homes constructed in Novato over the last five years are located on large lots, are themselves large, and are extremely expensive.

The residential districts established by the Novato zoning ordinance are distinguished from those in San Rafael chiefly by the existence of large-lot single-family districts. Responding to farming and ranching interests, the Novato zoning code designates two types of residential-agricultural districts in which minimum lot sizes vary between 7,500 square feet and two acres, as well as two restricted residential districts that allow for varying types of agricultural use.

Recent trends in townhouse construction have increased the importance of planned districts. In Novato, the three types of planned districts are differentiated by the types of uses permitted. Planned Single-Family Districts may be established only on parcels at least five acres in size, and though units may be clustered, they must also be detached. More flexible is the Planned Residential District (R-P), where approved uses include single-family homes, duplexes, apartments, or an appropriate mixture of all three. Although residential densities are not specified, they must conform to guidelines included in the Novato General Plan. Most flexible is the Planned Community District (P-C), in which residential uses may be mixed with commercial, business, and even certain light industrial uses.

Charting the Plan Approval Process

Novato's system of land use controls differs from San Rafael's not in the controls themselves, but in the way they are administered. For a small project in San Rafael (less than five units), the builder must first submit a tentative subdivision map showing all existing property lines and easements, and specifying proposed lot locations. All grading must be specified and proper erosion and draingate control must be assured. In addition, the builder must obtain a negative declaration from the San Rafael Planning Commission, exempting the project from the requirement of an Environmental Impact Report (EIR). Except for very large projects, negative declarations are virtually automatic. After a brief review by the San Rafael Planning Department, the subdivision application is then referred to the Planning Commission, which, in a meeting open to local citizens, either approves or rejects the builder's tentative subdivision map. Assuming that the map is accepted, the application next goes to the San Rafael City Council for final approval.

Review of the tentative subdivision map process is the primary point for local citizen input and city-builder negotiation. Except in rare instances, approval of the final subdivision map and building permits automatically follow the city council's approval of the tentative subdivision map. The timing of these various approvals depends largely on the builder. If the tentative subdivision map application is complete, and the project is in conformance with local zoning codes, the entire approval process—from initial subdivision application to building permit approval—can take as little as three months. When delays occur in approval of small projects, they are generally the fault of the applicant.

Although small projects are most frequent, occasionally the San Rafael Planning Department receives an application for a large planned-district development. Under San Rafael's zoning code, such proposals are subject to an entirely different approval process, but they are infrequent enough to receive the full attention of the Planning Department and Planning Commission. Although review and approval times do increase with project size, larger residential projects are delayed primarily by time requirements to prepare and certify an EIR.

Novato's single-family review process is comparable to the San Rafael approval procedure outlined above. Builders submit tentative subdivision maps and application forms to be reviewed by the Planning Department, the Planning Commission, and finally the Novato City Council. If the project is large or located in an environmentally sensitive area, an EIR may also be required by the Environmental Impact Review Committee, a panel made up of representatives from various city departments. As in San Rafael, once a tentative subdivision map has been approved, the builder may submit a final subdivision map and apply for a building permit. Based on past review times for similar Novato projects, the period between the tentative subdivision map application and building permit approval averages four to six months.

Because much of Novato's vacant land has been zoned into one of three planned districts, Novato builders commonly find themselves subject to a different review procedure from the one outlined above. If the parcel is not already zoned for a planned district, the developer's first step is to seek a rezoning. Two separate applications are required: a Master Plan in which the builder sets forth the development scheme for the parcel, and a Precise Development Plan (PDP) in which all eventual uses and dwelling units are clearly specified and documented. As its name implies, the Precise Development Plan is a more refined and specific version of the initial Master Plan. Although it is not recommended, Novato does allow builders to combine the Master Plan and Precise Development Plan into one submission. Table 18 profiles the submission requirements for both the Master Plan and the PDP.

Immediately after receipt of the builder's Master Plan, the Environmental Impact Review Committee meets to determine whether an EIR will be required. For example, if twenty units were being proposed for a hillside tract, an EIR would probably be required. The responsibility for researching and preparing the EIR rests entirely with the applicant, and the preparation of a Draft EIR may take two to three months. While the applicant has been preparing the EIR, the Novato Planning Department has been reviewing the Master Plan and suggesting changes to the builder. In its subsequent review of the Master Plan, the Novato Planning

TABLE 18

SUBMISSION REQUIREMENTS FOR NOVATO
PLANNED DISTRICTS

Master Plan	Precise Development Plan
1. Diagram of areas and streets to be developed, and boundaries of existing property	A. Documents showing: 1. The completed project, including all buildings and structures, streets, parks, pathways, patios, decks, pools, light fixtures, and similar improvements
2. Diagrams of topography and slope	
3. Location of all existing man-made improvements	
4. Location of existing trees	2. Preliminary grading plan
5. Location of all water areas	3. Preliminary landscaping plan
6. Location of contiguous properties and their degree and type of development, and surrounding street pattern	4. Geological hazard map 5. Preliminary utility plan B. Written statements describing: 1. Type and intensity of all uses
7. Single line sections of each building type proposed	2. Mitigation measures taken to address adverse environmental impact
8. Proposed densities	
9. Geologic map identifying potential hazardous areas	3. Parking computations and ratios, and trip generation figures
10. Statements regarding the development concept as they apply to public services and facilities, noise, traffic, soils stability, wildlife and vegetation, shopping opportunities, utility service and use of undeveloped areas	4. Detailed subdivision lot lines 5. Maintenance and management concepts for common areas 6. Use of undeveloped areas

SOURCE: City of Novato Zoning Code, 16 February 1960.

Commission uses four broad criteria to gauge the acceptability of the plan: (1) conformance with the General Plan, (2) conformance with Planned District zoning regulations, (3) existence of adequate public services and infrastructure to service the project, and (4) suitability of the project to neighborhood and site characteristics.

If the Planning Commission approves, the applicant's amended Master Plan goes to the Novato City Council for approval. Both the Planning Commission and the city council also check to see whether the amended Master Plan includes steps to mitigate any adverse environmental effects uncovered in the certification of the EIR.

An applicant's second major hurdle involves approval of the Precise Development Plan. Unless otherwise specified, the PDP need only be approved by the Planning Commission. Although PDP approval generally follows Master Plan approval, two or three months may be required for the actual review process, during which the builder and Novato planners hammer out final design details. Once the applicant's PDP is approved by the Planning Commission, he must still file a final subdivision map (to be approved by the city council) as well as apply for a building permit. Within the context of the planned district review procedure, these last two steps are largely pro forma and occur at the developer's discretion. Depending on the time elapsed between Master Plan approval and PDP submission, or between PDP approval and building permit application, the review process could vary in length from eight to twelve months.

The Push for Controls

Both Novato and San Rafael use a combination of open-space preservation and zoning to separate land uses, regulate residential densities, and limit the amount of developable land available to builders. Second, both use the project review process to regulate the quality of new residential development, ensuring that it is consistent with the aesthetic and environmental values of the community. Another increasingly important function of the plan approval process is to ensure that the full environmental, social, and fiscal costs of new development fall on the builder and thus presumably on the home buyer.

By the time San Rafael's citizens and government first focused their attention on the problem of "uncontrolled growth" in the early 1970s, the city had already been largely built out. Large developable parcels remained, as a result of San Rafael's geographic relationship with its unincorporated neighbors. However, these parcels were scattered throughout Point San Pedro and Terra Linda, and many were unsuitable for large subdivisions or single-family home tracts, due to soil conditions and public opposition. These conditions resulted in a growing land shortage that caused San Rafael's land prices to escalate rapidly, further discouraging large-scale suburban development. In an effort to reduce the city's growth potential and simultaneously preserve valued open space, San Rafael adopted three somewhat coordinated land use policies: (1) purchasing open space for greenbelt and recreational uses, (2) refusing to annex vacant parcels that lie within the San Rafael Planning Area but are under Marin County land use control, and (3) leaving many vacant parcels unzoned, thus making it more difficult for builders to receive development approval. The city also zoned substantial Point San Pedro acreage into Planned Community District status—a designation that increases city discretion over the form and intensity of development. If San Rafael's policies are judged in terms of how effectively they discourage the construction of single-family housing, they must be viewed as successful.

In the meantime, the city of Novato was experiencing a 4 percent annual growth rate, and was, if anything, more concerned about the problems of growth than its southern neighbor. Novato's land prices were lower than San Rafael's, and its rate of single-family home construction rose year after year, due partially to the lack of developable land in Marin County's southern cities. Most disturbing of all, if hillside and marshland acreage was included, Novato's supply of residentially developable land was immense—an indication that the city's recent growth rates might continue to accelerate. During the updating of the Novato General Plan, it became apparent that any new set of land use policies adopted should be aimed toward bringing Novato's rate of residential growth to a more manageable level, and preserving those hillsides, bay areas, and agricultural lands threatened by rampant development. Unlike San Rafael, where the acreage to be preserved was relatively small, Novato could not afford to buy land in quantities sufficient to slow down the rate of development. Accordingly, the city's few open-space purchases were calculated to secure a greenbelt at the Novato border. As an alternative to the purchase of land, Novato adopted a series of density guidelines as part of the Land Use Element of its General Plan. By restricting development of hillsides, water-related areas, and agricultural tracts to less than three dwelling units per acre (and in many instances less than one dwelling unit per acre), it was hoped that valued land could be preserved and growth could be reduced.

But the General Plan guidelines proved to be unequal to the task. As land capability data illustrate, they still left the more level and stable areas of the city unprotected. To further reduce the possibility of intense development in these areas, the Novato Planning Commission rezoned many of these vacant parcels into planned districts. As in San Rafael, increased discretion over builder's proposals through an open-ended process of master plan review was sought. As a final measure, the city of Novato has used Williamson contracts to preserve viable farms and horse ranches.

To some critics, the adoption of these various strategies for preempting intensive subdivision construction seems almost conspiratorial. But on the contrary, the various policies implemented by San Rafael and Novato enjoyed the full support of the citizenry. Voters in both cities overwhelmingly approved bond programs to finance open-space purchases, and in several instances the landholders of adjoining parcels agreed to increased property tax assessments in order to finance open-space acquisitions. Equally important, although these various policies were intended to reduce growth pressures and succeeded in doing so, they did not seem blatantly exclusionary, as did the land use and housing policies then being proposed in Petaluma, Novato's neighbor to the north.

Besides their explicit effects on land use, the policies adopted by Novato and San Rafael also discouraged construction indirectly. By constricting the supply of developable land, they caused the price of remaining developable parcels to rise rapidly. The ensuing land price inflation encouraged builders to shift to the production of expensive, custom-built homes on large lots. To recapture the increasing number of home buyers priced out of the single-family market, builders are now producing townhouses, which offset high land costs with lower land requirements per unit.

CONCLUSION

The six communities studied encountered varying types of growth pressures. Some were hardest hit by development in the 1950s and 1960s; others have been confronted by substantial land conversion only recently. Regardless of their stage in the development cycle, all these communities are greatly concerned with the impact of development, and all have devoted considerable effort to developing land use plans and sophisticated measures for shaping growth.

In the more mature cities, such as Concord and San Rafael, land use planning functions to maintain the quality of existing neighborhoods, minimize the fiscal impact, and preserve precious open space. Careful architectural review is now the rule in both towns, and planners take care to see that new projects do not arouse neighborhood opposition.

In a sense, the real issue is no longer growth per se, but how best to maintain the status quo. This is evident from the changing posture revealed by comparison of San Rafael's 1966 and 1974 General Plans. Why did San Rafael change its tack so emphatically? The shift can be attributed in part to fallout from Marin's countywide planning efforts, but also to the growing public perception that San Rafael was approaching the final chapter in its development history. As the supply of developable land dwindled, planners and residents increasingly focused on the importance of preserving the city's existing character. The result: more complex review procedures and more exacting and comprehensive criteria for judging projects.

These complicated review procedures helped to slow the pace of development in San Rafael to a crawl. Many developers were not sophisticated or financially capitalized enough to survive under a more complex regime. Some moved north to Novato and Sonoma County; others stayed, but adjusted by decreasing project size and decreasing the price and quality of units.

San Rafael is by no means an isolated example of the Bay Area's shifting development climate. Concord has also become more cautious and critical of new growth, for the same reasons observed in San Rafael: a perception that the city is reaching full build-out, and a keen interest in maintaining community character. Coupled with limited land availability, this stance has served to slow Concord's expansion considerably. Unlike San Rafael, Concord's growing skepticism toward continued land conversion is also based on fiscal pressure. Hard-pressed to provide sewer service to outlying areas, the city has imposed a moratorium on development until developers provide enough capital to pay for the extension of sewer trunk lines.

Land and housing markets in central Contra Costa County have not been adversely affected by Concord's development slowdown, because nearby unincorporated areas and the cities of Antioch, Pittsburg, and Clayton have picked up the growth passed off by Concord. Unfortunately, the same has not been true for San Rafael, Marin County's growth center for much of the late 1960s and 1970s. The growth pressures deflected as San Rafael slowed development to a trickle were never completely absorbed. The cities to the south were fairly well built-out, and developers ran into stringent controls in Novato, Sonoma County, and unincorporated portions of Marin to the north.

The other case cities have also heightened their scrutiny of development. For instance, Fremont has instituted stricter evaluation of projects, and like Concord it now places greater emphasis on Planned Unit Development districts. While these PUD designations increase developer flexibility, they also increase the scope of development control and add much additional time to the review of projects. Only in Santa Rosa have planners really assessed how complex review procedures affect the time required for project review. In other communities the time needed to obtain a permit has increased significantly in the past ten years. In Novato, for example, some projects are now tied up for as long as thirty-six months. In cities that have growth management programs, such as Napa, or accept development permits only twice a year, the review process is lengthy indeed.

Thus, communities have increased both the scope and depth of project evaluation, and for various reasons. In mature cities, development is viewed as having an important impact on the use of scarce land resources, while residents demand that new development not disrupt the community, nor cause an adverse fiscal and environmental impact. Citizen groups are more vocal and better organized. Consequently, the potential impact of projects is examined more carefully. For example, most cities are carefully assessing the fiscal impact of all residential project proposals. Proposition 13 has had a tremendous effect on local land use planning; there is a solidly entrenched perception that single-family housing does not pay its own way.

The case studies also revealed that preservation of open space, hillsides, and ridgelands is a goal of increasing importance to all of the cities. The two Marin County cities, Novato and San Rafael, have made particular efforts to identify and control open-space lands; the preservation of hillside and ridgeland areas has been a major planning issue in both communities. But such concerns are not unique to Marin County. In Fremont and Santa Rosa, citizen pressure to preserve hillside lands is very strong and has resulted in planning policies to protect such areas from development. In Fremont, several citizen groups have been pressuring the city to prohibit development in the bay plain area. Concern over the environmental impact of land conversion is common in rapid-growth areas, typically occurring once there is a critical mass of residents who have lived there long enough to perceive the adverse effects of development. It appears that Fremont has now reached this stage.

In Santa Rosa, on the other hand, though development still continues at a rapid pace, there is little sign that citizen groups are mounting opposition. Opposition may develop if the city doesn't act to preserve hillside and other sensitive lands. But Santa Rosa has already taken steps in that direction. The city has designated an urban limit line around it and is attempting to prevent further sprawl or, as it is called, "scatteration." These efforts may help counteract the frequent call for growth management.

Napa's transition to open-space preservation was predictable, since the county's economy is so completely dependent on winemaking and vineyards. Once the alarm was first sounded over the conversion of grape-growing land to residential developments early in the 1960s, it was easy to pass regulations and write plans to protect that land.

Another trend apparent in the six cities is the universal effort to make new development pay its own way. In the wake of Proposition 13, communities have been struggling to find ways of supporting new development. Most have turned to fees, charges, and dedications of land and facilities to offset development costs. Permit application fees, impact fees, and building permit charges have all increased dramatically. Besides higher fees, some communities have also begun placing much of the burden for new infrastructure on the developer. In Concord, for example, the developers must finance extension of trunk sewer lines before a project is approved.

Projects are now subject to cost-revenue impact assessment in the normal course of development review; each proposal is evaluated in terms of the tax revenues generated versus its impact on local public service costs. Cost-cutting modifications are frequently required in projects that would generate an excess of costs over revenues. These evaluation procedures affect the nature of development in other ways as well. For example, in estimating the local public service costs associated with a project, the largest variable is the number of bedrooms in each unit. The more bedrooms, the greater the number of school-aged children, and the greater the demand for public education. In many development projects, builders are reducing the number of four-bedroom units while increasing the proportion of townhouses. This kind of "fiscal zoning" will become more and more common unless there are major changes in the way state subventions are made to local governments.

Examination of the land use control systems of the six communities clearly indicates that the control of development is becoming more rigorous and demanding. As a result, developers' projects are not being approved as quickly as they were in the past, and in some cities new housing is being built at a slower rate than might be the case with more expeditious controls. The increased complexity of such development controls has had a major impact on the development industry. Smaller builders in particular are finding it very difficult to operate in highly regulated communities. In such communities the level of the builder competition tends to be very low, since only a few well-capitalized builder-developers can survive.

The six case communities have moved toward more aggressive preservation of open space at the same time that they have begun running out of land for urban development—ironic but logical timing. As the supply of buildable land becomes tighter, developers begin to convert hillside and ridgeland areas that were bypassed when flat, easily developed valley lands were readily available. As development begins to encroach upon environmentally sensitive areas, residents react by seeking action to have them preserved. This process has occurred in Fremont, San Rafael, Novato, and at least twenty other Bay Area communities.

Perhaps the most clear-cut of all of the case study findings is the trend toward making new development pay its own way. Pressed by Proposition 13, communities are forced to make fiscally motivated zoning and land use decisions. This dynamic is one of the major reasons why it is impossible to construct affordable housing in the Bay Area. Since almost every community is now armed with a cost-revenue impact model, new housing projects are forced to pass a fiscal acid test, and local governments have a powerful incentive to orient their planning more toward commercial development than in the past.

CHAPTER FIVE

The Direct Effects of Land Use Regulations on New Housing Costs

Controlling growth at the local level is difficult and frustrating. Postwar development pressures have had a severe impact on many Bay Area communities, leading them to respond with a variety of land use and environmental controls to shape, slow, or stop development. This chapter assesses how the land use control systems of the six case study areas directly affect the costs of producing new housing. There are four ways that local land use regulations affect residential construction costs: through land costs, requirements for the layout of subdivisions, approval time, and direct fees and charges. The more complex and difficult question of how local land use controls affect the pricing of new units is left to chapter 6.

Throughout California, the costs of constructing new housing have risen far more rapidly than the total rate of housing price inflation. Judging from our six case study cities (table 19), the average price of new single-family housing rose by an average of 71 percent between 1976 and the first half of 1979, a rate of increase well above that for housing prices in the six communities. Not surprisingly, the cities with the highest-priced housing, Novato and San Rafael, exhibited the greatest dollar increase in prices over the 1976–79 period ($83,800 and $65,300, respectively). On a percentage basis, however, homes in Fremont, Napa, and Santa Rosa also experienced large price increases. Clearly, the problem of rising production costs for new homes is a regional one.

Despite across-the-board construction cost increases, new homes are still more affordable in outlying cities such as Napa and Santa Rosa than in communities closer to San Francisco, or in cities such as Fremont where recent surges of demand have sharply pushed sales prices upward. Few

TABLE 19

SELECTED HOUSING CHARACTERISTICS IN THE SIX BAY AREA COMMUNITIES

	Fremont	Concord	Napa	Santa Rosa	San Rafael	Novato
New housing starts						
1976	1,145	1,251	—	1,112	—	—
1977	1,276	964	425	855	48	—
1978	1,127	372	499	763	38	—
1979	1,499	962	140		72	—
Average new single-family home price						
1976	$61,200	$62,300	$51,500	$49,100	$108,900	$76,900
1977	$75,600	$74,900	$70,700	$58,900	$131,700	$86,500
1978	$90,100	$87,900	$77,400	$65,100	$182,100	$109,500
1979	$113,800	$92,000	$97,800	$90,500	$172,200	$160,700[a]
Average new single-family home size (sq. ft.)						
1976	1,713	1,865	1,756	1,593	2,403	2,122
1977	1,716	1,907	1,896	1,524	2,502	2,071
1978	1,818	1,835	1,898	1,434	2,358	2,206
1979[a]	2,056	1,951	1,970	1,607	1,868	2,368
Average new home price per sq. ft.						
1976	$35.72	$33.40	$29.32	$30.82	$45.31	$36.24
1977	$44.05	$39.27	$37.28	$38.64	$52.63	$41.76
1978	$49.58	$47.90	$40.78	$45.39	$77.22	$49.63
1979	$55.35	$47.10	$49.64	$56.32	$93.25	$76.79
Average new home lot size (sq. ft.)	7,500–8,100	6,900–10,000	8,500–9,200	7,800–9,500	11,500–18,600	10,500–13,200

SOURCES: Housing starts from California Department of Finance Population Estimates, 1976–80. Price, square footage, and lotsize information from Northern California Society of Real Estate Appraisers.

[a]Data for 1979 only available for January through June.

Bay Area communities reported new home prices of less than $90,000 in 1979, and in most cities they easily exceeded $100,000. Although table 19 documents many of the recent trends for new Bay Area homes, it omits one that is very important—the substitution of townhouses and condominiums for detached starter homes, particularly in areas where supplies of flat, stable land are dwindling, such as Concord.[1] Priced below $90,000 and with less than 1,500 square feet of floor space, Concord's new townhouses are designed to appeal to younger families, first-time home buyers, and the single person desiring the tax/investment advantages of owning a home. The same kind of development is occurring in other Bay Area communities, including Hayward, Redwood City, San Mateo, and Vallejo. Townhouse and condominium construction has also increased in higher-income suburbs. Not only are Novato and San Rafael builders constructing condominiums to appeal to those priced out of the detached home market; by erecting high-quality, architecturally innovative townhouses, Marin homebuilders are also aiming for smaller families that want the benefits of owning a home while foregoing the chores of yardwork and home maintenance.

THE COST OF NEW HOUSING

How much should it cost to construct a new home? In 1976, Fox and Jacobs, a Dallas-based volume builder specializing in tract construction, could provide a finished home with 1,540 square feet of floor space for less than $30,000.[2] Although some Bay Area residents might look down on the Fox home—a one-story affair using preassembled, masonite sheathing walls—other Bay Area households would not, and the sales figures suggest that many Dallas families found them a tremendous value. At the other extreme, an official of the Novak Development Company, a large-scale Novato builder, noted that he could not build a new home in Marin County that would sell for less than $160,000.[3] But the typical Novak home offers 2,000 square feet, hardwood floors, a fireplace, a microwave oven, and a 7,500-square-foot lot.

This contrast between the Novak and the Fox and Jacobs homes illustrates two points, the first related to demand and the second to supply. First, builders produce what they think home buyers want. Even if Fox and Jacobs could get their "basic home" approved for construction by the Novato planning authorities, they would probably find substantially less demand for their stripped 1,540-square-foot home in wealthy Novato than in the rapidly growing Dallas suburbs. Second, Fox and Jacobs have a basic advantage over Novak: lower land costs. Even if their entire construction operation could be magically transported to the Bay Area, Fox and Jacobs would find it impossible to construct their basic home for anywhere near their Dallas costs.

Whether a 100-unit tract developer or the "spec" builder of a single custom home, every builder faces the same generic costs: land, subdivision improvements, construction materials and labor, interest and finance charges, planning and service fees, and overhead expenses.

THE MOST FUNDAMENTAL FACTOR: LAND

It all starts with land. The price and availability of this commodity ultimately determine where new housing is built—and how much. In cities where large tracts of raw land are still available, builders continue to provide new subdivisions of affordable single-family homes. Where land is not plentiful, or where local governments have restricted the supply of raw land, the new construction that does occur centers around dense townhouses and expensive custom homes on large lots.

The urban land market is a curious one. No standardized product exists; each parcel differs in size, configuration, environmental quality, and development potential as defined by local zoning ordinances. Unlike the stock market, in which thousands of transactions occur simultaneously and the flow of information is almost instantaneous, the land market sees only infrequent activity, and price information is difficult to come by. As a result, expectations play a key role in the determination of land prices. For example, a land speculator might act out of a long-term expectation that a parcel's land uses will shift from agriculture to urban activities. In the short term, a large landholder's decision to develop a particular site may rest on his expectation of its development potential and on assumptions about the availability of other buildable parcels in the area.

In a real estate market where land is viewed as being in tight supply, owners of developable property will attempt to keep their parcels off the market until prices have been bid to a maximum. Thus land prices are propelled upward by market conditions, government policies, or any other factors that either actually reduce the supply of developable land or give the impression that the supply of vacant land is dwindling. For example, in Novato a large parcel located in a designated floodplain and judged unlikely to be approved for development sold for the very low price of $1,500 per acre in 1979. In the same city, a two-acre parcel that had stable soils and was surrounded by expensive homes sold for $185,000. If the latter parcel were developed under R-1 zoning (10,000-square-foot minimum lot size), the raw land value per lot would exceed $25,000.

To understand the relationship between the price of undeveloped land and the price of a finished lot, consider the hypothetical case of a subdivider who pays $150,000 for a three-acre parcel on which he intends to develop twelve single-family detached lots. With individual lot improvement costs assumed to be $8,000, and total planning fees estimated at $600, development costs run to $21,000 per lot. But the developer also incurs other costs along the way. Even if the land were originally acquired on option, with purchase occurring immediately after the approval of a tentative subdivision map, the finance charges on a six-month, 80 percent loan at a 15 percent interest rate would exceed $900 per lot. Adding 10 percent for the subdivider's overhead and 15 percent profit, the developer charge would average $27,500 for any of the twelve lots. If instead of selling the subdivided lots, the developer were to undertake construction of single-family homes, the lot cost would still exceed $26,000. Although he would no longer add a separate profit margin to the land component of the completed home, increased interest charges and taxes over the home construction period would more than make up the difference.

In 1979, one of the Bay Area's hottest land markets was in Fremont, where raw land frequently sold in the range of $50,000 per acre. Considering the past and present abundance of raw land in Fremont, this price range was quite high—a condition that local real estate analysts attribute to continued growth in the South Bay area and the spillover of Silicon Valley households unable to afford housing closer to Santa Clara County job centers. Another fact in spiraling land prices was the realization that very large land parcels—those of fifty acres or more—were becoming scarce. Development companies building subdivisions as large as one hundred units or more began bidding up the price.

In contrast, Marin County has always boasted very high land prices, as one might expect given its unique natural environment, comparatively low residential densities, and excellent highway access to San Francisco. Residential land was fairly plentiful in San Rafael during the 1950s, and in Novato until the 1960s, but today local land use and annexation policies exacerbate the problem of a dwindling land supply. Raw land sales are now infrequent in Novato, and as in San Rafael, most transactions involve previously subdivided or improved lots. The buyer also pays a premium for Marin's popularity, location, and environmental amenities. The average price in 1978–79 for an acre of raw land in San Rafael was $75,000. In Novato, the comparable average land transaction was

$57,000. Land prices in both cities rose at an annual rate of 20 to 25 percent between 1975 and 1979—a rate nearly equivalent to the yearly increase in their housing prices. Two related conditions accounted for this rapid rise. First, as illustrated in table 20, undeveloped land is becoming increasingly scarce in Novato and San Rafael. Second, in a period of pronounced but erratic inflation, and in a local market characterized by a strong willingness to pay for housing, real estate is generally viewed as an inflation-beating investment. Investors and speculators are encouraged to raise their bid prices for valuable parcels, while potential sellers, reading the same set of signals, up their asking prices. The result is a long and steep land price spiral, fed by high Marin County incomes and even higher housing prices.

Despite widespread agreement that southern Sonoma County supply of vacant land is sufficient to accommodate expected population growth through the year 2000, land in the area (including Santa Rosa) is expensive and regarded by developers as being in tight supply. Until the recent credit-induced housing construction slowdown, land prices were increasing at an estimated annual rate of 15 to 25 percent, a rate of price inflation greater than that of Santa Rosa housing. Large land parcels suitable for single-family development and zoned R-1 (single-family detached) sold for roughly $25,000 per acre in the summer of 1979; appearing on the list of buyers were several large housing developers scrambling to bank sufficient land for future construction. Finished lot prices also reflected the boost in raw land prices. For example, Santa Rosa real estate appraisers report that during the summer of 1979, 6,000-square-foot finished lots (with utilities, roads, and other subdivision improvements) brought $20,000 to $30,000 on the land market. Larger, half-acre lots often sold for over $50,000.

Sonoma County will likely continue to be a major residential growth center. Although Petaluma instituted a residential permit allocation system in 1974, Santa Rosa does not seem inclined to follow Petaluma's lead. Expecting continued economic expansion in Santa Rosa, "bullish" real estate developers foresee a steady demand for all forms of housing through the end of the century. Larger builders also view the Santa Rosa market as the "last frontier." With communities to the south either employing growth controls or almost entirely built out, Santa Rosa and Rohnert Park are the only remaining North Bay communities in which developers can compete.

Napa's supply of developable land (within the RUL boundary) is much smaller than Santa Rosa's. At the same time, Napa's population and eco-

TABLE 20
LAND AND IMPROVEMENT COSTS

	Fremont	Concord	Napa	Santa Rosa	San Rafael	Novato
			Sample Lot Size (in sq. ft.)			
	8,000	10,000	9,000	8,000	12,000	12,000
Land	$9,100 (@ $50,000/acre)	$9,100 (@ $40,000/acre)	$3,100 (@ $15,000/acre)	$3,300 (@ $18,000/acre)	$20,500 (@ $75,000/acre)	$15,000 (@ $57,000/acre)
Lot improvements	$10,000	$12,000	$10,000	$8,000	$12,000	$12,000
Total lot cost	$19,100	$21,100	$13,100	$11,300	$32,500	$27,000

nomic growth have slowed in recent years (partially as a result of prior growth restrictions), and the demand for new housing has slackened. Despite a six-month building permit moratorium and the adoption of a growth management system, vacancy rates have been constant over the last five years. A year after the formal implementation of the Residential Development Management Plan, the outlook for Napa's land market remains cloudy. Unlike Santa Rosa, where large-scale builders still dominate, Napa home builders tend to be smaller and less willing to engage in what is seen as speculative construction. Coupled with the decreased supply of large developable parcels and the uncertainty of project approval under the RDMP, Napa's lack of large builders results in a relatively inactive raw land market. Acreage sales are less frequent than purchases of subdivided lots, which are exempt from the RDMP if developed individually. During 1979, Napa realtors reported a floor price of $20,000 for a single 6,000-square-foot lot located in an R-1 District.[4]

HOW PUBLIC POLICY AFFECTS LAND SUPPLY

City land use policies and ordinances affect the price of developable land—and ultimately, the cost of new housing—in two ways. First, cities can reduce the physical supply of land through purchase, condemnation, or other means of acquisition, and the effective supply through prohibitions on further annexation or the imposition of urban service boundaries. Second, zoning ordinances and general plans can be used to decrease the development potential of particular parcels. These policies change the supply of available land and reorder their prices, usually upward.[5]

The precise effects of local land development controls depend on the strength of the demand for land, the supply of developable land available, and the rate at which that supply is being depleted. For example, only nine hundred acres of developable land remained in Concord in 1978, and nearly 50 percent of that acreage was held by one landowner. But because surrounding communities such as Antioch and Pittsburg had ample low-priced raw land, Concord land prices did not escalate as quickly as in other constrained, fast-growth communities, such as Fremont.

Prior to 1978, governments in three of the six cities—Napa, San Rafael, and Novato—had adopted de facto policies aimed at limiting outward expansion. All three have discouraged annexation applications. Napa adopted its own version of a public service/utilities boundary, and Concord decided that future annexations would be limited to islands of unincorporated land wholly or partially contained by city boundaries.

Soon after Santa Rosa's designation of its urban services boundary in 1978, several builders submitted subdivision applications for lands outside the designated limit. Santa Rosa officials responded by saying that urban services would not be extended beyond the boundary in the foreseeable future, and thus residential development would not be permitted. These refusals told landowners and home builders that Santa Rosa's buildable land supply was for all practical purposes finite, despite a seemingly limitless supply of developable agricultural land. Builders seeking to secure or "bank" sufficient raw land for future housing projects quickly bid prices upward. Reading the same set of signals, owners of coveted parcels upped their asking prices. The result was a flurry of land acquisitions at inflated prices. Thus the private market reacted to a perceived decline in land supply, even though the undeveloped areas enclosed by the urban services boundary were projected as adequate to meet Santa Rosa's housing needs through the year 2000.

In Napa, which has much less vacant land than Santa Rosa, the 1975 introduction of the RUL did *not* cause any widespread increase in land prices. Creation of the RUL coincided with the second half of a nationwide housing recession, and the market was still bearish for both housing and land. Large-scale tract developers, who typically compete for vacant land supplies, had already abandoned Napa for cities with greater development potential. And though the Bay Area demand for housing rose in the years after adoption of the RUL, Napa was no longer regarded as a regional growth center. Together with the ongoing possibility of additional growth controls, these factors served to moderate land price increases. Napa's adoption of the RDMP in 1979 not only added to the uncertainties faced by builders, it also reoriented the market for vacant land. Consider the example of an acre of undeveloped land in the Brown's Valley area, a highly desirable neighborhood, but one in which development was difficult under the RDMP point system. Though this parcel would probably have sold quickly for $15,000 in 1977, its owner had difficulty selling it for $20,000 two years later. A 33 percent increase in asking price over a two-year period seems excessive, until it is contrasted with the 50 percent price increases seen over the same period for closer-in parcels favored by the RDMP. Napa realtors also reported that during 1979, price hikes for raw land were less than those for subdivided but unfinished lots, which are exempt from the RDMP. Napa officials concede that the RDMP had some effect on the distribution of land prices in the city. They correctly point out, however, that any meaningful estimate of that effect has been compromised by the coincident nationwide plunge in housing demand.[6]

Attempts to limit the supply of land available to home builders took a different form in Marin County: the acquisition of buildable land as permanent open space, the promotion of Planned District zoning, and the selective downzoning of vacant land parcels. In defense of his city's open-space acquisitions, Novato Planning Director Brian Mattson points out that most of the acquired areas consist of steep hillside, unlikely ever to be intensively developed. But at the same time Mattson concedes that some of the purchased lands are developable, and that taking them off the market has probably had an inflationary impact on land prices.

How much of an impact is difficult to assess. Because Marin's development-restricting policies evolved gradually during the course of the 1970s, and because land markets reflect changes in development potential fairly quickly, it is an extremely difficult task to identify price effects occurring ten or even five years after controls have first been imposed. That upper-income households have been willing to pay for the exclusivity of a home in Marin only makes it doubly difficult to isolate the factors in rising land prices.

Both the Concord and Fremont city governments have typically maintained a hands-off attitude toward the rate of land development. With the exception of the Northern Plains episode, Fremont has not attempted to reduce the supply of buildable land or construction densities. In the past, Fremont has zoned hillside areas for low-density agricultural purposes and used Williamson contracts to save working farms, but in no case have these steps been permanent. Rather, Fremont has attempted to impose some order on the flow of raw land into the development process. Given that city's supply of land, neither policy has been greatly inflationary. Concord officials have always been similarly hesitant to regulate the supply of developable land. The city did establish several large Planned Districts during the early 1970s, but given the Concord style of subdivision approval, that step was not viewed as an attempt to reduce residential densities. Large-scale builders have generally preferred raw acreage in Pittsburg or Antioch over Concord's remaining parcels, a factor that, when coupled with the Newhall Company's vacant land monopoly, has tended to limit land speculation opportunities and land price increases. Likewise, the fact that Concord's sewer-related development moratorium is effective at the building permit stage, not the subdivision approval stage, has reduced the moratorium's inflationary effects on individual lot prices. In fact, by increasing the uncertainties of development, the moratorium may actually be helping to hold land prices down.

A diminishing supply of developable land, along with land use controls that limit development, have greatly affected the urban land markets of Concord, Fremont, Novato, San Rafael, Napa, and Santa Rosa. In the more mature cities of Concord and San Rafael, historical development has consumed most of the developable land. In Novato, Napa, and Santa Rosa, rising land prices have followed controls limiting the conversion of outlying parcels. In Fremont, the combination of dwindling large land parcels and strong demand pressures from Santa Clara County have heated up the land market.

SUBDIVISION IMPROVEMENTS

Between 1968 and 1976, the cost of constructing a finished lot in a typical Bay Area subdivision rose from slightly more than $2,300 to over $6,300. By January 1980, according to the Bank of America, the costs approached $8,300 per 6,000-square-foot lot.[7] In all likelihood these estimates are on the low side, as per-lot improvement costs vary widely depending on slope, soil stability, and the number of finished lots over which fixed costs are distributed. A recent study of Bay Area subdivision costs by Ecumene Associates (table 21) attaches some numbers to these factors. For a 10,000-square-foot hillside lot, the costs of site preparation, street and utility construction, engineering services, and fees run as high as $25,000. For an equivalently sized lot in an inland valley or along the flat coastal bay plain, the costs total only $17,000. Not only are hillside lots more expensive to prepare, but Ecumene estimates that hillside construction techniques can add an additional $25,000 to the cost of a home. True, these estimates include the expense of constructing finished lots as well as the extra costs attributable to topography. But why have subdivision costs escalated so rapidly in ten years' time, and, perhaps more important, what portion of the increase is due to local restrictions?

The tasks necessary to construct finished lots and make required improvements have varied little since the early 1960s, or even in some areas since the mid-1950s; nor do they vary much among Bay Area communities. Builders are required to grade home pads (the section of the lot on which the home is constructed), install drainage and erosion controls, construct necessary sewer and water submains to serve the home or tract, and provide streets, curbs, and usually sidewalks. Depending on location, home builders may also be required to provide street lighting, trees, acoustical barriers separating the tract from major traffic arteries, some minimal landscaping, and connecting links to existing sewer and water mains (table 22). The one "improvement" added to the list only recently is land dedication for neigh-

TABLE 21

COMPARATIVE COSTS PER UNIT FOR HILL AREA AND
BAY PLAIN DEVELOPMENT
(ASSUMES 10,000 SQ. FT. SUBDIVISION LOTS AND
A 2,000 SQ. FT. HOUSE)[a]

Cost Component	Hill Area	% of Total Sales Price	Bay Plain	% of Total Sales Price
	Cost		*Cost*	
Land purchase	$4,500	3%	$12,000	10%
Site preparation, street and utility improvements, engineering, fees, etc.	$25,000	17%	$17,000	14%
Total cost per lot	$29,500	20%	$30,000	25%
Spread footings, subdrains, and special hill area building techniques	$27,000	18%		
Other home construction	$90,000	61%	$90,000	75%
Sales price of home	$146,500	100%	$120,000	100%

SOURCE: *Walpert Ridge Environmental Impact Report,* Ecumene Associates, Hayward, Calif., 1979.

NOTE: Figures may not add up due to rounding.

[a]Figures are taken from representative projects or plans and *are not site specific.* Likewise, interest and carrying costs are not considered. Note that the figures are based upon a specific type of single-family home and are not necessarily representative of other forms of residential development.

borhood park space, but in most instances cities encourage builders to substitute a cash payment in lieu of actual dedications.

Thus, escalating subdivision costs cannot be attributed to changes or variations in the improvement process. The primary reason why subdivision costs have increased so dramatically is deceptively simple: inflation. In 1977, the price (nationally averaged) of a ton of asphalt for street and driveway construction was $73, delivered. By January 1980, the price of a ton of asphalt had jumped to $108, a 48 percent increase.[8] During the same period, the costs of the twenty-four inch concrete pipe typically used in the construction of sewer submains jumped 21 percent. Labor costs

TABLE 22
REQUIRED SUBDIVISION IMPROVEMENTS

Improvement	Concord	Fremont	Napa	Santa Rosa	San Rafael	Novato
Noise barriers (generally walls)	varies with location	X	varies with location	varies with location		
Streets and thoroughfares	X	X	X	X	X[a]	X
Curbs, gutters, and sidewalks	X	X	X	X	X	X
Utility lines (sewer, water, and electrical)	varies with location	X	X	X	X[a]	X
Lots in conformance with applicable zoning standards	X	X	X	X	X	X
Drainage and erosion controls	X	X	X	X	X	X
Fire hydrants and water delivery system	hydrants only	X	X	X	X[a]	X
Utility hookups for each lot	X	X	X	X	X	X
Street lighting	X	X	X	X	X	X
Street trees and mailboxes	X	X				
Telephone hookups for each lot		X				
Railroad crossings		X				

SOURCE: Local Subdivision Ordinances.
[a]Because of the shortage of buildable acreage, these improvements are rarely necessary.

also figure into materials cost increases. According to Lee Saylor, Inc., a Bay Area construction estimator, the cost of union labor nationally rose by 36 percent between 1974 and 1977, and by 15 percent between 1977 and January 1980. In total, Saylor estimates that labor and materials costs increased by about 200 percent between 1967 and 1980, which goes a long way toward explaining higher subdivision costs. Saylor's estimates are corroborated by a study undertaken for Citation Homes, which reports that the cost of a typical subdivision in the South Bay (including the Fremont area) rose by 33 percent between 1968 and 1972, and by an additional 200 percent between 1972 and 1976. While certain items such as street and sidewalk construction rose at less than the total rate, others, such as clearing, grading, utility construction, and landscaping, registered excessive price hikes.

Another factor in increasing subdivision costs is the quality and location of developable land. In the 1950s, 1960s, and early 1970s, much of the region's new housing, including the bulk of new construction in each of the six case study cities, took place on flat, stable bay plain or in inland valleys. Despite the occasional "leapfrogging" tract, new subdivisions were generally added along the border of an existing tract. As a result, sewer and water lines and streets were constructed as increments to the existing system. This helped to keep down subdivision improvement costs. In the case of Santa Rosa, where it was the city's policy to extend services on demand, or Fremont, where new construction was a tool to unify five independent centers, utility districts helped underwrite the costs of sewer and water line extensions.

But this situation began changing in the 1970s, as available valley and bay plain acreage close to existing activity centers was built out. Some developers searched farther and farther from urban centers for inexpensive flatland, investigating cities such as Vacaville, Gilroy, and Tracy. Others began developing hillside areas. But in either case, home builders found their costs escalating sharply. Those who chose to build along hillsides faced not only citizen or even governmental opposition, but also higher costs to develop sewer lines, water lines, and especially streets. Moreover, local zoning codes frequently specified reduced densities on hillsides, which meant fewer new units over which builders could distribute their improvement costs. Finally, hillside construction often demanded extensive pad preparation or special foundation work. Those builders who had moved to the urban fringe were not necessarily any better off.

Even when building on flatland kept onsite construction costs down, some builders found themselves required to construct expensive connecting links to existing streets and utility networks, or occasionally even to subsidize new sewage treatment facilities. Partly in the name of fiscal responsibility (a common phrase since Proposition 13), and partly through a renewed desire to minimize sprawl, municipalities and special assessment districts were becoming increasingly reluctant to subsidize new infrastructure. As a result, home builders in Fremont, Napa, Santa Rosa, and a host of other growing cities were forced to shoulder a bigger share of the costs of providing improvements. The concept of assessing builders the full cost of development has perhaps been carried to its logical conclusion in Concord, where as a condition for obtaining a building permit in the sewer moratorium area, home builders must agree to privately underwrite a major sewer capacity increase that ultimately will serve not just those who financed it, but additional growth as well. The trend toward making developers provide infrastructure such as roadways, water, and sewer trunk lines probably adds 5 to 10 percent to the cost of new housing.

In his study of the impact of local government on housing costs, Steven Seidel claims that many communities enforce excessive subdivision improvement standards: unnecessarily wide streets and rights-of-way, the provision of sidewalks and curbs in rural environs, overdesigned sewerage systems, and unnecessary landscaping. All of this costs home builders and thus home buyers hundreds of additional dollars, Seidel maintains, based on his own survey of 2,327 builders and 80 cities, as well as a variety of independent engineering reports.[9]

But although some of the Bay Area builders interviewed felt that the costs of producing new homes could in fact be reduced by loosening subdivision standards, most admitted that given current practices and the current market, the reduction would not be that great. Unlike the majority of Seidel's respondents, who were drawn from a nationwide sampling, Bay Area builders have been dealing with essentially the same set of subdivision improvement standards for twenty or more years; most have completely incorporated these standards into their design/construction practices.

THE DELAY PROBLEM

Lengthy subdivision review periods cause much of the delay in constructing new housing, and therefore add considerably to the cost. Depending on a proposed housing project's size, location, and initial zoning, the entire subdivision approval process can take as little as two months or as long as three years. At first glance the review process may seem straightforward, but this is deceptive. Any Bay Area developer, whether large or small, will confirm that there are countless possible permutations, convolutions, and delays.

In practice, four factors differentiate the subdivision review process among cities:

1. *The number of review agencies involved in each approval.* In Fremont, for example, the review process is two-tiered—both the Fremont Planning Commission and the Fremont City Council review any and all subdivision and master plan applications. Not surprisingly, Fremont's project review periods for residential construction are among the region's longest. In contrast, Concord's project review process is single-tiered, with the city council reviewing subdivision or planned district applications only on appeal from the Concord Planning Commission. Project reviews in Concord are among the region's speediest, averaging just two to three months.

2. *The threshold project size beyond which a detailed Environmental Impact Report is required.* Most smaller residential projects receive "negative declarations" that exempt developers from preparing a detailed Environmental Impact Report. The threshold beyond which an EIR is required varies widely among communities. In Fremont, where the average residential project might include fifty units, EIRs are rarely required for projects smaller than twenty units. In Novato, where land is in shorter supply and projects tend to be smaller, the Novato Environmental Impact Review Committee might require an EIR from an applicant proposing only fifteen units. Communities also vary in the detail they require in an EIR.

3. *Reliance on conventional zoning versus planned districts.* Planned district applications, which involve detailed site plans, full environmental and social impact evaluation, and construction scheduling, are considerably more detailed than tentative subdivision applications. Accordingly, the planned-district review process tends to be more time-consuming than conventional subdivision review. To the extent that local governments either create planned districts themselves or encourage builders to apply for such rezoning, project approval times will tend to increase.

4. *The ratio of review staff to project applications.* Review staff work load greatly affects review times, particularly in fast-growing cities where the number of major proposals may exceed one hundred per year. The problem of insufficient review staff has been aggravated by Proposition 13 cutbacks and is most severe in cities with a two-tiered review process.

The review process is a means to perform several valuable functions. It allows local government to act as a watchdog, ensuring that local builders comply with the plethora of relevant zoning codes, general plan restrictions, subdivision ordinances, and requirements to mitigate unavoidable environmental impact. Most often the combination of close government scrutiny and delays associated with subdivision review will automatically shake out projects that are poorly designed or tenuously financed. Local government gains its bargaining power from the ability to reject a builder's proposal or stipulate costly design changes. Cities negotiate with builders over parkland dedication, the provision of infrastructure, site designs, and, in rare instances, housing densities. The popularity of planned-district zoning is at least partly explained by the fact that it increases the administrative discretion of local government officials.

And yet, among both city officials and home builders there is a growing consensus that something has gone wrong—the subdivision approval process simply takes too long. In Novato, where approval periods range from several months to several years, builders charge that unreasonable and unnecessary delays add several thousand dollars to the cost of each new unit. Santa Rosa planning officials agreed with local builders who complained about extreme delays, and in 1978 responded by streamlining the subdivision approval process. In the space of one year, tentative subdivision map approval time dropped from an average of 240 days to under 100. In Fremont, even the larger small builders who know full well how to play "the development game" often find themselves waiting two to three years for a construction go-ahead. Cognizant of the problem, the California Legislature passed AB 884, putting a limit of twelve months on the local subdivision approval process; unfortunately, many communities have managed to circumvent the requirements of AB 884.[10]

Why do some builders encounter lengthy delays while others speed through the approval process? In truth, part of the blame for approval and processing delays must be shared by project applicants. In addition to the factors listed above, other specific causes of delay include:

1. *Improper submissions.* Many builders simply do a poor job of preparing plans and proposals. Needed information on site geology, potential traffic effects, and the impact on neighborhoods may be misstated or omitted. Site plans may be poorly considered, easements not noted, or land dedications not specified. Although builders may believe that such detail is superfluous, valuable review time may be required to bring a plan up to minimum acceptable quality.

2. *Design disagreements between builder, planner, and city council members.* Frequently, design features specified by builders are not acceptable to the various review agencies. Builders and government officials may negotiate over final plans; other times proposals are initially rejected. In each case, project redesign time is needed. This problem may be particularly severe when, for example, the city council adds, at the end of the project approval process, a design stipulation not required earlier.

3. *Midstream design changes initiated by builders.* Redesigns based on better market research, changing consumer preferences, and availability of financing are common and often occur midway through the approval process. Such redesigns themselves take time, and may also add to approval delays as the revised plans are evaluated.

4. *Increased citizen participation.* Homeowner's associations and other interested parties have claimed a larger role in the plan approval process.

5. *Environmental Impact Report requirements.* If a builder has not prepared an EIR, but learns that one is required, an additional two to six months may be added to the process, depending on the scope of the EIR.

The extent to which these factors come into play will vary according to project size, type, and location, municipal attitudes toward development, and the sophistication of the builder.

Table 23 summarizes subdivision approval times in each of the six case study cities. For most projects, the crucial step is the tentative subdivision map review or, in the case of planned districts, the preliminary development plan review. Once a builder has gained city council approval of his tentative map or preliminary plan, subsequent changes or delays are generally minor. The review times shown in table 23 are for projects proposed under R-1 zoning; planned-district review times are considerably more varied.

Delays of all types affect the cost of producing new homes in several ways. A 1978 study by the Rice Center presented a delay-cost model with four components: (1) additional land-related costs (land interest costs, property taxes, overhead rates); (2) development loan interest costs; (3) inflation costs; and (4) costs of capital tie-up.[11]

Even with the Rice model, however, it is difficult to pinpoint the costs of delay. Numerous assumptions must be employed, because overhead rates and capital tie-up costs are hard to determine empirically, and builders rarely reveal their financing arrangements or land acquisition costs.

The Rice Study has also been faulted for offering few normative guidelines as to how long subdivision and plan review times *should* take. We cannot know, therefore, what portion of delay costs (estimated by Rice at $140–$200 per month in 1978 dollars) is avoidable. This is not a trivial criticism. Delay costs are most burdensome when they are unexpected. Some developers are prepared for lengthy delays—for example, those who finance land or construction internally have longer-term labor and materials contracts, and are therefore less vulnerable to inflation, or they budget a substantial contingency fund. Typically, these "prepared" home builders are large-scale tract developers, who construct the majority of

TABLE 23
SUBDIVISION MAP APPROVAL PERIODS, 1978–79
(ASSUMES R-1 ZONING)

Project Size	Fremont	Concord	Santa Rosa	Napa	San Rafael	Novato
Less than 10 units	4–6 mo.	3 mo.	3 mo.	3–4 mo. under RDMP[a]	too few projects to sample	less than 6 mo.
10–25 units	6–12 mo.	3–6 mo.	3–6 mo.[b]			6–8 mo.
25–100 units	12–18 mo.		6–8 mo.[b]			12 mo.
100+ units	24+ mo.					
Primary causes of delay	two-tiered review process	design disagreements	design disagreements		review process	two-tiered review system
	design disagreements	EIR preparation	EIR preparation		design disagreements	EIR preparation
	midstream design changes				EIR preparation	design disagreements
	public opposition					
	EIR preparation					public opposition
	too small review staff					

[a]Prior to passage of RDMP, review periods varied between 6 and 18 months.
[b]Review periods were somewhat reduced in 1978.

new homes in Fremont or Santa Rosa. In my interviews with Fremont builders, several commented that subdivision approval delays, although perhaps excessive, were not unexpected or particularly burdensome.[12] However, this was not the case in Novato, where large and small builders compete. Several developers bitterly complained about the costs of delay, especially the small builders who typically operate on a tight cash-flow basis and are therefore more vulnerable to delay.

CALCULATING THE COSTS OF DELAY

For the purpose of computing delay costs, I assumed that home builders obtain construction loans only after all relevant local government approvals have been given. A serious difficulty in estimating the costs of delay is deciding how long the review and approval process should take; ten months would be unreasonably long for a ten-unit project but speedy for a hundred-unit planned district. For sample single-family housing proposals of ten, thirty, and fifty units, I have assumed minimum approval periods of four, eight, and twelve months, respectively, with the builders coordinating their planning and financing activities accordingly. In each case the units are similar in size and location to the 2,100-square-foot home profiled in table 24. Raw land costs at the time of acquisition are assumed to be $10,000 per unit, and interest charges on the land acquisition loans an average of 12 percent per year. Inflation is pegged at 10 percent, and construction costs are estimated to be $95,000 per unit, including both subdivision and home construction activities. In these examples the property tax rate is $4.36 per $100 assessed property valuation (a representative rate), and the homes take nine months to complete.

Table 24 presents estimates of how a doubling of time consumed in the subdivision/master plan approval process would increase the construction costs of three sample housing projects. For the ten-unit project, doubling the approval time from four to eight months would add roughly $4,000 (3.4 percent) to the cost of construction; an additional eight months of approval time would add $8,000 (6.8 percent). In the fifty-unit example, construction costs would rise by roughly $12,000 per unit (10.2 percent) if the plan review process consumed two years instead of one.

By far the biggest factor in the added costs is inflation in construction materials and labor costs, which accounts for roughly 85 percent of delay-related cost increase. Increased interest charges can add up to $2,000 to the cost of new housing, but the impact of additional property taxes is relatively minor. As table 24 indicates, delays increase the cost of building new housing at roughly the rate of inflation.

TABLE 24

EFFECTS OF APPROVAL DELAYS ON NEW HOME CONSTRUCTION COSTS
(PER UNIT COST)

Cost Item	Ten-Unit Project		Thirty-Unit Project		Fifty-Unit Project	
	No Delay	4 Mo. Delay	No Delay	8 Mo. Delay	No Delay	1 Yr. Delay
Land	$10,000	$10,000	$10,000	$10,000	$10,000	$10,000
Interest on land loan	400	800	800	1,600	1,200	2,400
Construction costs	95,000	98,150	95,000	101,350	95,000	104,500
Interest on construction loan	7,900	8,175	7,950	8,475	7,950	8,750
Fees	2,300	2,300	2,300	2,300	2,300	2,300
Additional property tax		150		300		450
Subtotal	$115,600	$119,575	$116,050	$124,025	$116,450	$128,400
Additional cost percentage attributable to delay		3.4%		6.8%		10.2%

For large Fremont and Santa Rosa developers, the delay costs shown in table 24 are probably borne out in reality. In Concord and San Rafael, where lengthy delays are rare, delay-related costs average about 4 percent. Theoretically, Napa's RDMP review process totally eliminates approval delays, but in practice there are delays of four to six months, which add about 5 percent to costs. In Novato, the range of reported subdivision approval times varies widely, and delay costs can range from 4 to 10 percent.

The dollar costs included in table 24 are not the only costs associated with plan approval delays. Although developers and home builders are typically highly leveraged—that is, they use a small amount of their own capital as collateral for land and construction loans—many still operate on a positive cash-flow basis. Expectations of project profitability are therefore directly linked to project scheduling. To a highly leveraged builder, the line between profit and loss may be a fine one directly related to meeting a loan deadline. Large builders can absorb these temporary losses, repay outstanding loans from other income, or perhaps renegotiate the loans. Others must liquidate some or all of their projects in order to meet financial obligations. But in all cases, the risk and uncertainty posed by possible delay is capitalized into higher profit. To what extent is risk capitalized in the home building industry? That question remains unanswered, but in cities such as Novato, where approval periods range from six to sixteen months, the effect on prices is undoubtedly significant.

FEES AND CHARGES

It is frequently argued that the increasing planning and development fees assessed by local governments are a major factor driving up the cost of housing and land. That may be true in some communities. For example, in Vallejo, Livermore, and Fairfield, locally assessed fees exceed $5,500 per dwelling unit. But a recent study by ABAG revealed that in the expanding suburban areas of the region, 1979 local government fee assessments per new dwelling unit averaged $4,033—about 4 percent of the price of a typical new home.[13]

Historically, development fees have been assessed to pay for the additional public services a local government or special-assessment district provides to buyers of new homes. Fees have always varied widely within the Bay Area, some cities assessing builders according to the marginal costs resulting from new construction, and other cities and special districts choosing to subsidize new housing through property tax revenues. In the wake of Proposition 13, the loss of property tax revenues led many of the latter cities to revaluate their fee schedules and, in several instances, to institute large, unprecedented jumps in development fees. A 1979 study by the Institute for Business and Economic Research at the University of California, Berkeley, estimated that local government assessments on new housing increased by an average of 70 percent between 1976 and 1979. [14] The IBER researchers note that only four of the sixty-five cities surveyed imposed fees of $2,100 or more in 1976, but that by 1979 twenty-two communities listed fees above this level.

Table 25 profiles 1976 and 1979 fees for the six case study cities, dividing fees into four categories: planning and plan review, building permit and review, utility hookup, and growth impact.

Planning fees generally pay for staff review time and administrative work, and therefore vary with project size. For example, in the case of a large planned district with a hundred units, planning fees might average only $50 per dwelling unit. For a smaller, conventionally zoned, twenty-unit proposal, the average per-unit fee might total $120. Neither of these estimates includes the cost of preparing an EIR; if an EIR is required by the reviewing agency, its cost is borne solely by the applicant. The most notable rise in planning fees between 1976 and 1979 occurred in Fremont and Concord, as those cities shifted from partial subsidization of planning activities to fee schedules reflecting staff review times and salaries. Though planning-related fees have risen substantially, they add relatively little to the cost of new housing, particularly in large projects.

Building permit fees and plan check fees are assessed on a sliding scale that varies with home size and value. Five of the six case study cities base their building permit review charges on the value-based fee schedule suggested in the Uniform Building Code. Accordingly, the increase shown in table 25 reflects inflation-related increases in valuation, not higher plan review rates. Averaging $500 per dwelling unit in the Bay Area (based on a 1,500-square-foot tract home), building permit fees contributed less than 1 percent to the cost of a new home in 1979.

Utility hookup fees cover both the capacity increases needed to serve new development (i.e., reservoirs and sewage treatment plants) and the costs of servicing a particular property. They do not pay for main trunk-line extensions or expansions, which, if necessary, are financed by the builder. Table 25 reveals that water and sewer hookup fees vary widely among the six study cities. Between 1976 and 1979, sewer hookup fees were more stable than water hookup fees, which may reflect the use of septic tanks in outlying areas. In all six of the study communities, sewer and water charges together constitute the largest component of fees as-

TABLE 25

RESIDENTIAL DEVELOPMENT FEES AND CHARGES

Fee Classification	Concord		Fremont		Napa		Santa Rosa		Novato		San Rafael	
	1976	1979	1976	1979	1976	1979	1976	1979	1976	1979	1976	1979
Planning department	25	150	35	100	25	25	25	25	25	25	25	50
Building department	300	375	300	375	300	375	225	301	260	356	325	425
Water hookup	975	975	950	1,255	285	590	550	655	655	1,050	760	1,700
Sewer hookup	1,050	1,050	580	802	900	900	340	600	435	510	200	300
Construction tax	0	0	550	566	125	125		709				
School impact fee	0	0	0	645	400	400		—[a]				
Park impact fee	300	300	300	600	250	250			275	275	725	380
Total fee	2,650	2,850	2,715	4,350	2,285	2,665	1,140	2,300	1,650	2,200	1,535	2,855
Average new home sale price	62,300	92,000	61,200	113,800	51,500	97,800	49,100	90,500	76,900	160,700	108,900	174,200
	4.3%	3.1%	4.4%	3.8%	4.4%	2.7%	2.3%	2.5%	2.1%	1.3%	1.4%	1.6%

[a] Varies with school district.

sessed, varying from a low of 47 percent in Fremont to a high of 71 percent in Concord. In general, water and sewer services are provided not by local municipalities, but by state-chartered special-assessment districts. Generally, these special-assessment districts increase their capacities to accommodate local growth trends, but in extraordinary circumstances, such as the 1976–77 drought, they may refuse to provide new hookups. The cost of providing new capacity is divided between new customers and existing rate payers according to formulas determined by the various utility boards of directors—a fact that helps to explain the wide descrepancy in hookup fees.

Fees covering such services as school expenses, street construction, or park maintenance go by a variety of names: growth impact fees, construction taxes, bedroom taxes, and special growth assessments. And as table 25 shows, they vary widely among cities. In slower-growing communities, typified by Napa, Proposition 13 revenue losses were made up without increasing growth impact fees. In expanding cities such as Fremont or Santa Rosa, existing fees were boosted or new fees imposed to pay for school construction and parkland expansion. Regionwide, growth impact fees contributed an average of $2,000 to the cost of a new home in 1979.

This discussion points out that although planning and building permit fees are often seen as excessive, they are for the most part service-related and actually contribute very little to the cost of constructing new housing. Such fees could justifiably be termed excessive only if it were reasonable to believe that comparable service could be provided at a lower cost by a private builder or developer. Otherwise, sewer and water fees should be seen as reflecting the marginal costs of servicing new development. Whether these costs should be split between existing residents (through the property tax or rate base) and buyers of new homes (through fees) is a political decision made by city councils and assessment-district boards of directors.

CONCLUSION

This chapter has examined how local land use regulations directly increase the cost of new home construction by affecting land acquisition, subdivision development, project review time, and fees and dedications.

In Novato and San Rafael, where high demand for housing coexists with a dwindling supply of buildable land, land costs are well above the levels in other areas. Either by exhausting their developable land or by erecting barriers to the development of vacant land, these cities have driven land prices upward. While the impact on costs is difficult to determine, local land use policies (including Marin County's) probably add 30 percent to land costs in Novato and San Rafael. In Santa Rosa and Fremont, the scarcity of large parcels of vacant land has already pushed land prices up by 5 to 10 percent. Because the level of housing demand is lower in Concord and Napa, land prices there have probably risen no more than 5 percent.

All of the case study communities have fairly complex and expensive subdivision requirements. Materials and labor costs have risen rapidly, forcing up lot preparation costs. Increased requirements for the dedication of land and public services have also increased costs. None of the communities studied absorbs the cost of extending services to new development. These costs are shifted to developers, adding between 5 and 10 percent to the cost of new housing, depending on the location and capacity of existing sewers, water lines, and streets.

With the growing use of permits and multistep project reviews, the time required to gain approval of a development has increased markedly in most communities. Requirements for detailed environmental impact reports and other specialized studies appear to be slowing down the review process, as are staff cutbacks due to Proposition 13. These trends add up to significant delays. But despite this problem, of the six communities only Santa Rosa has streamlined its review process. According to the developers interviewed, approval processes in Novato, Napa, and San Rafael are subject to excessive delays that add between 4 and 10 percent to the cost of new housing.

TABLE 26

COMBINED DIRECT COST EFFECT ESTIMATES OF LOCAL
LAND USE CONTROLS AND FEES ON NEW HOUSING

| | Additional Cost | |
Cost Component	Low (%)	High (%)
Land	5	10
Subdivision improvements	5	10
Delay costs	4	10
Fees and charges	4	4
Total	18	34

Development charges have also risen considerably since the passage of Proposition 13. All six communities levy fees and charges that are above the regional average, though not extraordinary. Recent ABAG estimates indicate that fees add about 4 percent to the cost of housing.

The combined effect of these four factors is presented in table 26. It is estimated that local land use controls, delays, fees, and charges add between 18 and 34 percent to the cost of a new house in the Bay Area—between $18,000 and $31,000 in dollar terms.

CHAPTER SIX

More Subtle Effects: Market Readjustments and Spillovers

This chapter goes several steps beyond identifying the direct effects of local land use controls on the cost of new housing construction. In it, I attempt to assess the indirect effects of local land use and environmental controls on the prices of new and existing housing units, as well as their spillover effects on surrounding communities.

Direct effects of regulations are those that affect the cost of producing new housing (land costs, subdivision costs, delay costs, and fees and charges), while indirect effects are those that secondarily influence the prices of *all* units, both new and existing.

Thus, an understanding of the characteristics of housing supply, demand, and their interaction is crucial in determining the indirect effects of local land use regulations. In areas where the demand for housing is very strong, such as Belmont, San Rafael, and Marin County, supply restrictions can be extremely inflationary. This was the conclusion of a study of San Jose, another strong housing market, conducted by the Urban Land Institute and Gruen, Gruen and Associates.[1]

On the other hand, even if local development is greatly restricted, the inflationary effects may not be substantial if the demand for housing is weak. In a study of Jacksonville, Florida, the Urban Land Institute found that restrictive land use controls did not significantly contribute to housing and land inflation.[2] Thus, indirect effects, since they are the result of price increases, are inherently tied to characteristics of both demand and supply.

THE TYPES OF INDIRECT EFFECTS

Indirect effects can be divided into four types: bottlenecks, monopoly power, market reorientation, and spillovers. The following section examines land and housing market performance in the case study communities to determine how and where these indirect effects have occurred.

Bottlenecks

What I've called a bottleneck effect takes place when the demand for land and housing exceeds current supply—a frequent occurrence. The best indication of a bottleneck is a vacancy rate below 5 percent. In the absence of local land use or development controls, the market quickly adjusts and supply increases to meet demand. But quite often bottlenecks occur because the community has not zoned for enough residential land to fulfill demand. If housing demand pressures continue in such cases, existing units will increase in price, and in the long term demand pressures will spill over into other communities, or else the economic forces creating demand will be cut off by rising costs. This is precisely what is beginning to happen in northern Santa Clara County. Silicon Valley cities want to attract clean, fiscally beneficial electronic industries, but most of these communities have little residentially zoned land to provide housing for employees of these new industries. Table 27 illustrates the severity of this imbalance between employment potential and residential development opportunities.

Housing prices in the county have increased tremendously over the past five years. The Santa Clara County Manufacturing Group has responded by expressing great concern over the lack of new housing construction in the area.[3] Industry officials fear that if housing prices continue to climb, the electronics industry will lose much of its ability to attract new employees at competitive wage rates. But while trade groups and concerned individuals describe the situation as a crisis, the process of market readjustment has already begun. Many employees, unable to afford housing near where they work, are looking instead to communities in southern Alameda County and, to a lesser extent, San Mateo County. Silicon Valley's lack of housing to meet job growth is a clear-cut example of a bottleneck effect.

Housing prices in Santa Clara and Marin Counties, in particular, are moving beyond per-square-foot price levels in other, less constrained areas. As indicated in table 28, the per-square-foot price of new single-family housing in Marin County cities (Fairfax, Novato, San Rafael, and

TABLE 27

JOBS AND HOUSING POTENTIAL IN SANTA CLARA COUNTY

	Job Expansion Based on Local Zoning	Housing Unit Expansion Based on Local Zoning
Palo Alto	3,000	1,300
Mountain View	18,620	3,600
Sunnyvale	12,350	1,680
Santa Clara	23,940	2,826
Cupertino	5,120	4,890
Los Altos	0	238
Los Altos Hills	0	322
Milpitas	29,700	3,648
San Jose	123,475	45,786
Campbell	500	200
Los Gatos	350	395
Saratoga	270	2,271
Monte Sereno	0	35
Morgan Hill	21,700	6,475
Gilroy	7,000	4,875
Total	246,005	78,541

SOURCE: Santa Clara County Manufacturing Group, *Vacant Land in Santa Clara County: Implications for Job Growth and Housing in the 1980s,* February 1980.

Tiburon) is greater than in prodevelopment areas in the East Bay (Livermore, Pleasanton, and Pleasant Hill).

Besides maintaining an imbalance between residential and industrial zoning, there are many other ways communities can create bottleneck effects, one being the use of growth controls. Traditional forms of local growth management regulate only the construction of housing, ignoring commercial and industrial uses. Planners may limit the number of housing permits issued annually, but they do not control the community's economic growth, nor the demand for housing. Few communities are willing to limit economic development, except the very exclusive residential enclaves, such as Los Altos Hills, Piedmont, and Tiburon. But in the absence of a comprehensive program to control the housing demand as well as supply, growth control programs are extremely inflationary, resulting in price increases for both new and existing units.

The lack of developable land can also contribute to rapid land and housing price inflation. This tends to occur in fairly dense urban areas, or

TABLE 28

PER-SQUARE-FOOT NEW HOUSING PRICES FOR SELECTED
BAY AREA CITIES, 1978–79

	1978	1979	% Change
Berkeley	72.00	80.00	11.1
Hayward	48.00	54.00	12.5
Livermore	50.00	55.00	10.0
Pleasanton	51.00	59.00	15.7
El Cerrito	56.00	66.00	17.9
Moraga	64.00	74.00	15.6
Pleasant Hill	62.00	72.00	16.1
Fairfax	60.00	85.00	41.7
Novato	53.00	67.00	26.4
San Rafael	74.00	87.00	17.6
Tiburon	89.00	180.00	102.2

SOURCE: Society of Real Estate Appraisers.

where substantial portions of land have been tied up in open-space or agricultural zones. In the face of growing demand, limitations on land supply (whether administrative or physical) will tend to drive up the price of housing.

Another way bottlenecks are created is to institute an administratively complex land use control process, making it difficult for outsiders to shepherd projects through the planning system. Byzantine growth management systems can slow the rate of development through direct controls or by making the process so complex that developers are scared off. Many communities have complex growth management programs that create substantial barriers to entry for developers, especially small firms. The only developers that will build in highly regulated communities are those large firms that can afford the risks of operating in an environment of uncertainty.

To summarize, bottleneck effects occur when the supply of development does not meet the demand. This imbalance can occur under a variety of circumstances: when economic development is rapid and unanticipated; when local communities do not zone enough land to meet housing demands; when communities enact restrictive supply-oriented land use regulations, such as growth controls; when the amount of land suitable for development is limited because of past development or physical characteristics; or when communities institute complex and time-consuming regulatory systems that slow down development and limit entry of new firms. If any of these situations is accompanied by strong demand for housing, prices of new and existing housing units will increase. Should the imbalance remain uncorrected, demand will eventually fall off in the long run, as housing consumers are priced out of the market and move to other communities, or as businesses relocate to lower-cost areas.

Monopoly Power

According to the standard economic definition, monopoly power is achieved when an entity has sufficient control of the market to both adjust the level of production and set prices that maximize profit. The most important qualification is size: a monopolist must be large enough and produce enough to control most of the market—theoretically, the entire market. The owner of the only gas station between Dawson Creek and Whitehorse has a monopoly on gas.

Applied to the housing market, the concept of monopoly is a bit different. In an isolated company town—for example, Pullman, Illinois in its heyday—the provider of housing did have extreme monopoly power. It is difficult to imagine such an extreme case of monopoly in urban or suburban areas, since in most towns there are at least a few developers building homes. Even if one developer controlled a town's entire housing market, he still might not have substantial monopoly power. Consumers could still buy existing units, or housing in neighboring towns and villages—opportunities that greatly dilute the monopoly power of a developer. Thus, the range of substitutes available—in this case, the types and locations of housing units available—is the key determinant of monopoly power.

The degree to which these other opportunities affect the level of monopoly power depends on how housing consumers perceive the total housing market. The more narrowly they define it, and the more it coincides with the type of housing produced by the developer, the more monopoly power the developer will have. For example, if housing consumers define the market as luxury condominiums in San Francisco, the developer is able to exert more monopoly power than if the market were defined as all condominiums in the Bay Area. The smaller the market, the easier it is to control. But to the degree that consumers perceive other types of housing, communities, or neighborhoods as acceptable substitutes for the developer's product, monopoly power will be limited.

Translated into simpler terms: if all houses and communities were identical, to obtain monopoly power a developer would have to control all of the housing stock. If he raised prices while controlling only 10 percent, consumers would shift to other identical but lower-priced units. A good example would be milk: no one dairy farmer can differentiate his product from others enough that consumers would be willing to pay higher prices. In the housing arena, monopoly power comes into play because neighborhoods and housing units are highly varied. Under conditions of strong housing demand and restricted supply, developers operating highly differentiated markets can earn excess profits. An extreme case occurred in Edmonton, Alberta, where the city had restricted residential land development to six areas. An examination of housing production in these areas found that four of the largest developers controlled 64 percent of the single-family units produced between September 1973 and August 1976. Each of the six areas was controlled by a single developer and was located in different sectors of the larger metropolitan region. Each area constituted a separate housing market. Not surprisingly, housing prices in all six areas escalated rapidly between 1973 and 1976.[4]

How do local land use regulations help to confer monopoly power on developers? By limiting the amount of land available for development, they make it easier for developers to control local land markets. As in the Edmonton example, the city's policy of limiting development to six targeted areas greatly facilitated developer efforts to control local residential planning areas. While planners decry the environmental impact of "leapfrog development," it is clearly a response by less fortunate developers to monopoly power exerted by others. If one or more developers ties up land, other builders must move out to less centrally located land. If local land use ordinances prohibit leapfrogging, these developers that do control land can act as monopolists.

Regulatory systems that rely on complex administrative procedures also act as barriers to market entry. The greater the level of complexity, the more reluctant developers will be to enter the local markets, for the costs of adjusting to unfamiliar administrative programs are high, and developers who already have good working relationships with local planners are more likely to obtain development permission. Developers who successfully shepherd housing projects through the review process can charge monopoly prices as long as local procedures effectively block increased competition. In a study of developers operating in San Jose, California, Gruen, Gruen and Associates found that after holding constant for labor, materials, and land costs increases, as well as changes in public requirements and housing quality, gross profits of the two developers analyzed increased from 158 to 231 percent between 1967 and 1976 (in constant dollars). The researchers concluded that these excess profits were attributable in part to constrained housing supply and the exercise of monopoly power.[5]

Another way local development policies reduce competition is by shifting public service costs to developers. While in high-demand areas these costs can easily be passed on to the consumer, increased front-end costs make it both more difficult and more expensive for the developer to obtain capital financing. For example, Cook estimates that Edmonton's decision to shift the financing of services onto developers added $7,800 per unit to front-end financing costs.[6] And as front-end costs increase, it becomes more difficult for smaller developers to operate. Particularly in light of Proposition 13, this cost shifting is having a dramatic effect on the structure of California's housing industry. When escalating front-end costs are compounded by increased local development fees and user charges, only well-capitalized firms can survive in the market.

In some parts of the San Francisco Bay Area, particularly Marin County, Napa, and Fremont, the lack of developable land and substantial development fees have allowed larger developers to control major portions of the housing market.

Market Reorientation

The reorientation of residential projects from moderate-priced to high-priced luxury units is a commonly occurring indirect effect of regulation. In the absence of clear-cut zoning and subdivision regulations, developers are often forced to negotiate the elements of a project with planning staff and community groups, with negotiations frequently revolving around demands for lower density and more luxurious subdivision improvements. The result is that developers planning to build a fairly large-scale project of moderately priced units are forced to realign their projects to higher-priced markets. What's more, unit prices are generally increased far beyond what is necessary to cover higher subdivision and per-unit land costs. After the developers calculate what negotiated plan changes will mean in terms of costs, they often decide that it is better marketing strategy to completely reorient their projects to high-income clientele.

This is exactly what happened to the Caballo Hills project in Oakland, developed by a real estate subsidiary of Kaiser Aluminum. The developer's original proposal, first put forward in 1971, was to construct 2,200 units on a 685-acre site located in the hill area of the city. In 1979—eight years later—the developer was granted permission to develop approxi-

TABLE 29

AVERAGE SIZE OF NEW HOUSING IN SELECTED
BAY AREA CITIES

	1978	1979	% Change
Albany	1682	1914	13.8
Fremont	1822	2056	12.8
Livermore	1484	1689	13.8
San Leandro	1580	1687	6.8
Clayton	1947	2516	29.2
El Cerrito	1397	1782	27.6
Pleasant Hill	1879	2220	18.1
Larkspur	1338	2158	61.3
Mill Valley	850	1119	31.6
San Anselmo	1086	1809	66.6
Tiburon	3174	2193	−30.9

SOURCE: Society of Real Estate Appraisers.

mately 150 units, after giving the East Bay Regional District over 400
acres of the site for parkland. Back in 1971, the developers planned to sell
the single-family units for $33,500 and the condo units for $23,750. At a
project review hearing in 1979, the developer estimated the selling prices
of the new units at $175,000 to $200,000. The developer also said that
higher densities were not being sought because the project was being
aimed at a high-income clientele, and also because Kaiser, the parent
company, did not want to "make waves" in its hometown.

It is difficult to measure systematically the extent to which market
reorientation occurs as a result of local planning. But one approach is to
determine whether the size of new homes is changing in Bay Area communities. Table 29 presents data on median size for new homes by year for
selected communities, and shows wide variation in the extent of change.
In Clayton, El Cerrito, Larkspur, Mill Valley, and San Anselmo, new units
have increased substantially in size. This is probably due to the fact that
these communities are largely built out, and new development now tends
toward larger, custom-built homes on infill lots. Tiburon's substantial
decline in average unit size is probably due to a shift toward townhouse
and condominium construction.

Spillovers

This indirect effect crops up when a community's housing market is so
constrained that demand pressures spread out into neighboring towns.

This is precisely the argument that Claude Gruen made in his brief on the potential economic effects of Petaluma's growth control plan. Gruen argued that no city can shut off growth; it can only be shifted to surrounding towns. Gruen also contended that growth may shift to those towns least capable of handling additional development.[7] While this has not happened in all parts of the Bay Area, the problem is acute in some areas. Many communities in Sonoma County, including Cotati, Rohnert Park, and Sonoma, have been affected by spillovers resulting from the Petaluma growth management program. Similarly, the lack of housing opportunities in the Silicon Valley has pushed demand over into southern Alameda County, particularly Fremont.

Spillovers force surrounding communities to either erect their own barriers to growth or face the prospect of intensified development. Cotati, Rohnert Park, and Sonoma have all recently enacted local growth-control programs or have downzoned substantial acreage to low-intensity residential use. Santa Clara County cities have become extremely combative, fighting back with a variety of growth-restricting mechanisms that have made each community a "tight little island."

GAUGING INDIRECT EFFECTS

These four kinds of indirect effects—bottlenecks, monopoly power, market reorientation, and spillovers—alter the local housing market by influencing the quantity, type, and quality of new housing produced, or by pushing development off onto other communities. As these effects become more pronounced over time, the pricing of existing housing units in the area will be affected. How much it is affected depends, both in the short and the long run, on the level of demand for housing. If demand pressures are strong, and few opportunities for additional housing exist in other communities, the effect on prices will be substantial.

It is difficult, however, to precisely quantify the effect on the price of new and existing housing. Accurate data on land prices, profits, and appreciation on resale units are largely unavailable. I have attempted to document the indirect effect on prices by identifying price levels that are in excess of normal construction costs and profits for new units. I have also examined each city's land use development trends during the past three years, and attempted to explain variations in the prices of new units.

Table 30 presents the average price of new units constructed in each case study community for the years 1976 through 1979. Prices have increased substantially in each of these six cities. The greatest appreciation was in Novato, where the price of new units rose by over 100 percent in

TABLE 30

AVERAGE PRICE OF NEW HOUSES IN THE SIX CASE STUDY
CITIES, 1976–79

	1976	1977	1978	1979	% Change 1976–79
Concord	$62,300	74,900	87,900	92,000	47.7
Fremont	61,200	75,600	90,100	113,800	85.9
Napa	51,500	70,700	77,400	97,800	89.9
Santa Rosa	49,100	58,900	65,100	90,500	84.3
Novato	76,900	86,500	109,500	160,700	109.0
San Rafael	108,900	131,700	182,100	174,200	60.0
Average	71,800	81,300	98,400	109,100	51.9

SOURCE: Society of Real Estate Appraisers

TABLE 31

PER-SQUARE-FOOT PRICE OF NEW HOUSES IN THE SIX CASE
STUDY CITIES, 1976–79

	1976	1977	1978	1979
Concord	33.40	39.28	47.90	47.15
Fremont	35.73	44.06	49.56	55.35
Napa	29.33	37.29	40.78	49.64
Santa Rosa	30.76	38.65	45.40	56.32
Novato	36.24	41.77	49.64	67.86
San Rafael	45.32	52.64	77.23	93.25

SOURCE: Society of Real Estate Appraisers.

four years. Three cities experienced increases of well over 80 percent during that time: Fremont, Napa, and Santa Rosa. San Rafael, which already had high housing prices in 1976, experienced a price increase of 60 percent. Only Concord, with a 48 percent increase, had a price rise less than the region's average of 52 percent.

Why have new housing price increases varied so much in these six communities? According to economic theory, if demand is uniform across all submarkets, and if the supply characteristics are identical, price changes should be similar. But as table 30 clearly indicates, price trends were not at all similar. In San Rafael (the highest-priced city), the 1976 average for new housing prices was 122 percent higher than the average in the lowest-priced city, Santa Rosa. By 1979, the gap between the two cities had diminished to 92 percent.

Much of the price variation is due to differences in the quality of new units. A comparison of per-square-foot prices for new houses, presented in table 31, shows this price measure to be 55 percent greater in the highest-ranking city (San Rafael) than in the lowest (Napa). By 1979, the gap in price per-square-foot was even wider, with the highest city (San Rafael) showing price levels 98 percent greater than the lowest city (Concord). Table 31 suggests that in 1976 and 1977 much of the price variation among communities can be explained by differences in the size of the new units. If San Rafael is excluded, the same would hold true for 1978. But by 1979, both Novato and San Rafael had housing prices substantially higher, on a per-square-foot basis, than the other four cities. Why?

To answer this question, it is necessary to examine closely both housing prices and the costs of producing new housing units in each of these cities. My approach is to subtract from the average house price the cost of constructing new units, the costs of land preparation, and required fees and charges. Since construction and land preparation costs include normal profit and overhead, the resulting residual value is what is left to account for land and land-holding costs, marketing costs, and excess profit. The variation in residual value among cities provides a clear indication of where housing prices have been driven up by land scarcity, monopoly power, and other indirect effects. Table 32 presents this information for each of the six cities, covering the years 1976 to 1979.

In 1976, residual values were similar across all communities, with the exception of San Rafael. The residual value in Napa was a negative $2,069, indicating low land values and a low profit rate. Santa Rosa's residual value of $1,072 suggests low per-unit land costs.

By 1977, the range of residual values began to widen. Napa and Santa Rosa were at the low end, with values in the upper $6,000 range. Increasing residual values in Concord, Fremont, and Novato indicate a rise in demand accompanied by increasing land prices and profit rates.

Concord's average residual value increased by nearly 60 percent in 1978. In contrast, Fremont's residual value, which had increased substantially the previous year, grew by only 18 percent, bringing it to $20,279. The divergence between Fremont and Concord is due in large part to the slowdown of construction in Concord during that time. Napa's falling residual value reflects a weakening of demand. Santa Rosa experienced substantial residual-value growth (about 35 percent) between 1977 and 1978, but the greatest value increases occurred in Marin County, reflect-

TABLE 32

RESIDUAL VALUES FOR SIX BAY AREA CITIES, 1976–79

Concord	1976	1977	1978	1979
Average new house price[a]	$62,300	$74,900	$87,900	$92,000
construction cost[b]	45,935	53,034	57,894	67,310
lot improvement cost[b]	6,514	7,157	8,051	9,959
fees and charges[c]	2,600	2,675	2,800	2,850
Residual value	$7,251	$12,034	$19,155	$11,881

Fremont	1976	1977	1978	1979
Average new house price	$61,200	$75,600	$90,100	$113,800
construction cost	42,191	47,722	57,358	70,932
lot improvement cost	7,031	7,747	8,338	10,247
fees and charges	2,715	2,905	4,125	4,350
Residual value	$9,263	$17,226	$20,279	$28,271

Napa	1976	1977	1978	1979
Average new house price	$51,500	$70,700	$77,400	$97,800
construction cost	43,250	52,728	59,882	67,965
lot improvement cost	8,033	9,188	10,452	17,149
fees and charges	2,285	2,460	2,590	2,665
Residual value	$−2,068	$6,324	$4,476	$10,021

Santa Rosa	1976	1977	1978	1979
Average new house price	$49,100	$58,900	$65,100	$90,500
construction cost	39,236	42,382	45,243	55,442
lot improvement cost	7,652	8,136	8,678	11,014
fees and charges	1,140	1,165	1,450	2,300
Residual value	$1,072	$6,855	$9,266	$21,744

(Table 32, cont.)

Novato	1976	1977	1978	1979
Average new house price	$76,900	$86,500	$109,500	$160,700
construction cost	52,265	57,595	69,599	81,696
lot improvement cost	12,432	10,707	11,210	13,565
fees and charges	1,650	1,785	1,945	2,200
Residual value	$10,553	$16,413	$26,746	$63,239

San Rafael	1976	1977	1978	1979
Average new house price	$108,900	$131,700	$182,100	$174,200
construction cost	59,186	69,581	74,395	64,446
lot improvement cost	13,717	14,593	15,566	17,030
fees and charges	1,535	2,140	2,495	2,855
Residual value	$34,464	$45,386	$89,644	$89,869

[a]Analysis of Society of Real Estate Appraisers' data tapes, 1976–79.
[b]Bank of America Appraisal Department, *Cost Study,* San Francisco, 1976–79.
[c]Association of Bay Area Governments, *Development Fees in the San Francisco Bay Area: A Survey* (Berkeley, 1980).

ing burgeoning housing demand. Novato's residual value increased by 63 percent, and San Rafael's by 98 percent.

By 1979, San Rafael's growth in residual value had flattened out. Residual value increased by less than 1 percent that year, and housing prices fell in absolute terms. Novato, on the other hand, continued to experience upward price pressure and rapidly rising residual value. Santa Rosa also experienced substantial demand pressure, reflected by a 135 percent increase in residual value.

Figure 6 graphs the residual-value trends for these six cities between 1976 and 1979. The figure illustrates that in comparison to San Rafael and Novato, Fremont, Concord, Santa Rosa, and Napa have all had fairly flat growth in residual values. Of those cities at the lower end of the scale, Fremont and Santa Rosa experienced the greatest increase in residual value.

EXPLAINING RESIDUAL VARIATIONS: HOUSING AND LAND MARKET PERFORMANCE

Concord and Fremont

Figure 6 raises some interesting questions about what happened in specific communities in the last half of the 1970s. For example, residual values in Concord and Fremont were about the same; Concord's average was $7,251 and Fremont's $9,263. By 1978, residual values stood at about $20,000 in both cities, representing a 164 percent increase for Concord and 119 percent for Fremont. But between 1978 and 1979, residual values fell by 38 percent in Concord, while increasing by 39 percent in Fremont. Why?

Developable, residentially zoned land is a precious commodity in both Concord and Fremont. Surprisingly, developable acreage is less expensive in Concord, where large parcels are extremely rare, than in Fremont, which boasts considerably more developable land.

In October 1978 the Concord Planning Department completed an inventory of vacant lands and underutilized parcels in the Concord planning area. A tabulation of the results of that study (table 33) indicates that Concord has, given current land use designations, an ultimate dwelling unit capacity of 44,000. This represents an increase of approximately 7,600 units over the 36,360 dwelling units existing in Concord in 1979.

In addition to the approximately 1,500 acres of developable residential land within Concord city limits, there is a limited amount of potential residential land that is outside city boundaries but inside Concord's "sphere of influence." Little of this land is serviced with either sewer or water facilities, and servicing is not likely in the near future. With the passage of Proposition 13 and the city's current sewer supply problem, Concord has adopted a cautious, conservative attitude toward further annexations.

Only 25 to 30 percent of Concord's remaining residential land supply consists of large parcels (50 or more acres) suitable for tract development, and much of this acreage lies in the sewer moratorium area. The largest single landholder in Concord, the Newhall Land and Development Company, owns over 1,400 acres of developable land, of which nearly 400 acres has been earmarked for residential construction. According to Newhall's own master plan, roughly 200 of the 400 acres are scheduled for development by 1983; 900 dwelling units are planned at various densities.

Of Concord's residentially developable acreage not owned by Newhall, the majority consists of parcels of ten acres or less. Discussion with Concord developers reveals that in 1979 these parcels ranged in price

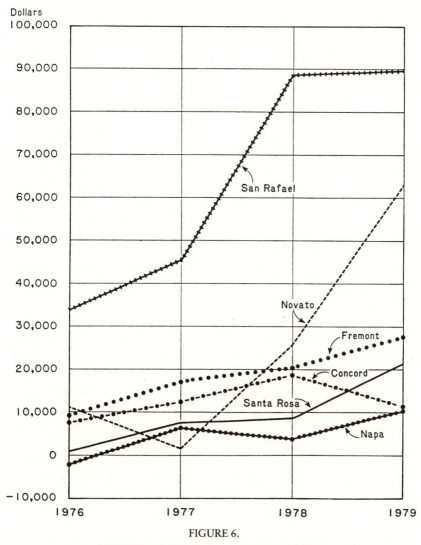

FIGURE 6.

RESIDUAL VALUE TRENDS IN THE SIX CITIES.

TABLE 33

CONCORD LAND SUPPLY AND HOUSING UNIT CAPACITY, 1978

Land Use Designation	Developable Land Area (acres)	Housing Unit Capacity
Single-family density	1,032	3,402
Low density	255	2,442
Medium to high density	43	1,264
Residential reserve	173	573
Totals	1,523	7,681

SOURCE: Concord Planning Department, 1978.

from $40,000 per acre, for tracts in the sewer moratorium area, up to $60,000 per acre. Several reasons were offered for these unusually low raw land prices. First and foremost, the current sewer hookup moratorium has reduced the development potential of many parcels, and thus reduced their asking prices. Second, there is little land speculation occurring. Most landowners, including Newhall, have been in the area for many years and intend to undertake their own construction. Finally, except for small infill parcels, most of Concord's vacant land is near the city's periphery, relatively close to Antioch or Clayton, where land prices have historically been lower.*

Concord prices for finished lots, the other source of buildable land, have been more in line with regional averages. According to several Concord real estate appraisers, in 1979 the cost of an improved lot (graded and serviced with all utilities, including roads) ranged from a low of $20,000 for a 6,000-square-foot lot to $50,000 for larger lots with better access. Infill lots intended for townhouse construction started at $5.00 per square foot.[8]

Fremont's remaining vacant land parcels fall into four categories: large agricultural tracts, industrially zoned land, sensitive Northern Plains land, and infill parcels. Over half of Fremont's agricultural lands are protected under Williamson contracts and could be removed only with a sizable property tax penalty. Moreover, many such parcels are on hillside areas too steep for intense residential development. There is a substantial supply of industrially zoned acreage along the Nimitz Freeway, but with Santa Clara County's supply of industrial land almost exhausted, Fre-

---

* Clayton's land prices are comparatively low per square foot, but because lots average more than one-third acre, individual lot prices are high.

mont's acreage is of increasing value. The Northern Plains area contains several large parcels suitable for residential development, but that area is environmentally sensitive, and the city is currently preparing plans that may limit further residential development opportunities. Of the vacant infill parcels in Fremont's built-up areas, most are zoned for multifamily development.

Did Fremont's residual values increase because the community is running out of developable land? Smaller infill parcels are expected to be available well into the 1990s and beyond, while large parcels zoned exclusively for single-family detached housing are likely to be built out by the late 1980s. Both developers and planners conclude that the supply of vacant land, though consisting mostly of small parcels, will be adequate through the current decade.

But Fremont's scarcity of large, buildable parcels has not gone unnoticed by existing landholders and potential land buyers. Nor have the profit opportunities available to well-financed developers gone unrecognized. As a result, between 1976 and 1979 land prices in Fremont escalated far more rapidly than general inflation. According to one independent appraiser, flatlands that sold at $15,000 per acre in 1977 commanded prices in excess of $50,000 per acre by 1979. Lands with less improvement potential were correspondingly less expensive. For example, the 1979 price of hillside land currently in agricultural use ranged from $20,000 to $30,000 per acre, up from $10,000 per acre in 1977. Land prices have also been affected by zoning and access to utilities and services. According to one appraiser, raw land that was zoned for residential use and had access to water and sewer facilities was priced at $1.50 per square foot in 1979, equivalent to roughly $60,000 per acre. Previously subdivided and serviced parcels sold for up to $30,000 per lot. Note that because they are in greater supply, serviced lots in Fremont sold for less than comparable lots in Concord.

As in Concord, the land costs for new homes constructed in 1979 were not necessarily as high as the figures quoted here, since many larger builders have owned or optioned developable land for a number of years. But it seems safe to presume that builders have not asked less than the going rate for homes, no matter what their original land acquisition cost.

Several factors differentiate Concord's land market from that in Fremont. First, Fremont's supply of large parcels suitable for tract development is expected to last at least through the end of the current decade. Second, unlike the Concord area, where the search for inexpensive land has led to subdivision construction in Antioch and Pittsburg, Fremont's neighbors are closer to full build-out than Fremont itself. Third, the pattern of landownership in Fremont remains diverse and unconcentrated. Last and most important, the city of Fremont has not acted to impede the flow of land into the development process, while Concord has adopted a variety of growth-limiting policies, as well as refusing to annex land outside city limits. In fact, Fremont's step-density system provides builders with incentives to develop single-family housing tracts at high densities (lot sizes below the conventional minimum of 6,000 square feet). Because Fremont has traditionally maintained a "hands-off" attitude toward the rate of land development, large-scale builders are resisting the city's recent efforts to adopt a Northern Plains area master plan that stipulates specific uses for individual parcels.

Going strictly on the basis of land supply and ownership characteristics, Concord should have higher land prices than Fremont, but information from real estate appraisers indicates the opposite is true. It appears the reasons for this are demand factors, along with the housing market characteristics of neighboring communities. While Concord is largely built out, many other communities in Contra Costa County provide ample development opportunities. Concord land prices cannot rise too much, or demand will quickly spill over into other areas. In Fremont, on the other hand, surrounding communities provide few alternative opportunities for development. Another constraint is the surrounding hillsides, which limit development and block access to eastern Alameda County. As a consequence, demand pressures are focused on Fremont, with prices rising accordingly. This price differential between the two cities is perhaps their most significant difference revealed in the study.

These pressures have been intensified by Silicon Valley's tremendous employment boom over the past few years. Since Santa Clara County's housing opportunities have not kept pace with new jobs, many electronics workers have turned to Fremont. Land prices have risen rapidly over the past three years, and because Santa Clara County workers are relatively affluent, builders in Fremont have not found it necessary to cut back size or quality in order to keep costs down. In Concord, where cost competition is vigorous, townhouse construction has proliferated.

With the escalating costs of land, construction, and approval process delays, smaller Fremont builders that lack the financial reserves of their larger counterparts may find the going increasingly rough. In 1978 and 1979, over 50 percent of the building permits issued for single-family housing went to four large development firms. In some areas, the concentration levels are even higher. For example, in Fremont's northern neighborhoods (those north of Thornton Avenue), 81.4 percent of the 474 building permits issued in 1978 and 1979 went to Fremont's largest builders—Shapell, Citation, and Ponderosa. In the Mission San Jose and Warm Springs Districts, 54.4 percent of the 732 building permits issued in 1978–79 were given to four developers, again including Citation. However, my surveys of project approvals found no relation between developer size and approval rate; the larger builders gain more approvals because they propose more housing units, not because Fremont regulations favor larger builders. As for the Concord area, except for developers such as Newhall, most large builders have shifted their activities eastward to Pittsburg and Antioch.

Santa Rosa and Napa

Santa Rosa's average residual value (presented in table 32) has increased by over 1,900 percent since 1976, but is still well below 1979 values in Novato, San Rafael, and Fremont. In contrast, Napa has had very low residual values and actually experienced a decline in 1978. Despite efforts by the city and the county to control development, rapid housing price inflation has not occurred. To understand the indirect effects of land use controls in Santa Rosa and Napa, it is necessary to look again at land supply and housing demand.

In Santa Rosa, the supply of vacant developable land is determined by the location of the urban area boundary. In 1978, an inventory was conducted of vacant parcels that consisted of more than two acres and were not located in designated hillside areas. According to this inventory, Santa Rosa's urban area boundary contained 3,887 vacant acres, 1,605 of them under city jurisdiction, and 2,285 under county control but within Santa Rosa's sphere of influence. Another, more detailed land inventory conducted the same year lists vacant acreage by planning area and by General Plan density classification (see table 34). Note that of the 11,031 acres listed as vacant, 6,336 (58 percent) are earmarked for development at very low densities. According to table 34, the planning areas with the greatest acreage available for low- and medium-density development include West Santa Rosa, Piner, Rincon Valley, Petaluma Hill, and Calistoga Road. Other outlying districts encompassing expanses of hillside, such as Mark West and North Santa Rosa, must be developed at substantially reduced densities.

Table 34 also includes the expected number of housing units to be developed in each of Santa Rosa's planning areas by the year 2000. The planning areas targeted for the greatest percentage increase in residential

TABLE 34
SANTA ROSA LAND AVAILABILITY BY PLANNING AREA AND GENERAL PLAN DENSITY CATEGORY

Planning Area		Vacant Acreage			Total Acreage Housing	Projected Additional (units/gross acre) Units	Projected Density
	Hillside Density[a]	Very Low Density[b]	Low Density[c]	Medium Density[d]			
Petaluma Hill	0	237	226	212	675	2641	3.9
Bennett Valley	75	331	132	113	651	1593	2.4
Valley of the Moon	150	391	178	58	777	1363	1.7
Howarth Park	0	178	128	5	311	611	2.0
Montgomery Village	0	0	9	96	107	797	7.4
South Central	0	0	0	9	9	73	8.0
Central District	0	0	0	13	13	100	7.7
Mendocino	0	0	0	19	19	152	8.0
Junior College	0	0	0	0	0	0	—
Montecito	0	45	13	0	58	74	1.3
North Santa Rosa	375	1307	200	113	2305	2500	1.1
Rincon Valley	0	49	312	91	452	1855	4.0
Calistoga Road	0	936	432	0	1368	2121	1.6
Mark West	248	292	94	30	1080	792	.8
Northwest Santa Rosa	0	31	202	70	303	1287	4.2
Piner	0	420	429	110	959	2655	2.7
West Santa Rosa	0	400	613	284	1297	4678	3.6
Roseland	0	0	40	154	193	1364	7.0
Bellevue	0	500	30	0	530	430	.8
South Wright	0	400	186	65	651	1431	2.2
Total	848	5518	3225	1440	11031	26517	2.4

SOURCE: Santa Rosa General Plan, March 1978.
[a] Hillside density: .133 dwelling units per acre.
[b] Very low density: .65 dwelling units per acre.
[c] Low density: 3.5 dwelling units per acre.
[d] Medium density: 8.0 dwelling units per acre.

uses include Petaluma Hill, North Santa Rosa, Calistoga Road, Piner, and West Santa Rosa—the same planning areas having the greatest development potential. The new housing allocation in Santa Rosa's General Plan assumes that 26,517 new dwelling units will be added to the city's housing stock by the year 2000. According to this forecast, the average gross residential density of the additional construction would be 2.3 units per acre, a density comparable to that of existing residential development. Nonetheless, average residential densities would vary quite widely among individual planning areas. For example, new construction in north Santa Rosa would be at a gross residential density of only 1 unit per acre, compared to 4 units per acre in Rincon Valley.

Unlike most other Bay Area growth centers, Santa Rosa has not planned additional open-space preservation within the boundaries of the city or the urban area. Acreage designated for open space in the Santa Rosa region lies outside the city's northeastern and southern borders. West of the city, great expanses of land will remain in agricultural use, even though no formal agricultural preservation ordinances have been adopted. Five new local park areas have been proposed inside the urban boundary, but the total acreage required for their development is small.

Although there is sufficient acreage to accommodate Santa Rosa's expected population growth, land is expensive in southern Sonoma County and is regarded by developers as being in short supply. Until recently, when housing construction slowed due to high interest rates, land prices were rising faster than housing prices in the area, increasing at an estimated annual rate of 15 to 25 percent. Large land parcels suitable for single-family development and zoned R-1 (single-family detached) sold for roughly $25,000 per acre in the summer of 1979; the list of buyers consisted primarily of large housing developers scrambling to bank sufficient land for future construction. Finished lot prices also reflected the boost in raw land prices. Field interviews with Santa Rosa real estate appraisers during the summer of 1979 revealed that 6,000-square-foot finished lots (with utilities, roads, and other subdivision improvements) brought $20,000 to $30,000 on the land market. Larger, half-acre lots often sold for over $50,000.

What caused this recent surge in Santa Rosa's land prices and the accompanying rush to obtain developable land? As Santa Rosa real estate analysts point out, large developers continue to believe that Sonoma County will remain the Bay Area's residential growth center. Although Petaluma instituted a residential allocation system in 1974, neither Santa Rosa nor Rohnert Park, the county's other two growth communities, seems likely to follow suit. Many also foresee continued economic expansion in Santa Rosa and steady demand for all forms of housing through the end of the century. In a sense, the Santa Rosa market is viewed as the "last frontier." Since communities to the south are either employing growth controls or approaching total build-out, Santa Rosa and Rohnert Park represent the final North Bay arena in which developers can compete.

Government controls have also been a factor in rapidly increasing land prices. Since the designation of Santa Rosa's urban boundary in 1978, several builders seeking approval of land subdivision outside the urban area boundary have been refused, on the basis that urban services would not be extended beyond the urban boundary within the foreseeable future. Landowners and developers concluded that there would be only a limited supply of land available for residential development in Santa Rosa. Builders quickly bid land prices upward as they sought to secure sufficient land for future construction projects, while owners of converted vacant land parcels increased their asking prices. The result: a flurry of acquisitions at higher prices.

Santa Rosa's experience illustrates a fundamental dilemma facing land-use planners in rapidly growing cities. Confronted with reductions in revenue after Proposition 13, along with an increasing demand for roads, utilities, and other costly urban services, many communities have designated urban service boundaries. But by prioritizing land development, or limiting the supply of developable land altogether, they push competing builders into bidding wars for what is correctly perceived as a decreasing supply of buildable land. Large housing developers perpetuate the cycle because they are able to meet high asking prices for desired parcels. It doesn't matter whether builders bid against each other for the same parcel; each land transaction sets, in effect, a new floor price for developable acreage. Compounding the problem of spiraling bids is the phenomenon of "speculative chaining," in which a single parcel is sold and resold several times. In each instance, the land seller prices the parcel to realize a "reasonable" rate of return. Ultimately, it is the home buyer who pays the price for these multiple profit margins.

Napa's supply of developable land is limited to that within the Residential Urban Limit (RUL) boundary, and is much smaller than Santa Rosa's. However, Napa's land supply is projected to be adequate to meet the city's housing needs through the end of the century. Table 35, prepared by the Napa Planning Department, indicates the potential for development of nearly 7,000 additional dwelling units within the RUL under

TABLE 35

NAPA DEVELOPMENT POTENTIAL BY PLANNING AREA

Number of Parcels

Planning Area	One Acre or More	Less Than One Acre	Potential Dwelling Units
Salvador	156	12	168
Dry Creek	214	3	217
Linda Vista	414	18	432
Crescent	494	58	552
Sarco	8	7	15
Alta Heights	435	84	519
Beard	1501	128	1629
Lincoln	23	25	48
Central Napa	200	25	225
Pueblo	331	229	560
Brown's Valley	750	—	750
Foster	336	42	378
Shearer	46	79	125
Coombsville	591	—	591
River West	387	58	445
Hove Hill	300	—	300
Total	6,186	768	6,954

SOURCE: Napa Planning Department, 1978.

current zoning. (Note that this figure includes several hundred units which have been completed since the inventory was compiled several years ago.) These data also reveal that the largest percentage of Napa's developable acreage is in the districts of Linda Vista, Crescent, Brown's Valley, and Shearer, which have inferior access to downtown commercial areas and urban services, and are therefore penalized under Napa's current project evaluation system. As in Santa Rosa, Napa's designated open-space preserves are outside the RUL and therefore do not affect the city's supply of vacant land.

But less than three years after the implementation of the Residential Development Management Plan, the future of Napa's land market remains clouded. Unlike the large-scale builders who predominate in Santa Rosa, Napa developers tend to be smaller and less willing to engage in what is seen as speculative construction. In light of Napa's decreasing number of large vacant parcels, and the uncertainty posed by the RDMP, Napa's lack of large developers means a less active land market. Purchases of finished lots (which are exempt from the RDMP when developed individually) are considerably more frequent in Napa than elsewhere. Realtors report a floor price of $20,000 for a 6,000-square-foot lot located in an R-1 district.

Passage of the RDMP ushered in a new phase in Napa's residential development. Builders are no longer so free to build what they want where they want. To accumulate the evaluation points needed for construction approval, they must now provide a wide variety of dwelling units as close as possible to existing services. Opponents of the RDMP— the Napa building industry among them—are quick to point out that growth controls that restrict housing supply generally cause housing prices to rise. Moreover, by taking away their discretion over project design and location, restrictions make the development process less efficient and more costly.

Actually, there are several ways in which the RDMP may indirectly increase the price of new housing in Napa. First, if the market demand for additional housing exceeds the allocation limit of 350 units (1980 allocation), competing home buyers may bid prices upward. This is especially true for new single-family detached homes, as only 158 permits for detached homes were awarded in 1979 and 1980. Second, in order to gain needed evaluation points, builders may add features to their plans, the costs of which are then passed on to home buyers. Third, by promoting the development of infill parcels, the RDMP encourages construction on higher-priced land. Fourth, the RDMP's potentially costliest effect is to accelerate the shift from construction of moderately-priced homes to larger, premium homes. This is due to a variety of reasons, including rising land costs, changing consumer preferences, and the fact that Napa has never been a tract development city. But most developers also acknowledge that when the supply of housing is even slightly restricted, they have a greater ability to choose what they produce. What many are choosing to build is the larger, more expensive detached home or townhouse.

The price effects of demand outstripping a constrained supply deserve a closer look. For supply-demand mismatches occur not only in terms of housing types (e.g., single-family versus multi-family), but also in timing (short run versus long run). In the next few years, taking into account the yearly allocation of 350 new units under the RDMP and the several dozen individual single-family housing starts exempt from controls, the yearly total of new housing starts should exceed 400. Although this level of construction activity is less than the 673 building permits issued in 1978, it is comparable to Napa's housing growth rate during the mid-1970s. With mortgage rates at current high levels, the demand for all types of housing has softened throughout the Bay Area, and construction activity in Napa has slowed accordingly. Thus, it does not appear that a drastic shortfall of new housing will occur in Napa because of this situation.

The long-run market outlook is much murkier. Although the allocation formula was originally intended to ensure a permanent ceiling of 350 new units annually, subsequent reductions in Napa's average household size would alter the formula to permit yearly starts exceeding 500 by the mid-1980s. In that case, the allocation formula will probably be adjusted if necessary, so for the foreseeable future housing starts are likely to remain below 400 per year. But the surge in housing demand that Napa experienced during the mid-1970s resulted less from population in-migration than from a decrease in household sizes. This trend toward smaller families meant relatively higher housing demand, and some upward pressure on prices, particularly for new homes. Since both household sizes and in-migration trends have leveled off, it now appears that if kept at 350 units per year, the RDMP subdivision/building permit allocation would allow the construction of enough new housing to meet expected household demand (though that is not to say demand might not outstrip supply in any single year). This scenario might be altered by a renewed surge in housing demand, due to spillover growth from expanding cities such as Santa Rosa, but that seems unlikely to occur. As past history clearly shows, the demand for new housing can be extremely uneven.

Although the RDMP has not been in place long enough to evaluate its effect on land prices, a spot check of Napa real estate assessors revealed that fringe lands are selling more slowly and at a lower price than would otherwise be expected. As currently constituted, the RDMP evaluation scale discourages development in areas with the greatest number of remaining vacant land parcels, because those areas tend to be at the city's periphery. For example, of the sixteen single-family detached housing projects submitted for 1979–80 RDMP evaluation, fourteen were located outside of Napa's central corridor. Only four of the fourteen were approved, and of those four only one received less than thirty-nine (out of a possible fifty) locational points. The lesson is clear: builders proposing projects in less accessible areas must offer outstanding designs, or their plans are unlikely to gain approval.

Not only has the RDMP caused a reorientation in the vacant land market, it has also driven up prices of smaller, single lots, which are exempt from the allocation. Napa realtors report that an unimproved but previously subdivided lot needing sewer hookup now sells for a minimum of

$20,000. Floor prices on larger one-acre lots, which are also exempt from the RDMP, now range between $35,000 and $45,000. Lot prices have registered one-year increases of as much as 25 percent.

In analyzing the effects of Napa's RDMP on the city's housing stock, the biggest question mark is the extent of product reorientation. New single-family detached homes in Napa increased in size and cost, averaging more than 1,900 square feet in size and $95,000 in price as of the summer of 1979. The trend is similar for newer townhouses and duplexes. Regardless of future unit mixes, the trend toward large and more expensive homes will continue. As a result, first-time home buyers will be increasingly priced out of the market for new homes.

However, the trend toward premium housing is somewhat offset by an increase in the supply of townhouses and duplexes. Because they are easier to construct on the infill lots favored by the RDMP, and because they keep land costs down by occupying less lot area per unit, townhouses are becoming increasingly popular among developers who want to stay active in the Napa market. Of the 452 units approved for construction in 1979 and 1980, 203 were townhouses (versus the minimum 45 units suggested as part of the city council's development guidelines). Thus far, home buyer reaction to townhouse developments has been mixed. Well-designed, moderately priced units have sold quickly, but several poorly constructed and managed complexes have not been well accepted. The "American Dream" of a single-family home dies hard, but as the price of housing continues to rise, townhouses may be substituted more and more for detached housing.

Given Napa's only moderate level of housing demand, these rising land prices and relatively limited development opportunities suggest that developer profits are low. Since demand is not strong enough to push prices up dramatically, builders must pay higher land prices without gaining from correspondingly higher home prices.

Until the passage of the RDMP Napa had no specific mechanism other than the RUL for constraining residential development. Beyond design constraints imposed during the subdivision approval process, city agencies did little to regulate the number of new units constructed. Adoption of the RDMP has led to a number of indirect price effects on Napa's housing and land markets. Prices of outlying land parcels not favored for development under the RDMP have not risen as rapidly as the prices of single-family finished lots or larger infill parcels. For example, the builder purchasing a 6,000-square-foot lot exempt from the RDMP pays as much as $5,000 more than he would have in the absence of the RDMP—a result of the intensified competition for exempt parcels. For nonexempt parcels, the RDMP has had the opposite effect. Lack of certainty over project approval has fostered a "wait and see" attitude among builders, particularly in light of today's higher interest rates. Land transactions have slowed, and the smaller developers who operate in Napa have been less willing to engage in speculative development. As a result, Napa's raw land prices are no longer increasing rapidly.

With only limited experience on which to base judgments about the RDMP, other conclusions about its cost effects must be regarded as speculative. The current RDMP evaluation system encourages the construction of close-in multifamily units at the expense of single-family construction. The long-run effects of this trend remain unclear, but one expected result is a continued shift toward the development of larger and more expensive single-family homes, insofar as such projects are approved under the RDMP.

Unlike Napa, Santa Rosa has not experienced a slowdown in the housing demand, particularly in the moderately-priced, single-family detached segment of the market. Projections from most Bay Area forecasting units, including ABAG, indicate that the demand for housing along the Highway 101 corridor will remain strong through the year 2000. Until the recent rise in mortgage interest rates, builders were continuing to construct short-term speculative housing projects. In addition, the Santa Rosa vacancy rate, currently estimated at 1.5 percent, is expected to drop below 1 percent and remain there through the mid-1980s.

Given Santa Rosa's "tight" housing market, government policies that greatly restrict the supply of housing or land could have drastic price consequences. Fortunately, as has been shown, Santa Rosa's development policies reflect a willingness to accommodate residential development. However, the city recently established an urban service limit line, known in Santa Rosa as the urban area boundary, and subsequently disapproved several projects outside this area. Although projections indicate that there is enough land in the contained urban area to accommodate expected residential development at a fairly low average density (2.3 units per acre), those active in the Santa Rosa land market view the urban area boundary as a direct limitation on the city's land supply. Predictably, the large and well-funded developers who operate in Santa Rosa, Rohnert Park, and Petaluma rushed to secure acreage for future projects, driving the price of raw land from about $15,000 per acre to over $25,000 per acre.

Depending on the density of housing eventually developed on those properties, and taking into account effects on property tax and loan interest, these raw land price increases may push unit prices up by as much as $3,500. Finished lot prices in Santa Rosa have also escalated, reflecting some shortfall in supply. On the whole, finished lot prices in both Napa and Santa Rosa now average $25,000, which is comparable to prices in other Bay Area growth centers, but still less than in the developed communities of Marin, Alameda, and San Mateo counties.

As was the case in Napa, increasing costs for land, labor, and materials have pushed developers to construct larger homes than in the past. Measured on a per-square-foot basis, the cost of producing some new 1,800-square-foot homes may actually be less than that for more modest, 1,500-square-foot homes. But because the larger units generally sell for prices in excess of $100,000, the trend toward bigger, costlier units has a negative effect on housing affordability.

Novato and San Rafael

There is a growing body of circumstantial evidence indicating that the system of land use and development controls currently in place in Marin County (and Novato in particular) has led to housing price increases greater than those in other Bay Area cities.

Novato's residential density guidelines have accelerated the shift away from moderately-sized single-family homes, toward a combination of large, expensive single-family homes and smaller, more affordable townhouse units. In late 1979 the city was considering proposals for roughly 1,500 townhouses and 2,450 single-family homes. Many of the townhouse units were proposed not for infill parcels, but for areas that five years ago would have been considered for single-family construction. This is attributed to Novato's policy of limiting residential development in outlying areas, and allowing higher density development in central locations. For one thing, these policies have helped to raise land prices beyond the level at which the construction of affordable single-family homes would still be profitable.

In the strictest sense, Novato and San Rafael's regulatory systems have not increased the monopoly power of any specific builder or set of builders. In 1979 twenty-nine residential developers had proposed projects in Novato that varied in size from 5 to 1,250 units. Of these developers, only Debra Homes of Santa Rosa had a dominant position in any geographical section of the city. Additionally, because of the homogeneity of housing in Novato in terms of both size and age, existing homes are close substitutes for new homes, further diminishing the monopoly power of builders.

Between 1975 and 1979, the average price of all Novato homes rose by roughly 90 percent, from approximately $60,000 to more than $112,000. The price of new housing rose even more sharply, reaching $160,000 in 1979—an average that would have been much higher if lower-priced townhouses had been excluded. Quite clearly, much of the price increase is attributable to construction costs, which increased by 41 percent between 1976 and 1979. A tightening housing market, as reflected by a drop in vacancy rates, also contributed to the price increase. Yet, even in combination these two factors cannot account for the fact that between 1976 and 1979 housing prices in Novato and San Rafael increased 57 and 80 percent faster, respectively, than the regional average.

Much of this extraordinary increase is indeed due to county and city land use controls. At the county level, policies reducing the supply and increasing the cost of land in Marin's southern cities have accelerated Novato's residential growth. Development has been channeled to those few areas where land is comparatively inexpensive: Novato and some unincorporated pockets. Novato's new, higher-income residents have bid up housing prices and pushed middle-income households into southern Sonoma County. Not only does this trend show no sign of abating, but it is likely to be exacerbated by city land use controls.

The Marin County system of land and development controls is the most comprehensive in the Bay Area. In cooperation with the Marin County Planning Department, cities attempt to buy or otherwise control vacant land for open space, reduce the residential densities of new construction, and strictly review all aspects of residential projects. Partly as a result of these policies, Marin County's population grew by only 19,000 between 1970 and 1980, a smaller increase than any other of the nine Bay Area counties, except San Francisco. Since the adoption of the Countywide Plan in October 1973, ten of Marin's eleven cities have either lost population or added fewer than 300 new residents; only Novato has seen its population expand by more than 1,000 (table 36).

Why has growth slowed in Marin County, and what role have county-initiated housing and land use policies played in reducing growth? In 1970, according to the Marin Countywide Plan, the urban corridor contained roughly 9,000 acres of vacant, residentially developable land (table 42). Of this land, 25 percent was located in the Richardson Bay communities of Belvedere, Mill Valley, Sausalito, and Tiburon, 10 percent in Larkspur and Corte Madera, and another 5 percent in the inland communities of Fairfax, San Anselmo, and Ross. The remaining 5,400 vacant acres were distributed evenly between San Rafael and Novato. According to the

TABLE 36

MARIN COUNTY GROWTH, 1975–80

	1980 Population	% Growth since 1975
Belvedere	2,470	−.8
Corte Madera	7,775	−6.4
Fairfax	7,500	−4.6
Larkspur	12,850	+4.2
Mill Valley	13,500	+.5
Novato	42,550	+14.1
Ross	2,520	−5.7
San Anselmo	12,450	−4.3
San Rafael	44,300	−2.3
Sausalito	6,850	+8.2
Tiburon	7,600	−1.0
Unincorporated areas	65,400	—
Total	225,200	—

SOURCE: California State Department of Finance, *Census Report* (Sacramento, 1981).

Countywide Plan these 5,400 acres would accommodate an additional 20,000 dwelling units by 1990. But how much of this land was genuinely developable? In projecting land totals, the county planning staff had included all parcels either zoned for residential construction or left unzoned but expected to be residentially developed; the county had not investigated the holding capacities of particular parcels.

ABAG's 1975 inventory tried to remedy this shortcoming. All vacant land, not just residentially zoned land, was divided into one of two categories: "prime developable land" (parcels zoned or committed for development, which could be economically provided with services and infrastructure) and "secondary developable land" (other vacant parcels). ABAG found far less economically developable land in Marin County than the county itself had estimated five years earlier (see table 37). Although all eleven incorporated cities maintained large reserves of vacant (secondary developable) land, most was on ridgelines, had unstable soils, or was too far from existing services to be feasible for development.

The already dwindling supply of vacant land in Marin's urban corridor was further eroded by purchases of unincorporated land as open space, coupled with city land acquisitions during the early 1970s. By 1975, all vacant residentially zoned parcels in the urban corridor south of Point San

TABLE 37

VACANT LAND SUPPLY IN THE MARIN URBAN CORRIDOR

Area	Marin Countywide Plan, 1975	ABAG, 1975	
	Total Acres	Prime Developable Acres	Secondary Developable Acres
Richardson Bay (Belvedere, Tiburon, Sausalito, Mill Valley)	2180	618	674
Lower Ross Valley (Larkspur, Corte Madera, Kentfield)	980	512[a]	182[a]
Upper Ross Valley (Fairfax, San Anselmo, Ross)	560	234	2768
San Rafael (San Rafael, Lucas Valley, Santa Venecia)	3220	1088[b]	5751[b]
Novato	2220	4389	10,117
Total	9160	6841	19,492

SOURCES: 1973 Marin Countywide Plan; Association of Bay Area Governments, *Series II Projections* (Berkeley, 1976).

[a]Does not include unincorporated city of Kentfield.

[b]Does not include incorporated villages of Lucas Valley and Santa Venecia.

Pedro consisted of smaller, infill-type parcels, except for a few large tracts in San Rafael, Larkspur, and Corte Madera. As land supplies decreased, land and housing prices escalated; yet the demand for housing in southern Marin County still did not diminish, and as vacancy rates dropped, prices rose even further.

By the early 1970s, much of San Rafael was almost completely developed, particularly the areas south of Point San Pedro. Despite the paucity of development opportunities, the city of San Rafael acted to further limit development through a series of land purchases, planned district rezonings, and decisions not to annex vacant parcels. The few new single-family homes constructed in San Rafael in the last half of the 1970s sold at record prices.

Because other Marin County cities had acted to export growth, Novato, with its large supply of developable land, quickly became the focal point for Marin County's residential expansion. And accordingly, it is in Novato that land use controls and other local regulations have had their greatest effect. When Novato instituted a system of density guidelines to restrict residential construction in hillside, bay plain, agricultural, and "water-related" areas, there were three market responses:

1. Land prices escalated sharply, particularly prices for residentially zoned land with allowable densities of three to five units per acre. In many instances, raw land prices in Novato are now comparable with those in San Rafael.

2. Lot prices, which reflect the pricing of raw acreage, also rose.

3. Production shifted to larger, and thus more expensive housing.

Although the number of development proposals increased and the plan review process became more complex, the city of Novato did not greatly expand its review staff or otherwise expedite the plan approval process. Combined with the trend toward planned district rezonings, and the perennial problem of incomplete project submittals, this lack of action has meant serious problems with delay in the approval process. From the builder's perspective, delays may be tolerable when construction costs are increasing at a rate below 10 percent per year. However, when a year's delay means a 15 percent increase in construction costs, as was the case in 1977 and 1978, the problem begins to have a substantially greater impact on the financial stability of builders, and ultimately on the price of new housing.

In both San Rafael and Novato, land use controls have been designed to limit the aggregate supply of raw land, to restrict the flow of land into development, and to reduce residential densities. But because they have not served to reduce the demand for shelter, these policies have led to sharp increases in the price of land and new housing.

Figure 7 shows housing start trends in San Rafael and Novato between 1970 and 1980. What is most noticeable in San Rafael's case is the sharp drop in starts after 1973. Although 1974 and 1975 were poor years for housing construction nationwide, Novato recovered from the slump, while San Rafael did not. Faced with escalating land prices, a scarcity of large vacant tracts, and public opposition to growth, developers left San Rafael even before the 1974–75 national downturn, and never returned. Instead, development activity shifted northward to Novato, where relatively large tracts of undeveloped land were still available.

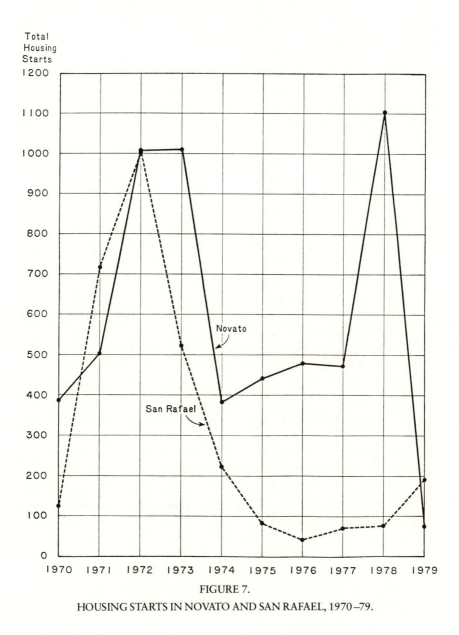

FIGURE 7.

HOUSING STARTS IN NOVATO AND SAN RAFAEL, 1970–79.

What would have happened to land prices, and by extension, to housing construction costs, if San Rafael had been able to maintain pre-1974 construction levels? In this case, the demand for housing in Novato would have been reduced, because home buyers would have purchased units in more accessible San Rafael. The effect of a "decontrolled" situation on housing prices is more difficult to estimate. But all else being equal, greater land supplies would mean a reduction in land prices and an increase in the supply of new units.

Throughout the early and mid-1970s, Novato's supply of economically developable acreage zoned at single-family densities (three to five units per acre) was sufficient to accommodate the influx of potential home buyers. But in the latter part of the decade, the supply of valley acreage began to dwindle. As a result, the bid prices for buildable lots and tracts zoned at single-family densities climbed quickly, rising, according to Novato realtors, at a rate approaching 25 percent per year. As noted previously, some builders turned to the construction of expensive, large-lot hillside homes, while others entered the townhouse market. Unlike the situation in San Rafael, where large tracts really were in short supply, Novato's seeming shortage of developable land was the direct result of the city's density guidelines. To illustrate the potential extent of this price distortion, realtors reported that a parcel that could not be residentially developed under city policy would sell for less than $1,500 per acre. Other parcels, because they were zoned for residential construction, would sell at more than $50,000 per acre.[9]

This analysis is limited by the lack of reliable land price data (particularly for San Rafael) as well as by uncertainty over what would have occurred if these two communities had had a greater supply of developable land. The demand shifts that would have taken place, both within and between San Rafael and Novato, can only be hypothesized. In San Rafael, an expansion of the housing supply accompanying land decontrol would have ultimately led to some decrease in housing prices through a reduction in excess demand. Although decontrol of land development densities in Novato would not have produced an increase in housing starts, it probably would have encouraged production of smaller, and hence more affordable, single-family homes.

CONCLUSION

This chapter has explored the more subtle ways that local land use policies affect land and housing markets. Four types of indirect effects were identified and discussed: bottlenecks, monopoly power, market re-orientation, and spillovers. These effects come into play when local policies significantly alter the operation of competitive land and housing markets. Generally, the result of these indirect effects is to drive land and housing prices above the level that would otherwise prevail.

Each of the six case study communities provides a unique perspective on how suburban land and housing markets are affected by growth pressures and systems of land use control. For example, both Concord and Fremont face dwindling supplies of vacant and developable land, yet only in Fremont do land prices appear to be moving upward. There are various reasons for this, but two factors stand out. First, because there is ample vacant land surrounding Concord, developers and builders will take advantage of these other development opportunities rather than paying higher prices for Concord land. Few alternatives exist near Fremont, because of the lack of developable land in surrounding areas and the physical constraints imposed by the foothills. Second, Fremont's land and housing markets are being strongly affected by housing demand spillovers from Santa Clara County. By pushing up the demand for land and housing, these growth pressures cause land and housing inflation, in light of limited land supply. The main lesson of the Concord and Fremont comparison is that the indirect effects of land use controls depend in large part on a community's relationship to surrounding land markets; the availability of alternative lands near Concord greatly moderates the inflationary effects of land scarcity within the city itself. The comparison also shows that demand spillovers, such as those from Santa Clara County, can have a profound effect on local land and housing markets. Fremont is well connected with the Santa Clara County market, but the connection only works one way: demand pressures flow toward Fremont, and Santa Clara County offers no supply alternatives to offset Fremont's excess demand.

The Napa/Santa Rosa comparison showed that restrictive urban limit lines can cause substantial adjustments in the land market. While both cities have adopted urban limit lines, Napa's poses a much greater constraint, having driven a wedge between lots more proximate to developed areas and those farther out. Santa Rosa's urban boundary designation allows development of considerable land over time, and as a result the land market has not been greatly affected. The Napa situation also highlights the role of demand in forcing up housing prices. Even though Napa has a highly restrictive program of land use controls, the effect of these policies has been moderated by limited demand for land and housing.

The Novato/San Rafael comparison illustrated how countywide land use restrictions can influence land and housing markets. The county General Plan channeled housing development into the urban corridor along Highway 101, pushing growth northward to San Rafael as the more mature cities in southern Marin County were built out. San Rafael then began to run out of land, and acted to slow down its growth rate, again using land use controls to limit development of the city's few remaining vacant land parcels. These conditions have placed extreme development pressures on Novato, where the inflation of land and housing prices has been tremendous. Besides illustrating how supply limitations fuel inflation, the comparison also demonstrates how readily demand can spill over from one community to another.

This in-depth look at six Bay Area cities suggests that local actions to limit development opportunities not only accelerate inflation of land and housing prices in local markets, but have regional implications as well.

CHAPTER SEVEN

Are the Same Land Use Constraints Showing Up in Other Metropolitan Areas?

Many land use commentators are quick to suggest that the brand of environmentalism and local land use regulation seen in the San Francisco Bay Area is unique to California and unlikely to spread to other metropolitan areas. This notion is incorrect and presumptuous. Restrictive land use regulations have currency in many areas across the country. Moreover, as in the Bay Area, they are affecting land conversion and the delivery of housing.

Skepticism about the relevance of the Bay Area's experience to other areas stems in large part from the fact that many of the northeastern and north-central metropolitan areas are losing population. But even in the regions that are shrinking in population as a whole, suburban communities continue to feel growth pressures as urban dwellers flee the central cities. And many of these suburbs, such as Westchester County, New York, are trying to fight back. Communities concerned with the conversion of farmlands and the adverse environmental effects of growth are restricting development through sophisticated growth control systems, as well as through more conventional means such as zoning or sewer and water service limits.

Fiscal zoning is also becoming popular in communities across most of the United States. Many communities began zoning out growth because they found rapid expansion too costly. For example, in the case of suburban Washington, D.C., a shortage of sewerage treatment capacity led to the adoption of a growth moratorium in Montgomery County, Maryland.[1] Many towns and counties zone land so as to maximize property tax revenues, creating large-lot residential zones and emphasizing commercial and industrial development.

CONCERNS WITH REGULATORY IMPACTS: NOTHING NEW

Constraints on suburban land conversion have become commonplace since the 1960s, when developable land was no longer so easy to come by, and communities began to control development aggressively. Several national commissions studying housing and urban problems looked at these trends and explored ways to provide more housing opportunities in suburban areas.

Both the National Commission on Urban Problems and the President's Committee on Urban Housing argued that local governments in metropolitan areas often practice discriminatory zoning and subdivision control to limit growth and exclude the poor. As one report stated, "Zoning, which is barely a body of law, very effectively keeps the poor and those with low incomes out of suburban areas by stipulating lot sizes way beyond their economic reach."[2] Continuing, the report stated:

Removing zoning practices which prevent planned unit developments, and which restrict land supply and raise the cost of site improvements through excessive large-lot zoning, would help cut costs. More objective standards for site improvements and subdivision regulations could also reduce some excessive costs now required.[3]

Over the years, particularly since the passage of the National Environmental Protection Act (NEPA) in 1968, local land use controls have become progressively more restrictive. Even before NEPA, the National Commission on Urban Problems expressed alarm over this trend, arguing that public awareness of the potential adverse effects of land conversion was increasing, and that land development needed to be more closely regulated. This increased awareness closely coincides with the rapid pace of postwar land development in the nation's metropolitan areas. In many areas, as urban pressures threatened prime agricultural and hillside areas, citizen pressure to control growth crystallized.

In the 1970s, communities responded to the environmental impact of development with sophisticated growth management programs, but in the late 1950s and 1960s most communities simply used large-lot zoning to regulate growth. Often, vacant land that had been zoned for moderately dense residential development was rezoned to large-lot residential estates. Such rezoning did slow the rate of land conversion, but it also guaranteed that only very expensive housing would be constructed. The practice of zoning vacant land at exceedingly low densities became the modus operandi for many towns. Called "wait-and-see" zoning, this approach effectively removed land from development pressure and required developers to approach local governments if they sought rezoning of land.[4]

The National Commission and the President's Committee concluded that these national trends have a profound effect on housing and land markets across the country. In several studies done for the National Commission, Manvel and Milgram documented how land development constraints and strong demand pushed raw land prices upward. Between 1956 and 1966, the market value of privately owned land in the United States more or less doubled. As an indicator of the effects on housing production costs, consider that on average the cost of land represented 12 percent of total housing costs in 1956, but by 1966 the land component accounted for 20 percent of the total.[5]

The President's Committee addressed how land use planning and regulation limit housing production, particularly for low-income subsidized units. One study by McGraw-Hill Company determined that between 1950 and 1967 the price of FHA-insured single-family home lots increased by 300 percent, from $1,035 to $2,766.[6] This rate of increase far outstripped that of any other component of housing production. In high-growth areas, such as Staten Island, New York, and Montgomery County, Maryland, lot prices skyrocketed by as much as 500 percent.[7]

A study by the Regional Plan Association (RPA) examined zoning practices in the New York metropolitan area. RPA found that of vacant land within the 500 zoning jurisdictions in the New York area, 90 percent was zoned for residential use; outside of New York City, only 0.4 percent of this residential land was zoned for multifamily development. In 1960, the median minimum lot size permitted in the zoned suburban communities outside of the city was one-third of an acre. These zoning patterns differ greatly from those of the 1930s and 1940s, when homes were frequently constructed on lots as small as one-eighth of an acre. The RPA's conclusion: if suburban communities in the New York area do not change the zoning policies that were in effect as of 1960, the region will be unable to house its projected 1985 population.[8]

These prestigious national studies did a thorough job of mapping the housing problems created by restrictive land use controls. Their statements of basic problems and issues are still valid. But something has changed: once considered a burden only to low-income households, these problems have now fallen squarely on the shoulders of the middle class.

MORE RECENT NATIONAL STUDIES

While earlier research efforts emphasized the effects on the poor and ethnic groups, the studies of the 1970s took a broader approach. This reflected awareness that local land use controls were beginning to have a dramatic effect on land conversion in general, not just on the production on low- and moderate-cost housing.

Research was also spurred by a rapid increase in housing prices nationwide. As described in chapter 1, housing prices began to escalate in 1975, first in California and then elsewhere. This phenomenon coincided with a surge in housing demand as those born in the postwar "baby boom" aged and began to need housing, and with the spreading use of growth controls throughout the United States. Several studies completed in the late 1970s and early 1980s illustrate the national scope of the land use policy problem.

For example, in examining community land use policies, Dowall identified 228 cities and counties across the country that were controlling population growth.[9] Predictably, all these communities had been confronted by fairly intense growth pressures. Their average population growth rate between 1960 and 1970 exceeded 30 percent, and substantial housing construction had already taken place. In fact, over 25 percent of the communities' housing stock had been added during the 1960s. Dowall's empirical analysis of these communities identified several kinds of growth pressures most likely to spur imposition of local growth controls. The largest group of communities was very rural and was motivated primarily by the desire to limit conversion of agricultural land. Other cities imposed growth controls because of concerns with the fiscal impact and rising taxes. A number of communities located in metropolitan areas were being overwhelmed by population emigrating from central cities. Finally, about 10 percent of the communities were wealthy and exclusive residential enclaves that appeared bent on blocking new development in any form.

A U.S. General Accounting Office survey of localities discovered that many communities had established excessively large minimum lot sizes, and concluded that this was a prime cause of housing cost inflation. Table 38 presents the range of lot sizes in the eighty-seven communities surveyed. The survey results show considerable variance in lot sizes, which ranged from a minimum of 4,500 square feet to two acres. The average size was

TABLE 38

LOT SIZE RANGES OF GAO SURVEYED CITIES

Minimum Lot Size (sq. ft.)	Number of Communities	% of Total Communities
5,000 and under	7	8
5,001–7,500	25	28
7,501–11,000 (1/4 acre)	25	28
11,001–22,000 (1/2 acre)	20	22
22,001–44,000 (1 acre)	7	8
Over one acre	3	3
Subtotal	87	97
No minimum requirement	3	3
Total	90[a]	100

Source: U.S. General Accounting Office, *Why Are New Housing Prices So High? How Are They Influenced by Government Regulation and Can Prices Be Reduced?* (Washington, 1978).

[a] Three zoning officials cited two areas in their community where an equal amount of development was taking place.

about 15,000 square feet and the median 10,000 square feet. According to land price data, reductions in minimum lot sizes could yield considerable savings in terms of housing costs. A 1981 Homer Hoyt Institute survey of land prices found that residential lots were priced between $1.05 and $2.07 per square foot.[10] Thus, if minimum lot size requirements were reduced by one-third, land cost savings could range from $3,500 to as much as $10,000 per unit.

Another pertinent national study was that done by the U.S. Department of Housing and Urban Development's Housing Costs Task Force. Created in 1977, this group surveyed local land use and housing regulations and assessed their impact on housing production costs. The task force found that severe land supply bottlenecks were occurring in many of the nation's metropolitan areas, and were caused by many factors, of which the most important was the dearth of finished, "ready-to-go" residential lots. According to the task force, it is

governmental action—through regulation and investment decisions—which, more than any other factor, has constrained land supply. Limitations in the capacity of infrastructure, such as sewers and roads, can preclude development in certain areas. Supply can also be limited by zoning or other special ordinances which effectively prohibit development in designated areas. In addition, property tax practices, either by design or inadvertence, sometimes work to keep raw land off the market.[11]

The task force report concluded that these problems were not likely to ease, since pressures to limit fiscal obligations and increase environmental standards were intensifying. The report also pointed out the growing difficulty of finding land for higher-density housing.

A third study assessing the effects of land use control on housing costs was conducted by Seidel at the Center for Urban Policy Research.[12] Seidel's work is based on surveys of 26,000 builders, 7,000 land developers, and 86 communities across the country; the surveys dealt with the effects of building codes, energy conservation codes, subdivision regulations, zoning, growth controls, environmental regulations, and settlement and financing costs.

Results of his builder-developer survey show just how much the delay problem worsened in five years. In 1970, 28 percent of the land developers interviewed indicated that they completed their projects in less than four months, 41 percent completed them in four to six months, and 17 percent in seven to twelve months. In fact, no respondent had required more than twenty-four months to complete a project. By 1975, the picture was quite different. Only 2 percent of builders reported completion of a project in less than four months, 8 percent needed between four and six months, and 31 percent between seven and twelve months. Another 35 percent indicated that it took between thirteen and eighteen months to complete a project, and for over 14 percent it took more than two years.

Seidel concluded that building codes, energy conservation requirements, and subdivisions add substantially to the costs of housing. His study showed that there is wide variation in building codes and subdivision regulations, and that communities could lower housing production costs by using more standardized codes and lowering subdivision requirements. He also found that energy conservation requirements do indeed yield energy savings, but add to the sales price of new units, so much so that this factor alone may exclude many first-time buyers from the new home market. Zoning policies were found to have a considerable impact on the type, cost, and location of residential development. Of the builders Seidel surveyed, zoning requirements cause 60 percent to build more expensive units and 40 percent to seek development opportunities in less populated areas.

Seidel's national survey of municipal zoning ordinances revealed that most communities have an aversion to multifamily development. In fact, 64 percent of the zoned land in sampled communities was designated for single-family units. Of the remainder, 72 percent was zoned for low-density garden apartments and townhouses. These findings are consistent

TABLE 39

SINGLE-FAMILY MINIMUM LOT SIZE BY REGION

Percentage of Single-Family Zoned Land

| Lot Size (sq. ft.) | Region | | | |
	East N = 18	North Central N = 16	South N = 18	West N = 23
0–6,999	15.8	18.7	47.1	50.0
7,000–9,999	24.0	40.0	14.0	35.4
10,000–19,999	26.9	38.6	11.8	5.5
20,000–39,999	10.0	2.0	18.0	5.5
40,000–79,999	15.6	0.0	4.6	3.7
80,000 or more	7.8	0.0	4.5	0.0
Unrestricted	0.0	0.7	0.0	0.0
Total[a]	100.0	100.0	100.0	100.0

SOURCE: Stephen R. Seidel, *Housing Costs and Government Regulations: Confronting the Regulatory Maze* (New Brunswick, N.J.: Center for Urban Policy Research, 1978).
[a]Due to rounding, total may not add to 100.0.

with the results of a 1972 New Jersey study, which found that only 6 percent of net residential land in the state was zoned for multifamily use, and of that land almost two-thirds was zoned to permit only efficiency and one-bedroom apartments.[13]

Much of land the surveyed communities had zoned for single-family development was restricted by large minimum lot sizes. As table 39 indicates, Seidel's national survey shows an interesting geographic pattern: minimum residential lot sizes appear to be larger in the eastern portion of the country. Of land zoned for single-family homes in the West, 15 percent was subject to minimum lot sizes of 10,000 square feet or more, as compared to over 60 percent of land in the Eastern region.

Environmental controls were another area of local regulation assessed by Seidel. His survey of state and local governments revealed that use of environmental regulations and such requirements as environmental impact statements and coastal zone controls was widespread and still increasing. As of 1975, seventeen states required environmental impact statements, and thirty-seven had imposed controls over development in wetlands, floodplains, or critical areas.

The proliferation of these special environmental requirements has made the review of land development proposals much more cumbersome and time-consuming. It has also made compliance with regulations more expensive. For example, Muller and James found that in Florida the preparation of required environmental impact statements added approximately $400 to the cost of each new housing unit.[14]

A recently published study of land price inflation and its causes sheds much light on the suburban squeeze now confronting many metropolitan areas.[15] A joint research team of the U.S. Department of Housing and Urban Development (HUD) and the Urban Land Institute (ULI) used panels of local real estate appraisers to estimate single-family lot prices and per-acre raw land prices in thirty metropolitan areas. The results of this study, presented in table 40, show that the average price of a finished single-family lot rose from $10,320 to $18,750 between 1975 and 1980—an 81 percent increase in five years. The price of raw land suitable for residential development increased by an enormous 157 percent, going from $8,370 to $21,520 per acre. These rates of inflation are well above those reflected in the national consumer price index, which rose 53 percent during this period.

Closer inspection of table 40 reveals that improved lot and raw land price increases were highest in the western portion of the nation, where housing demand has been strongest. In the West, for example, the price of improved lots increased by 130 percent between 1975 and 1980, well above the average for the north–north central and southern regions. The comparison is similar for raw land price increases. In the western region, prices increased nearly 300 percent, far outpacing the 73 and 82 percent increases seen in the north–north central and southern regions respectively.

Though average increases in the north–north central and southern regions were modest, several metropolitan areas within these regions experienced large five-year increases. In the north–north central region, Hartford, Pittsburgh, and Minneapolis all registered significant increases. Of metropolitan areas in the South, Miami, Oklahoma City, and Raleigh had lot price increases over 65 percent. And raw land prices increased by over 100 percent in Chattanooga, Dallas, Fort Lauderdale, Lexington, and Oklahoma City. Clearly, the Bay Area has no monopoly on land price inflation; nor, for that matter, does California.

Economic theory offers an explanation for the land price inflation seen in metropolitan areas all across the nation: the combination of strong housing demand and limited land and housing supply increases land prices. Thus, any actions to limit land supply—be they land use controls, limits on street, sewer, or water systems, or special efforts to protect unique resources—will exert further upward pressure on land prices.

TABLE 40

MEDIAN SINGLE-FAMILY LOT AND RAW ACREAGE PRICES IN
SELECTED METROPOLITAN AREAS, 1975 AND 1980

SMSA	Improved Lot			Raw Acreage		
	1980	1975	5-year %	1980	1975	5-year %
North–North Central						
Boston	$23,750	$18,176	30.7	$16,250	$10,500	51.8
Cincinnati	15,000	—	—	6,000	—	—
Hartford	20,000	12,000	66.7	7,250	3,000	141.7
Indianapolis	12,000	7,000	71.4	4,000	3,000	33.9
Kansas City	14,000	10,000	40.0	8,550	5,000	71.0
Minneapolis	20,000	9,500	110.5	9,750	2,664	266.0
Pittsburgh	16,950	10,000	69.5	5,250	2,500	110.0
St. Louis	15,000	10,500	42.9	15,500	10,000	55.5
Average	17,088	11,025	55.0	9,069	5,238	73.1
South						
Atlanta	13,250	8,000	65.6	6,750	5,000	35.0
Charlotte	9,500	6,000	58.3	5,500	3,750	46.7
Chattanooga	7,500	4,500	66.7	2,500	1,165	114.6
Dallas	16,000	9,500	68.4	20,500	8,500	141.2
Fort Lauderdale	21,250	13,875	53.2	35,000	15,068	132.3
Houston	12,000	7,850	53.8	10,000	7,004	42.8
Jacksonville	12,000	8,500	41.2	7,750	5,250	47.6
Lexington	14,000	10,000	40.0	8,000	4,000	100.0
Louisville	15,125	9,900	52.8	7,750	4,000	93.8
Miami	25,000	11,750	112.8	60,000	35,000	71.4
New Orleans	31,428	20,000	57.1	28,751	18,551	54.0
Oklahoma City	13,000	7,300	78.1	8,500	3,500	142.9
Raleigh	14,500	8,582	69.0	6,375	3,250	96.2
Average	15,735	9,674	62.7	15,952	8,772	81.8
West						
Albuquerque	21,250	11,651	82.4	21,000	11,400	84.2
Boulder	25,000	11,500	117.4	15,000	5,000	200.0
Phoenix	20,000	10,000	100.0	27,500	10,000	175.0
Portland	22,000	10,000	120.0	27,500	8,500	223.5
Salt Lake City	16,625	8,375	98.5	26,250	10,000	162.5
San Diego	40,000	15,000	166.7	35,000	10,000	250.0
San Jose	40,000	14,500	175.9	187,500	27,500	581.8
Seattle	20,000	8,000	150.0	20,000	7,000	185.7
Tacoma	16,500	7,500	120.0	6,000	2,552	135.1
Average	24,597	10,725	129.9	40,639	10,277	297.8
Total Averages	$18,750	$10,320	81.7	$21,520	$8,370	157.0

SOURCE: Jim Hoben and J. Thomas Black, "Residential Land Prices: Variations Between Metropolitan Areas" (unpublished manuscript, 1982).

The authors of the HUD-ULI study attempted to determine the causes of rapid land price inflation in these metropolitan areas by using a statistical approach based on the following factors:

Demand Factors

1. 1980 population (U.S. Bureau of the Census). A measure of size is used to indicate demand pressures associated with large size, such as suburbanization and decentralization.

2. Percentage change in population, 1975–80 (U.S. Bureau of the Census). A measure of demand for land by new households.

3. Percentage change in employment (U.S. Bureau of the Census). A measure of new development pressure.

4. Per capita income, 1979 (U.S. Bureau of Economic Analysis). A measure of regional wealth and, therefore, of demand for land.

5. Percentage change in per capita income, 1975–79 (U.S. Bureau of Economic Analysis).

Supply Factors

1. Single-family building permits issued per 1,000 population, 1980 (U.S. Bureau of the Census). A measure of the amount of new residential development approved, proportional to total population.

2. Ratio of employment income increase to single-family building permits issued, 1975–80 (U.S. Bureau of the Census and Department of Labor). A measure of the relationship between income increases and permitted residential development.

3. Ratio of new to existing home loans, 1975–80 (U.S. Federal Home Loan Bank Board). A measure of new capital for residential development.

4. Rating of physical restrictions, 1980 (Urban Land Institute Survey estimate). A measure of physical limits to urban expansion, such as mountains, swamps, or oceans. Metropolitan areas were rated: 0 = few, 1 = severe on one side, and 2 = severe on several sides of Standard Metropolitan Statistical Area (SMSA).

5. Rating of regulatory restrictions, 1980 (Urban Land Institute Survey). A measure of the extent to which local government policies seek and support growth, are neutral, or attempt to restrict and control growth. A select panel of land use experts from across the country was asked to rate the growth policies of each metropolitan area on a ten-point scale.

The HUD-ULI team collected these data for all thirty areas and combined them with the land and lot price data contained in table 40. Several regression analyses were conducted for twenty-seven of the thirty metropolitan areas. Models were generated for 1982 lot prices, lot price increases between 1975 and 1980, and 1982 raw land prices and raw land price increases. The results are presented in table 41.

The T-ratios presented in table 41 suggest that four factors were closely associated with variations in the price of improved lots: (1) regulatory rating, (2) five-year changes in population, (3) 1975 lot or raw land prices, and (4) 1980 median home prices. These four factors are also clearly associated with raw land prices and their rates of increase. Increases in raw land prices were also linked with two other factors: the increase in employment and the ratio of jobs to building permits.

While these results are far from conclusive, they do indicate that local land use policies have a great deal of influence on land prices and, in particular, lot prices.

These recent studies present a powerful body of evidence that land use and development controls add to the cost of constructing housing. They also confirm that restrictive controls are used by communities in all areas of the country, particularly in the East, as well as in Florida, Illinois, Minnesota, Oregon, Washington, Arizona, and New Mexico. The next section takes a closer look at some of these metropolitan areas.

PROFILES OF SEVERAL METROPOLITAN AREAS

Northeastern New Jersey

The northeastern counties of New Jersey have been a focus of the New York metropolitan area's postwar housing growth. While Connecticut, Long Island, and upstate New York counties have also provided opportunities for suburban development, most housing built there has been aimed at upper-middle and upper income households, particularly in Connecticut. Another reason northeastern New Jersey is such an important housing market is its growing industrial development and employment base. The result of economic decentralization from New York, these increases in basic employment have created additional economic activity and strong demands for housing in the area.

At the same time, local land use controls are greatly constraining the construction of moderate-cost housing. Various motivations for these restrictive controls could be suggested, but according to Williams and Norman, fiscal concerns, racism, and the desire to preserve the rural environment are the most likely reasons.[16]

Williams and Norman based their analysis in large part on information generated by the New Jersey Department of Community Affairs,

TABLE 41

LAND PRICE MODELS: SUMMARY OF REGRESSION ANALYSES

Explanatory Variables	Short Models (T-ratios)				Long Models (T-ratios)			
	Improved Lot Price 1980	Lot Price Increase 1975–80	Raw Land Price 1980	Raw Land Price Increase 1975–80	Improved Lot Price 1980	Lot Price Increase 1975–80	Raw Land Price 1980	Raw Land Price Increase 1975–80
1975 lot or acre price	7.10	−2.76	15.31	0.55	4.44	−1.15	5.33	1.19
Regulatory rating	−5.23	−7.30	−4.01	−1.85	−3.84	−5.37	−1.43	−2.94
5-year % population increase	2.91	3.50	4.16	−1.67	1.57	2.02	0.08	−0.69
Median home price 1980	4.29	2.56	1.58	3.05	2.31	1.67	2.54	1.93
1980 population						−0.50	−1.26	−0.56
4-year % increase in income per capita			1.49			2.46		1.73
5-year % increase in jobs				2.73	−0.67	−1.45	0.94	1.86
Building permits per 1000 population					−0.79	−0.54	−2.13	−1.31
Income/population 1979					0.70	0.79	0.19	1.00
New loans/existing loans					−0.46	−0.51	0.95	1.23
5-year increase in jobs/ building permits				−2.37	−1.22	−0.80	−1.56	−1.98
Physical restrictions					−0.27	0.51	−1.62	−1.08
Number in sample	27	27	26	27	26	26	25	26
Adjusted R^2	.901	.805	.934	.642	.885	.826	.775	.668

Source: Hoben and Black, "Residential Land Prices."
Note: All regressions include San Jose data.

which in 1970 surveyed the land use policies of all local governments in the state. Using the survey results, they focused on four counties: Morris, Somerset, Middlesex, and Monmouth.

The two northernmost counties, Morris and Somerset, are located in country dominated by rolling hills; the other two counties are within the coastal plain. In terms of land use patterns, Morris County is the most diverse, containing semiretired industrial towns, exclusive estate areas, new suburban divisions, and new job centers. Somerset County has a split personality. The northern portion is hilly, and estates are common; much of the southern county is still quite rural, but new subdivisions are developing. The recent construction of interstate highways through both counties has opened much land to development pressure. Pressure to convert land to urban uses, especially industrial development, will increase over time. Middlesex County is traversed—and dominated—by the main transportation corridor between New York and Philadelphia. It has captured a considerable share of industrial employment decentralized from New York. Monmouth County, historically a resort area, has only recently been pulled into New York's sphere. While it is not as well linked with New York as the other counties, its ample supply of vacant land makes it safe to predict that much residential development will soon take place there.

Despite these growth pressures, the likelihood is that future residential development of these counties will be skewed toward expensive homes. For, like other communities in New Jersey, these counties use a variety of land use controls to permit only the more exclusive types of residential development.

The Department of Community Affairs survey identified six devices commonly used to restrict development in the state: (1) minimum building sizes, (2) outright exclusion of multifamily development, (3) restrictions on the number of bedrooms per unit, (4) prohibition of mobile homes, (5) lot width requirements, and (6) lot size requirements.

The extent of exclusionary zoning and land development controls in the four counties is set forth in table 42. The survey results make it clear that local land use policies are effectively blocking the development of multifamily dwelling units in these four counties, and that even in the areas designated exclusively for single-family homes, only large-lot subdivision of land is permitted.

The extensive use of large-lot zoning by these New Jersey counties is similar to the pattern found in the San Francisco Bay Area. While new and complex growth management programs have garnered much attention

TABLE 42

EXCLUSIONARY ZONING IN SUBURBAN NORTHEASTERN
NEW JERSEY

Residential Land Available for Development	Morris Acres	Morris %	Somerset Acres	Somerset %	Middlesex Acres	Middlesex %	Monmouth Acres	Monmouth %	Total Acres	Total %
Kinds of residential use										
Multifamily	1,322	0.8	0	0.0	307	0.6	633	0.4	2,262	0.5
Mobile homes	0	0.0	0	0.0	0	0.0	0	0.0	0	0.0
Single-family	105,287	99.2	87,479	100.0	56,477	99.4	154,290	99.6	403,531	99.5
	106,609	100.0	87,479	100.0	56,784	100.0	154,923	100.0	405,793	100.0
Minimum building size, single-family										
Under 700 sq. ft.	0	0.0	14,156	16.1	83	0.1	0	0.0	14,239	3.5
700–999	13,769	13.0	6,406	7.2	6,572	11.4	1,757	1.1	28,504	7.1
1000–1199	21,604	20.6	1,689	1.8	17,921	30.9	1,375	0.9	42,580	10.6
1200–1599	64,059	60.8	62,776	72.3	10,392	20.0	120,019	77.7	257,246	63.8
1600 & over	5,760	5.5	1,971	2.1	21,499	37.6	26,627	17.4	55,857	13.8
No requirement	95	0.09	481	0.5	19	0.0	4,512	2.9	5,107	1.2
	105,287	100.0	87,479	100.0	56,477	100.0	154,290	100.0	403,531	100.0
Minimum lot width, single-family										
50–99 linear ft.	1,728	1.5	11,700	13.4	5,194	9.0	1,918	1.2	20,540	5.0
100–149	47,680	45.3	4,439	5.0	37,496	66.6	14,006	9.0	103,621	25.5
150–199	30,885	29.3	30,438	34.8	7,150	12.6	11,977	7.7	80,450	20.1
200 & over	24,994	23.9	40,901	46.8	6,637	11.8	122,101	79.4	194,633	48.3
No requirement	0	0.0	0	0.0	0	0.0	4,288	2.7	4,288	1.1
	105,287	100.0	87,479	100.0	56,477	100.0	154,290	100.0	403,531	100.0

Minimum lot size, single-family	No.	%	No.	%	No.	%	No.	%	No.	%
Under 10,000 sq. ft.	359	0.2	218	0.3	2,796	4.9	1,600	1.0	4,973	1.2
10,000–19,999	4,464	4.1	359	0.4	5,183	9.0	6,033	3.8	16,044	3.9
20,000–39,999	14,141	13.3	12,140	13.8	26,618	47.1	19,573	12.8	72,472	17.9
40,000–79,999	52,012	49.8	52,550	60.0	21,880	39.0	98,745	64.0	225,187	55.6
80,000–119,999	11,277	10.6	658	0.7	0	0.0	26,912	17.4	38,847	9.6
3 acres & over	23,034	22.0	21,554	24.6	0	0.0	1,427	1.0	46,015	11.8
	105,287	100.0	87,479	100.0	56,477	100.0	154,290	100.0	403,531	100.0

Source: Norman Williams, Jr. and Thomas Norman, "Exclusionary Land Use Controls: The Case of North-Eastern New Jersey," in *Land Use Controls: Present Problems and Future Reform*, ed. David Listokin (New Brunswick, N.J.: Center for Urban Policy Research, 1974).

from the planning profession and environmental groups, it is still by placing undeveloped land into large-lot zones that communities most commonly control population growth and land conversion. This practice en-
sures that land either cannot be developed economically, or can be used
only for the most expensive type of structures. The New Jersey example
differs from California in that it does not add an overlay of more sophisticated growth controls. While the reason for this is unclear, it is probably
due to differing state laws relating to land use control and environmental
protection. But complex growth controls are by no means unique to California. Across the New Jersey border in upstate New York, the town of
Ramapo has been a pioneer in growth management.

Ramapo, and Westchester County, New York

The town of Ramapo is located in Rockland County, on the western
bank of the Hudson River. With the completion of the Tappan Zee Bridge
over to Westchester County in the 1960s, Rockland County and Ramapo
were pulled into the commuting orbit of New York. The town saw substantial population growth during the 1960s, expanding from 35,000 to
76,000 residents in the course of the decade. This growth placed tremendous pressures on the town's sewer and water systems, schools, and
streets. In 1969, the town responded by passing a resolution to regulate
residential development. The resulting phased-growth plan attempted to
gear residential development to the capacity of the town's local services.

The Ramapo ordinance limited residential development to those proposed projects that scored a set number of points on a five-point evaluation of their access to, and demands upon, existing town services: sewers,
drainage, parks and recreation, streets, and fire stations.[17] Theoretically,
this system did not block growth, since all vacant parcels could be developed once community services were expanded. In short, the ordinance
was designed to control "leapfrog" development and limit the rate of
growth to match infrastructure capacity.

In contrast to the methods used by the four New Jersey counties, the
Ramapo ordinance does not attempt to control development by limiting
minimum lot sizes, nor does it limit or reduce the town's ultimate population. Rather, it slows the rate of growth. Proponents of the phased-growth
approach argue that it does not adversely affect housing or land prices by
distorting the land and housing markets. They also contend that, since
the density of residential development remains unchanged, the ordinance
is not exclusionary. But this argument is logical only if unfulfilled housing
can easily be shifted to other locales. As Claude Gruen has suggested,

local controls do not limit population expansion at the regional level; they merely redistribute it to other communities. If enough communities limit their own residential growth, the pressures on land and housing markets can be substantial, driving up housing prices accordingly.[18]

While few other communities in upstate New York have implemented growth controls of the Ramapo type, many have relied on large-lot exclusionary zoning to discourage land conversion and control the nature of residential development. Westchester County is a prime example. In a study done for the Westchester County Planning Department, Economic Consultants Organization, Inc., concluded:

In the towns, which contain the bulk of the County's undeveloped land, the density regulations are extremely stringent, and multiple dwellings, two-family dwellings, and mobile homes are virtually excluded. The town ordinances vary somewhat in the severity of their restrictions, but all reflect a clear policy to limit development to single-family dwellings on large lots.[19]

Table 43 illustrates the extent of large-lot zoning practiced by the ten towns in the developing northern portion of Westchester County. In these ten communities, which contain more than 60 percent of the county's

TABLE 43
DISTRIBUTION OF PERMITTED DENSITIES IN TEN
NORTHERN TOWNS COMBINED, 1969

Zone	No. of Acres	% of Total Residential Acres
One-family		
4-acre lot	26,674	16.6
2.0–3.99 acre	54,899	34.1
1.0–1.99 acre	46,250	28.7
30,000 sq. ft.–0.99 acre	14,836	9.2
20–29,999 sq. ft.	11,896	7.4
10–19,999 sq. ft.	5,048	3.1
less than 10,000 sq. ft.	497	0.3
Total one-family	160,100	99.4
Multifamily		
2–4 units	750	0.5
5 or more units	227	0.1
Total multifamily	977	0.6
Total all residential zones	161,077	100.0

SOURCE: Economic Consultants Organization, Inc., in "Zoning Ordinances and Administration," *Residential Analysis for Westchester County, New York* (New York, 1970).

total land area, over 50 percent of the residentially zoned land is limited to lot sizes of two acres or more, and nearly 80 percent to lots of more than one acre. Less than 1 percent of all residentially zoned land is designated for multifamily development. Clearly, these zoning ordinances limit land conversion and guarantee that only the most expensive type of development will be permitted in the northern portion of the county.

If this assessment of the New York metropolitan area were rounded out, similar patterns would be found in Connecticut and on Long Island. In the now developing suburban portions of this metropolitan region, residential development is occurring at very low density and is almost exclusively single-family in type.

Washington, D.C.

In terms of the widespread use of restrictive land use regulation, no metropolitan area comes closer to the San Francisco Bay Area than Washington, D.C. Like the Bay Area, Washington, D.C. experienced substantial population and employment growth during the 1960s and 1970s. This growth resulted largely from in-migration, spurred by expansion of the federal government and related private and public activities. The Washington Council of Governments estimates that 75 percent of the area's population growth in the 1960s was due to net in-migration. Migration remained a prime factor in the 1970s, but natural increases also added population. As in other metropolitan areas, the baby-boom cohort was coming to maturity, placing considerable pressure on the area's housing markets in the process. According to estimates by the Washington Council of Governments, the region needed to build approximately 39,000 new housing units per year during the 1970s, a level 30 percent above the previous decade's actual rate of housing construction.[20]

During the early 1970s, much attention was focused on the concept of "fair share" housing allocation as a way to meet housing demands. The idea was that communities would agree to provide the necessary services and zoning to permit the development of their "fair" share of the region's needed housing. While definitions of "fair share" varied, the construction of more housing in the Washington area hinged on the availability of adequate sewer capacity. But as of 1974, since most existing sewerage treatment plants lacked capacity, nearly the entire metropolitan area was under a sewer connection moratorium. Some communities used these capacity constraints to limit residential development. Fairfax County, Virginia, one jurisdiction that refused to expand sewerage treatment capacity, did so explicitly as a means of controlling population growth and land conversion. The county justified its actions as follows:

[This] slow growth policy is justified by the Supervisors on the grounds that Fairfax has taken more than its fair share of regional housing in recent years, and that this has caused overcrowding, poor standards of homebuilding and site planning, environmental pollution, and rising property tax burdens.[21]

Although examination of construction statistics indicated that Fairfax County received more than its share of regional housing development only during the first four years of the 1970s, county policy remained firm in the face of substantial political pressure.

Fairfax County's approach to land use control was based on its power as a provider of public facilities. As the Hirsts observed, the county used the following strategies to control development:

- Renegotiated earlier allocation agreements with other jurisdictions to reduce its share of sewer plant capacity.

- Designed smaller plants than contemplated by past elected officials.

- Planned undersized pipe collection systems leading to treatment plants, so that future expansion of capacity would necessitate the costly laying of parallel pipes.

- Shut down older treatment plants and pumped their flows to the new or expanded plants, thereby reducing the capacity available to serve new construction.

- Overstated the sewer treatment needs of independent communities served by Fairfax plants, again reducing the residual capacity for new development.

The impact of this five-point strategy was severe. The rate of home construction was cut back by more than 40 percent, with only 7,000 permits issued per year. Housing prices quickly reflected the restrictions on supply, and the median value of single-family homes approached $100,000.

The impact of Fairfax County's sewer moratorium extended beyond the county boundaries, as housing demand pressures shifted to other areas of the region. Shortly after the Fairfax County action, Montgomery County also imposed a sewer-related moratorium on residential development. This left only the District of Columbia and Prince George's County as possible growth centers. While Prince George's County considered imposing growth management in early 1974, after commissioning the firm of Hammer, Siler and George to outline a county growth control system, it did not move to limit the rate of development. In Washington, D.C., young professionals scrambled for affordable housing, looking especially to older areas such as Capitol Hill and Foggy Bottom. From the mid-1970s on, housing prices in the Washington area climbed sharply. In fact, it was the only metropolis where housing prices approached the stratospheric levels of San Francisco and Los Angeles.

The Washington area is a good example of how growth controls can spread as more and more communities are forced to stave off the growth forced on them by other growth-limiting communities. The Washington case also illustrates the point made by Claude Gruen: local growth control rarely limits growth; it merely shifts it to other portions of the metropolitan area.[22]

Boston

A recently prepared interim draft report, "The Real Estate of the Region," assesses land availability in the Boston metropolitan area.[23] Prepared by the Metropolitan Area Planning Council, the report examines zoning policies and inventories land suitable for development in 92 of the region's 101 cities and towns.

The zoning survey reveals that of the 626,000 acres of residentially zoned land in the region, 64 percent is zoned for a density of less than 2 units per acre, a pattern quite similar to that found in the northeastern portion of New Jersey. Another 27 percent was zoned for densities between 2 and 4.9 units per acre, and the remainder, 9 percent, was zoned for 5 or more units per acre.

Closer inspection of these zoning data reveals that in the outlying areas beyond the Route 128 highway loop, little land for high-density residential development remains. Communities located within the Route 128 loop highway contain 67 percent of all land zoned for 5 or more units per acre in the region. The suburban area contains 31 percent of the land zoned for 5 or more units per acre, most of it located in the western portion of the region (Hudson, Marlborough, Framingham, and Natick). Rural areas account for less than 2 percent of land zoned for 5 or more units per acre.

In assessing policies for commercial and industrial development, the report found that an increasing amount of land is being zoned for employment-generating uses, suggesting that the demand for housing will likely increase in suburban areas.

The study also assessed the availability of developable land in forty-two cities most likely to experience land conversion during the remainder of this century. This survey raised some disturbing questions about the future affordability of housing in the region. As shown in table 44, which presents land availability by use, the area's residential development process is highly oriented to the production of large-lot, single-family houses; little land is zoned for multifamily or cluster housing. As the report suggests:

Considering the impact of land costs, this presents some problems for housing opportunities. R-1, R-2, and R-3 land comprise twenty-seven percent, sixty-two percent and eleven percent of the residentially-zoned available land respectively. ... As this data is representative of the outlying cities and towns, the low amount of available R-4 land could be of future concern. First it does not contribute to the PLUMB's [Policies for Land Use in Metropolitan Boston] goal of promoting a diversity of housing types throughout the region, and secondly it is potentially indicative of zoning barriers to low and moderate income households who may desire to reside in these communities.[24]

Zoning and land-use control practices in the Boston area seem to closely parallel those in New Jersey. What about "free-market" Houston?

Houston

Houston enjoys the notoriety of being the nation's largest city without zoning. But that doesn't mean land conversion is unfettered throughout

TABLE 44

LAND AVAILABLE FOR DEVELOPMENT IN THE BOSTON
METROPOLITAN AREA

Use	Available Land (in acres)	% of Total	% of Residential
R-1 (less than one unit per acre)	53,907	24	27
R-2 (one to 1.9 units per acre)	123,622	55	62
R-3 (2 to 4.9 units per acre)	21,890	10	11
R-4 (5 or more units per acre)	759	0	0
Total residential	200,180	89	100
Commercial	3,494	2	
Industrial	18,980	9	
Total	222,725	100	

SOURCE: Metropolitan Area Planning Council, *The Real Estate of the Region,* Boston, n.d.

the metropolitan area; most of the other thirty-three cities in Harris County do have zoning. Furthermore, Houston relies on other tools to regulate land development—namely, deed restrictions and subdivision controls.[25] Such provisions are used to specify the use, height, bulk, and lot coverage of structures. Texas law allows the city of Houston to join in lawsuits to uphold existing deed restrictions, and the city's Planning Department assists property owners in drafting deed restrictions.

Another interesting feature of the Houston planning scene is that Texas law permits cities over 100,000 in population to exercise limited control over development proposals in unincorporated areas within five miles of the city limits.[26] That means that much development in Harris County is controlled by the city of Houston.

Population of the Houston area increased from 1.2 million in 1960 to 2.9 million in 1980, but this phenomenal growth has not been without costs. Traffic congestion, air and groundwater pollution, flooding, and subsidence head the list of growth-related problems, of which the public is increasingly aware. A 1975 study of Houstonians found that "flooding, drainage, and subsidence" was ranked by 22 percent of the respondents as the most important problem facing their community today, while "mass transit" and "pollution and decay" were ranked first by 17 percent.[27]

A recent report by the Rice Center, *Houston Initiatives*, discusses these problems and considers their possible consequences.[28] The report also reflects a level of concern sufficient to suggest that Houston's days of untrammeled growth may be drawing to a close. Sponsored by the business community, the *Houston Initiatives* project is a clear response to the potential threat of federal intervention in Houston's problems.

The level of citizen response to some of these problems is marked as well. For example, recent research by Barton Smith and Robert Ohsfeldt on the Houston housing market shows conclusively that traffic congestion is beginning to depress suburban housing prices.[29] Their statistical model estimates that in 1970, a hypothetical home increased in value 0.7 percent for each mile it was located closer to the CBD. By 1976, each mile of closer proximity would increase the house's value by a substantial 1.6 percent. The key finding is not the amount of the "proximity premium," but how dramatically it changed in seven years, coinciding with increases in traffic congestion and commuting times. In Houston, the suburbs are "squeezed" not by land use controls, but by the lack of infrastructure, especially roads.

Capacity constraints are not the only thing hurting Houston's housing production. The residents of some suburbs are beginning to behave like Californians: they are trying to stop development.

A Rice Center study (on which this author was a consultant) for Friendswood Development Company, the builders of Clear Lake City, is telling.[30] Clear Lake City is an emerging "new town" located on twenty-four square miles of southeast Harris County. The master plan for the city calls for a balance of single-family, apartment, condominium, retail, office, and light industrial development. This community was to boast a well-integrated, parklike environment, and the entire development was to have been largely independent of Houston.

This might have sounded idyllic to some, but not to nearby homeowners. Once Friendswood started to develop areas targeted for multifamily units, the homeowner's association was vocal in its opposition, alleging that multifamily housing would be visually disruptive, create traffic congestion, fail to generate enough taxes, and bring in a "different class" of people uncommitted to Clear Lake City. In the absence of zoning, the homeowners group could not seek rezoning of the land to block Friendswood's multifamily project. Instead, they exerted control over the municipal utility district to limit water and sewer extension to the project, forcing Friendswood Development Company to scale back its plans.

Thus, the combination of infrastructure limitations and citizen opposition is enough to restrict suburban development even in Houston, with its reputation as a freewheeling growth center.

CONCLUSION

This chapter has surveyed the extent of local land use regulations in metropolitan housing markets outside California, as well as their impact. Many of the nation's communities, particularly those on the East Coast, have for years practiced exclusionary zoning to fend off lower-income households seeking homes in the suburbs. Large-lot zoning is widespread in the New York and Boston metropolitan areas and has had a substantial impact on housing markets. In the Washington area, counties have relied on moratoriums to limit land conversion. Freeway constraints and growing citizen activism are also beginning to curtail housing in some areas of Houston.

Similar stories could be told about other areas of the country. For example, exclusionary zoning is prevalent in the suburbs of Philadelphia, as well as in districts near Chicago.[31] Even in growth centers such as Tucson, communities are using their power to withhold sewer and water service as a means to limit certain types of development. The Comprehensive Plan Policies that have been proposed by the city of Tucson would greatly reduce the supply of developable land.[32] Sophisticated growth-management programs implemented in other areas are already having an impact on land and housing prices. For example, Whitelaw found that prices for land inside the growth boundaries around Eugene, Oregon, have increased more rapidly than for land outside, suggesting that growth controls have shifted demand pressures to the areas targeted for development.[33]

Perhaps the main conclusion to be drawn from this survey of community land use policies is that since the 1960s, cities and counties across the country have begun to exert direct control over future development patterns. No longer do citizens want merely to accommodate development; they intend to control development in a way that meets their fiscal, environmental, and social objectives. The desire to preserve the status quo is particularly strong in communities that are located near large central cities. Close enough to be able to enjoy the cultural attractions of a major city, along with its business and financial services and transportation facilities, these communities also want to retain the benefits of small town living.

It is unlikely that these efforts to preserve the benefits of "smallness" will disappear in the future. On the contrary, they will probably increase in areas where land conversion pressures are strong, including small but growing metropolitan areas such as Charlotte, North Carolina, and Portland, Oregon.

Exactly how these communities will control land development is not clear, but they will probably rely on a combination of devices, among them sewer and water system moratoriums, designation of urban growth boundaries, agricultural or conservation zones, and, in high-growth areas, allocation systems similar to those of Petaluma, Ramapo, or Boulder.

The highly restrictive land use controls so popular in the San Francisco Bay Area are not unique to that region, nor to California. They enjoy popularity in a number of growth areas across the country, and are in fact more prevalent in northeastern New Jersey than in California. As this chapter has documented, California does not have a monopoly on restrictive land use controls.

CHAPTER EIGHT

Living with the Suburban Squeeze

The era of trouble-free, limitless suburban land is over. Across the nation, from San Francisco to Boston, from New York to Houston, it is becoming increasingly difficult to develop land in the suburbs. In some cases this is due to restrictive local land use policies, and in others, to limited freeway, water, and sewer capacity. Sometimes the key element is neighborhood groups that block suburban residential development. Some areas are simply running out of easy-to-develop land within commuting distance of downtown. Wherever the suburban squeeze is being felt, it has usually resulted from some combination of these factors.

The cycle of the suburban squeeze is always the same: first a high rate of suburban development, then constraints on residential growth, next an upward spiral in housing prices, and finally businesses begin to complain that they can't attract skilled workers when there is no affordable housing in the area. In the most acute stage, businesses begin to flee to lower-cost areas.

Once the suburban squeeze becomes chronic, land use planners find themselves on the horns of a dilemma: should they control development as strictly as neighborhood groups and environmentalists want or should they create affordable housing as the employers, housing advocates, and tenants urge?

What are the long-run consequences of the suburban squeeze? The clearest and most direct effect is a rapid rise in housing prices. Indirectly, this rise in housing prices also drives up labor costs, because firms must either raise wages and salaries or accept lower-quality employees. Firms today frequently limit recruitment to the local area, especially for middle-management employees. With this strategy, they can avoid having to underwrite housing assistance programs or meet extraordinarily high wage demands. It works well for some businesses, but has disastrous consequences for others. Imagine the University of California or Harvard University limiting its recruitment searches to the Bay Area or Boston. Enterprises in high-cost areas simply must pay higher wages if they are to attract the very best and brightest.

Some people might respond, "So what if employers have to pay more for new employees? That's the price they have to pay to operate here," or, "We don't want to destroy the environment just so corporations can make high profits." But these arguments imply that businesses *will* pay the higher prices, rather than trying to relocate. Higher prices don't just mean lower profits. They mean lower sales, loss of market share, and, eventually, a weaker market position. No wonder firms feel forced to offset higher costs of doing business by either increasing productivity or moving elsewhere.

Such concerns have been a prime impetus for business movement from the Frost Belt to the Sun Belt. While the corporate exodus from Manhattan has been observed for some time, San Francisco, Los Angeles, Boston, and other cities are beginning to experience the same phenomenon. Business firms are starting to view housing costs as one of the critical variables in location decisions. As symptoms of the suburban squeeze become common in various parts of the nation, the debates about the jobs/housing imbalance, so familiar in California, will be heard elsewhere.

Interestingly, the murmurs are already audible in Phoenix, the Sun Belt's shining star. In fact, the mayor of Phoenix has just established a task force to investigate ways that that housing prices can be held down.[1] The mayor and his fellow Phoenicians are well aware that low housing costs are one of the city's prime attractions, particularly to relocating California firms.

But hard-line environmentalists are not disturbed by the scenario of corporate flight. In fact, many see it as beneficial. To quote one environmental leader I've sparred with, "My daughter is ten years old. In the past year she grew two inches. At some point I want her to stop growing." The question is, are metropolitan areas like little girls? Should they stop growing at some point? And if so, what is their optimal size? On these matters, even the experts cannot agree. Clearly, the answers depend on your point of view.

My point of view is that all too often the issue of bigness gets confused with environmental quality or the quality of major transportation, water, and sewer systems. I would argue that issues of optimal city size are not very useful for formulating policy about housing, environmental quality, or economic development, at least not for U.S. cities.

What is important is maintaining the constant ebb and flow of business firms to ensure economic vitality in a metropolitan area. And growth is the only thing that can produce this ebb and flow. If the suburban squeeze induces an outflow of firms, or reduces the number of start-up businesses, the economic vitality of the region will be diminished, whether it be Boston, Washington, Houston, or San Francisco.

Even if it were possible to sustain a steady-state economy, I don't think that most people would enjoy it. In that situation, the prospects for a higher income and better standard of living are very dim indeed. Increasing the gloom would be the specter of Thurow's "zero-sum society," in which the disadvantaged will face some rough going.[2] For the poor and minorities, upward mobility is difficult enough in a growing economy, but just about impossible in a steady-state situation.

The steady-state vision is a seductive one. But it loses its allure when society's broader social and economic objectives are considered along with its environmental ones. Striving for optimal city size or a steady-state metropolitan economy is not the path to environmental quality and social well-being. Instead, planners must learn to manage land development well enough to minimize its environmental impact. The remainder of this chapter describes how local land use planners can learn to live with the suburban squeeze.

LEARNING TO COPE WITH THE SUBURBAN SQUEEZE

More and more, the suburban squeeze is forcing planners to perform a delicate balancing act. On one side are citizens, businesses, and tenants who want more affordable housing built, a group that is growing in size and power across the nation. On the other side are the environmental groups that have had a strong influence on planners for the past ten years. In the middle are planners, who are called upon to achieve that elusive balance between objectives. To do this, planners will need to address the key factors behind restrictive land use controls and their impact on housing inflation.

Financing Residential Growth

The financial constraints local governments are experiencing in the 1980s foster attitudes of ambivalence toward new residential development, if not clear-cut hostility. Across the nation, communities are closely examining the fiscal impact of new residential development. Planning commissions and city councils routinely ask whether a project will cost more to service than it provides in tax revenues. In general, any project suspected of being a fiscal albatross is denied, no matter what its other merits might be.

The current mood among suburbanites is that new development should pay its own way. This is a marked departure from the 1950s and 1960s, when many communities would gladly provide streets, sewer trunk lines, and water to new subdivisions. Back then, the developer paid only for the services contained in the subdivision. Sometimes he helped pay for service extensions, if the project were especially distant from town. But now developers are assessed for a share of all community services, and services cost a great deal.

In some cases, such as that of Fairfax County, Virginia, sewer trunk lines and treatment facilities are deliberately downsized to eliminate any opportunities for excess capacity and more residential development.[3] In other cities, extremely high fees and hookup charges are used to raise revenues for services benefiting the entire community. Unfortunately, the price of new housing is driven up in the bargain.

There are several ways that planners could reduce the fiscal disincentives now blocking affordable housing. For instance, special-assessment districts could be created to use tax-exempt bond financing for streets, water, and sewer systems, as well as other needed facilities such as schools and fire stations. In Texas, municipal utility districts are widely used as vehicles to finance growth. The establishment of more such public entities could greatly lower the cost of urban services to the home buyer.

Another big factor pushing up the costs of streets, sewer and water systems, and other facilities, is that they are overdesigned. We don't need "gold-plated" community services. Lowering subdivision standards could reduce housing costs by as much as 10 percent.

Even if public service costs cannot be trimmed, we could reduce the average cost to each new home buyer by building at higher densities. The cost of, say, a new fire station could be minimized if we allowed developers to build the maximum number of units that could be serviced from the station. Frequently, we require developers to pay for a new facility, but do not allow them to build enough units to support it.

The most radical change—but one that should be considered—would be for state or regional governments to take over the financing of local street, water, and sewer systems in metropolitan areas. In many metropolitan areas, cities only accept the most fiscally advantageous type of development, shunting residential growth off onto other communities. Since housing affordability benefits the entire metropolitan area, and in some cases the entire state, a shift in the financing of these services would reduce the excessive and counterproductive emphasis many cities place on the fiscal impact of residential development. A tax-sharing system might also help to reduce the mercantilist tendencies of cities.

Promoting Higher-Density and Mixed-Use Development

Residential density has been falling in suburban areas nationwide. Public attitudes about high-density living are largely negative, as is routinely reflected in the marketplace and at public hearings. Pollsters have found that high-density development is viewed as promoting crime and bringing in lower classes of people. Particularly in the case of rental units, neighborhood groups fear that newcomers will be transients who do not care about the neighborhood.[4]

One of the biggest problems in dealing with these perceptions is that the very phrase "high-density" conjures up images of high-rise apartment buildings and "Manhattanization." But in fact, the kind of high-density development needed is more on the order of clustered townhouses and small garden-style units built at twelve to eighteen units per acre. Land use planners are left with the difficult task of convincing citizens that well-designed, moderate-density cluster housing is the path residential development must take in the future.

Several groups around the country are trying to educate the public about alternatives to single-family detached housing, including the Metropolitan Institute in New York; the Urban Land Institute, the U.S. Department of Housing and Urban Development, and the National Association of Homebuilders in Washington, D.C.; the Bay Area Council and People for Open Space in San Francisco; and the 1000 Friends of Oregon. The National Association of Homebuilders has gone so far as to build a model subdivision of about forty cluster houses in Las Vegas, Nevada. The project has been visited by many people, and it serves as a clear example of higher-density, low-cost development. Another approach is the Urban Land Institute's project reference file, which catalogues and describes innovative projects.

In San Francisco, the Bay Area Council and People for Open Space are jointly developing a twenty-minute slide show on the benefits of higher-density development. The Bay Area Council, a business-sponsored organization, sees the slide show as a tool to promote more affordable housing; People for Open Space hopes to convince citizens, particularly environmentalists, that housing must be built at higher densities to preserve open space and farmlands. Such broad-based educational efforts are needed to alter attitudes about higher-density projects. These efforts should emphasize that higher-density projects can be attractive, can be well integrated into the community, and can help accomplish environmental objectives such as preservation of open space and farmlands. But promoting higher-density development is only one way to increase housing opportunities. The suburban squeeze needs to be confronted on other fronts as well.

One of the most important preliminary findings in the 1980s census is that household sizes are continuing to fall, and households are consuming even more space on a per capita basis than ever before. While this may seem paradoxical in light of rising home prices, high housing costs and interest rates are actually a major cause of this increased housing consumption. Older households—the empty nesters—are forced to remain in houses larger than they need because they cannot afford to move into a new, smaller unit. It's just too expensive. On top of that, local land use regulations prohibit these empty nesters from creating apartments in their homes. If more communities would allow remodeling of large older homes to provide second units, existing housing stock could accommodate many more households.

Fortunately, a trend in this direction is slowly gaining momentum. Secondary units have been popping up in Princeton, New Jersey, in Cambridge and Newton, Massachusetts, and in San Francisco. Westchester County, New York, recently adopted regulations on secondary units, and the city of San Anselmo, California, already allows them. Planners need to convince their planning commissions and city councils that secondary units, if appropriately regulated, make sense for the community, the homeowner, and the housing consumer.

Another subject on which education is needed is mixed-use developments. Over the past fifty years, the practice of combining residential with commercial or light industrial uses has gradually gone by the wayside. But with the suburban squeeze limiting land availability, we can no longer afford to ban housing from commercial developments. Here, as in the case of high-density development, inaccurate stereotypes are a major stumbling block. Planners should help articulate how mixed-use development can both provide affordable housing and help strengthen commercial areas.

Cities across the country appear to be more comfortable with mixed-use development than with secondary units. In Baltimore, Boston, New York, and Chicago, mixed-use developments have been widely approved. There have been greater difficulties in the smaller cities and on the fringes of metropolitan areas. Here, once again, educational efforts advocating well-designed examples of mixed use are needed.

Streamlining Local and State Land Use Regulations

A major cause of housing cost inflation is the tangle of overlapping and excessive land use regulations that slow the approval of new projects, and require developers to provide unnecessary amenities. Fortunately, in the past few years there has been considerable progress in simplifying regulations. A good deal of research on the effects of regulations was completed in the late 1970s, and the results have been widely quoted.[5] At the same time, many communities across the nation have made big strides in reducing the cost effects of unnecessary local development controls. One effort, involving the U.S. Department of Housing and Urban Development, the National Association of Homebuilders, local governments, and local builders, has already chalked up many successful reforms.

In Brattleboro, Vermont, the town's zoning ordinance has been rewritten to use a performance standards approach for environmental protection. The town has also adopted a wide range of techniques for streamlining regulations and speeding up the review process, including fast-track processing, simultaneous permit reviews, permit expediters, and developer checklists.[6]

Recently the city of Fort Collins, Colorado, eliminated its zoning ordinance, and substituted a land use guidance system. The city no longer designates use districts, but utilizes performance standards to assess project proposals on compatibility, design, and environmental impact. This new process is being heralded by developers and environmentalists alike for reducing review time and lowering the city's administrative costs.[7]

In Phoenix, Arizona, the city has revised its residential zoning ordinance to give developers greater flexibility in designing new neighborhoods. Phoenix also fast-tracks applications and uses administrative hearings to speed projects through the review process.[8]

WHAT IS THE ROLE OF THE LOCAL LAND USE PLANNER?

These are broadly defined ways of coping with the suburban squeeze. Alternative ways of financing public facilities, promoting higher density and mixed-use development, and streamlining local land-use regulations are all important and useful concepts. But what can one planner do?

The first order of business is to convince people that there is indeed a suburban squeeze. Even if all the housing advocates, tenants, employers, and economic development planners know your community is facing a housing crunch, you are still going to have to explain it to your council, your planning committee, and citizens. An essential step is to gather some information about the seriousness of the problem. Focusing your investigation on the following statements can help you assemble a comprehensive picture of local conditions:

- Available data and informed opinion indicate that local house prices or rents are higher than in comparable jurisdictions.

- Employers report difficulty in finding qualified personnel, partly because of housing cost.

- Many local government and public school employees have chosen not to live in the municipality in which they are employed because housing costs are too high.

- Local families have found that children who are now young adults are unable to live in the municipality, or, alternatively, that the housing situation is forcing such young people to continue living with their parents.

- Local social service organizations have reported increasing difficulty in finding housing for people of low and moderate income.

- Local economic development efforts have been frustrated by corporate concerns over high housing costs.

- Vacancy rates are unusually low. (This may be a sign of problems in the future.)

- Developers and municipal staff members report increasingly long processing times for zoning, subdivision, and other applications.

- Council and commission dockets are backlogged with development applications.

- The number of reviews and permits for residential development has increased in recent years.

- The community lacks a variety of housing types (e.g., townhouses or multifamily structures as well as one-family detached houses), and developers claim that this is a result of public policy, not the market.

- Realtors, developers, and the local assessor report that local land prices have been rising rapidly, and it is their opinion that this results in part from public policies relating to infrastructure and/or zoning.

- Local building codes are not based on updated national model codes, or are known to have costly, restrictive provisions.

- The community does not have an adopted program for financing, constructing, and maintaining all of the basic infrastructure (sewerage, water, transportation) needed to serve projected growth.[9]

After assembling all the information necessary to validate these statements, you can determine the extent of your suburban squeeze. If the statements turn out to be largely true, what do you do next?

You will need to develop some kind of plan for a community response to all these issues. While you might want to work most closely with your staff, it is often useful to have several kinds of people involved in the process, such as: (1) elected officials, (2) professional and business people with direct experience in residential development, (3) city staff, and (4) citizens representing various interests, such as future home buyers, environmentalists, and labor leaders.

Establishing this kind of task force would be one way to structure the process. The results of work done by the task force should be widely circulated and presented at several public hearings.

The most difficult task may be getting elected officials to take action aimed at overcoming the suburban squeeze. In some cases, recommendations for action will generate intense opposition from neighborhood groups or environmentalists. The planner's role is to inform all parties of the suburban squeeze and the problems that it creates, working with them to negotiate an acceptable compromise solution.

THE HIGH COST OF INACTION

If communities do not take decisive steps to provide more affordable housing, four possible scenarios seem likely. In the first scenario, the housing squeeze just gets worse, with some large-scale consequences. The high cost of housing helps to push U.S.-based manufacturing operations to offshore locations—meaning that Mexico, Singapore, Sri Lanka, Malaysia, and Latin America gain exported U.S. jobs. U.S. central cities become the exclusive domain of the wealthy, the way much of Manhattan and San Francisco already are. There is a critical shortage of rental units nationwide, and rents skyrocket. As tenants begin to realize that they may never afford to own a home, they succeed in instituting rent control all across the nation.

The second scenario is one in which housing affordability becomes a potent political issue in the metropolitan areas of the country. Tenant groups, labor organizations, and corporations coalesce into advocacy groups countering neighborhood and environmental groups that stridently oppose new housing. Local development reviews become highly political and controversial matters, and lawsuits are filed charging cities with failure to comply with state and federal housing laws. Most fundamentally, the haves (those who own housing) are pitted against the have-nots.

The third scenario is dominated by state governments. Progressive states, such as California, Massachusetts, and New Jersey, adopt legislation requiring localities to provide housing opportunities consistent with regional and statewide needs.

California's steps in this direction are revealing and suggest what may occur in other states that suffer from the suburban squeeze. In the 1980 session of the California Legislature, a number of housing bills were proposed and signed into law. The most significant of these, AB 2853, requires that local governments consider regional housing needs when preparing the housing elements of their general plans. Specifically, AB 2853 requires that local governments: recognize their responsibility to help meet a "fair share" of state and regional housing needs; implement housing elements that move toward the attainment of state housing goals; make determinations and take actions compatible with state housing goals and regional housing needs; and cooperate with each other to meet regional housing needs.

On paper this bill is very promising. If it is fully implemented and enforced, more housing units will likely be built as a result. However, it will take much effort and money to implement AB 2853. There are also serious political obstacles: many communities are ideologically opposed to this law as an unwarranted intrusion by the state into local affairs. Opposition also focuses on regional governments, such as ABAG, which must determine both the region's housing needs and each community's "fair share."

However, there is the potential for this bill to have a dramatic impact on California. Each local government must assess its housing needs and its regional share, state its community housing goals, and set forth a five-year program for meeting its housing needs and objectives—including how the administration of land use and development controls, provision of regulatory concessions and incentives, and the appropriate federal and state financing and subsidy programs will be used to meet the housing needs of all economic segments.

In the fourth and final scenario, the courts enter the fray. This is not at all out of the realm of possibility. If the suburban squeeze throttles metropolitan areas, the more progressive state courts will almost certainly attempt to impose a socially just solution. In fact, in its famous Mt. Laurel decision, the New Jersey State Court required New Jersey localities to consider regional housing needs. The case history is already written; it remains only to be applied in other states.

As a planner, I do not relish the thought that any of these scenarios might come true. Land use planning is a local matter. But unfortunately, in our pursuit of environmental quality we have ignored the housing needs of the local and regional populations. The solution is not to abolish all environmental controls and land use regulations, but to achieve a better balance of land use planning objectives.

This means making changes—some sweeping, some gradual—in the way our communities grow. Development must occur at higher densities, and housing must be better integrated with commercial and industrial projects. In cities across the nation, these actions would go a long way toward meeting future demand for housing without the conversion of any unserviced, open land. In order to solve the suburban squeeze, we must:

- Eliminate fiscal disincentives to new residential development.
- Protect reasonable housing projects from being torpedoed.
- Recycle older urban areas for high-density residential use.
- Show citizens, by way of concrete examples, that higher-density development can be both attractive and desirable.

Bringing about these changes will not be easy. It is the greatest challenge before land use planners in the 1980s.

Survey of Local Planning Departments

In the spring of 1979, a survey of Bay Area planning departments was undertaken. It was decided that a telephone survey, asking a series of questions about growth, local citizen concerns about land development, and current planning department policies about growth, would be the most cost-effective, and the approach most likely to have the highest response rate.

A telephone call was made to every Bay Area planning director. During this initial call, the researcher explained the nature of the study and that we wished to interview the director, or the member of his/her staff most knowledgeable about land development trends, citizen concerns, and local land use regulation. If the director agreed to be interviewed, we scheduled a day and time and explained that the interview would last approximately forty-five minutes. If the director referred us to a staff member, we called this person and explained the nature of the study, outlined the general nature of the questions we would ask, and then scheduled an interview.

We received excellent cooperation: ninety-one of ninety-four communities agreed to an interview. Interviews for all of these communities were completed over a three-month period.

Each interviewer had a two-page telephone questionnaire (see Exhibit 1) to guide the interview. Each question was asked and responses were recorded on the questionnaire. The questions required open ended responses.

The author analyzed each completed questionnaire, and a matrix of responses was developed, with each cell containing the summary response of each community informant to a specific question. After responses were classified by type, summary statistics were prepared. As outlined in Appendix B, the questions relating to the local land use policies were used to categorize communities according to their attitude toward growth.

EXHIBIT 1

Jurisdiction _____

LAND POLICY SURVEY . . . . Name of Respondent _____

Position _____

Spring 1979 . . . . Date _____

Interviewer _____

1. Which of the following land use regulations are in effect in your community?

	Yes	No	In Progress
a) Slope-density zoning	___	___	___
b) Regulations for watershed protection	___	___	___
c) Minimum lot sizes	___	___	___
What is minimum lot size for *new* single-family house development?		___	
d) Urban limit lines	___	___	___
e) Capital budgeting (to limit expansion)	___	___	___
f) Timing ordinance	___	___	___

How is it implemented? _____

	Yes	No	In Progress
g) Site review	___	___	___
h) Environmental review	___	___	___
i) Subdivision regulations	___	___	___

2. Is your General Plan up-to-date?   ___   ___   ___

If not, which elements are not completed? _____

3. Is zoning implementation adhering to the general plan? _____

_____

4. Has your community ever imposed any moratoriums on development? _____

   If yes, when? _____

   What type? _____

   For how long? _____

5. Have you implemented major (fifty or more units) zoning changes since 1975?
   _____ Up or downzoning? _____ Who initiated the change? _____

   _____

   If yes, when? _____

   How much area covered? _____

   How many units involved? _____

6. What are the land use issues in your community? _____

   _____

   _____

   _____

7. Are these political issues, i.e., issues in local elections? _____

   _____

   _____

8. What is the policy position toward General Plan changes? _____

   _____

   By what process are changes typically made? _____

   _____

9. Do you know the percentage of applications for *zoning* changes that are approved? (estimate) _____

   Comments: _____

10. Is your community annexing territory? _____ If yes, can you estimate the number of acres annexed since 1975? _____

11. Do you consider your LAFCO sphere of influence to be a realistic designation for planning purposes? _____

    If not, why not? _____

    Is it difficult to get changes approved by LAFCO? _____

12. Has there been residential development in unincorporated areas adjacent to your community? _____ Can you estimate the number of units involved? _____

    Is this considered a problem in your community? _____

    _____

13. Are development policies consistent with service provision policies in your community? _____

    _____

    If not, who controls conflicting services? _____

    _____

14. Which other agencies, in the following categories, play an important part in *development* in your community?
    Local jurisdictions and special service districts: _____

    _____

    _____

    Regional agencies (ABAG, BAAPCD, BCDC): _____

    _____

    _____

State agencies (CalTrans, State Water Project): _____

_____

_____

Federal agencies (Army Corps of Engineers, HUD, EPA): _____

_____

_____

15. Which are the most important influence on development, in your opinion and why? _____

_____

_____

16. How much land in your community is approved for development, i.e., with full services? _____

17. Do you know much land will be serviced within the next five years?

_____

18. Are housing units in your community being lost through conversion to other uses (commercial/office) or demolition to a considerable extent? _____ If yes, estimated number of units? _____

_____

19. If condominium conversions are occurring in your community (yes/no), can you estimate the number of units for which subdivision applications have been received since 1975? _____

Approximately what percentage are approved? _____

20. Do you have a housing code enforcement program in effect in your community? _____ If yes, how is it implemented? _____

_____

Is it assisted with federal or state funds? _____

21. Do you have an affirmative housing program in effect? E.g., inclusionary-zoning, subsidized housing program? _____

    Please describe: _____

    _____

    _____

22. Can you tell me what the average development fees are for:

	Typical s/f house (your area)	Typical 10 unit m/f (your area)	3-bed, 2-bath s/f house, 1500 sq. ft. in approp. zone w/util.
Building permit	_____	_____	_____
Sewer hookups	_____	_____	_____
Rezoning fees	_____	_____	_____
Bedroom taxes	_____	_____	_____
Park dedications	_____	_____	_____
Subdivision fee	_____	_____	_____
Plan review	_____	_____	_____
Others:			
_____	_____	_____	_____
_____	_____	_____	_____

23. Have these fees changed because of Proposition 13? _____ If yes, how have they changed? _____

24. Would you describe the typical development in your community to be by major builders or separate actors? Is it usually large-scale or small-scale? _____

25. What is the typical amount of time between application for development (rezoning or site review) to approval (building permit) for a single-family development of less than fifty units? _____

A development with fifty or more units? _____

26. What is the most common cause for delay in the application process?

_____

27. Has the review or land development process changed significantly because of Proposition 13? _____ Please explain: _____

_____

Has the percentage of approvals to applications changed? _____

Please explain: _____

_____

28. Can you tell me where in your community most of the new development is occurring? _____

29. Are there any other issues or factors concerning land development in your community that we have not covered that you feel are important or unusual? _____

_____

Choosing the Case Study Community Pairs

So many factors affect the cost and price of housing that it may seem close to impossible to isolate the effects generated by government regulation. A review of the literature has identified three types of research: anecdotal, econometric, and case study.[1] Anecdotal evidence provides the least insight into the range and magnitude of regulatory effects: it fails to account for nonregulatory forces and relies on mere correlation to suggest that government controls are responsible for housing cost inflation. Most available research can be characterized as anecdotal.

The second type of research is econometric. It relies on cross-sectional data to examine the relationship between various land use control techniques and housing costs. While econometric studies do attempt to control for the play of nongovernmental factors, the available research does not yield robust or insightful results. The control of exogenous factors is difficult, and problems of multicollinearity are widespread. In estimating the impact of regulation, the precise nature of the land use and environmental controls are not well specified. This lack of specification results in a failure to capture the effects of regulation, and places more emphasis on demand and other nonregulatory factors. In addition, most econometric studies use large pools of secondary data sources poorly suited to the question at hand: they rarely include land prices, only partially capture important neighborhood amenities, and often fail to include zoning and subdivision regulations.

The third and most promising type of research is the case study. Case studies have an advantage over econometric research in that they allow for a better specification of land use and environmental regulations. Detailed analyses of the cost components of residential construction can be examined and the regulatory effects isolated. The main disadvantage of this approach is that the results are always conditioned by the peculiarities of the local market. If the case is located in a high-demand area, the effects will be of one type and magnitude; if demand is lower, the effects will change. It is difficult to generalize the results to metropolitan areas or to larger contexts. These criticisms, however, are not aimed at the case study procedure per se, but at the scope of cases selected.

To overcome the problems of poor regulatory specification and control of nonregulatory factors, the author developed a research framework that paired communities that were as homogeneous as possible across all dimensions except for their land use and environmental programs. The approach typed communities in the San Francisco Bay Area into similar groups and then examined the land use and environmental regulations of each. Pairs of communities with varying land use and environmental controls were selected from these homogeneous groups of communities. The procedure generated three pairs of communities located in the northern, western, and eastern portions of the nine-county Bay Area.

IDENTIFYING COMMUNITY CHARACTERISTICS

The goal of the research design was to isolate regulatory from nonregulatory factors. Since we wished to determine the effects of government regulations on the costs of residential construction, we had to control all factors that affected the price and costs of housing units that were not associated with land use regulation. This was done in two steps. First, communities were grouped into homogeneous clusters. Second, based on land use and environmental policies identified in the telephone survey of ninety-one communities, pairs of communities with significantly different regulations were selected. The result of the two-step process was that the selected pairs were similar across all dimensions affecting housing price and costs with the exception of land use and environmental regulation.

To group like cities required us to first identify factors that affect housing markets and prices. A review of the social area and community taxonomy literature, and of the hedonic housing market models, pointed to several important dimensions of housing market and community characteristics.[2] Social area analysis identifies social status, life cycle, and ethnicity as being of key importance in differentiating communities; similarly, economic literature has identified characteristics of finance, neighborhood housing stock, location, employment, and income. Other characteristics include the physical and environmental attributes of the area. Table B-1 outlines the variables that were collected to measure the dimensions of community characteristics.

The nine-county region contains ninety-four communities. We attempted to obtain the best possible coverage. A major problem in data collection was that when we were selecting cases in 1979, the United States Census data were nearly ten years out of date. We examined other possible sources, particularly the State of California's Department of Finance surveys. These surveys were completed for two-thirds (sixty-one) of the Bay Area communities in 1975. However, all of San Mateo County and many communities in Alameda and Marin County were not surveyed. Two considerations prompted us to use the more recent, though less comprehensive data from the Department of Finance rather than the complete, but grossly out-of-date census figures. First, suburban development in the region has drastically altered many of the communities during the last ten years. To the extent that these changes would not be reflected in the 1970 U.S. Census data, their use for community typing would introduce considerable biases: communities that had developed rapidly since 1970 would be improperly typed with communities that had remained stable. Second, we felt that the excluded communities, that is, those for which Department of Finance data were not available, could be typed with updated 1975 estimates of community variables and merged with the statistical typing program. While the 1980 census data are now available, they add little to the present analysis. The six communities were selected in 1979, and by 1982, when the 1980 census data became available, all of the field research on the six communities had been collected. Reanalysis of the case selection method with 1980 data might generate slightly different results, but the outcome, in terms of paired communities, would most likely be the same.

The State of California's Department of Finance Population Research Unit is responsible for the State Census Program. The program was initiated in order to update federal census data at mid-decade. The 1975 Special Census, which is used in the analysis, was conducted for many of the state's county governments. The 1975 Special Census is based on a 100 percent enumeration of a locality's population. Variables, arranged according to type, are presented in table B-1. Those marked with an "a" are obtained from the 1975 Special Census enumeration. All variables are based on U.S. Census definitions. Other variables used in the analysis come from U.S Census, Society of Real Estate Appraisers, and Association of Bay Area Government sources.

TABLE B-1

DIMENSIONS AND VARIABLES SELECTED FOR IDENTIFYING
COMMUNITY CHARACTERISTICS

- Social and economic status
  Percentage of families with incomes above $15,000[a]
  Percentage of households owning homes[a]
  Median age of population[a]
  Percentage of persons over 65 years of age[a]
  Percentage of persons under 18 years of age[a]
  Average persons per household[a]

- Economic base and population size
  Population[a]
  Number of employed residents[a]
  Employment in basic industries[a]
  Employment in local-serving sector[a]
  Workforce size[a]

- Housing stock characteristics
  Mean house size per square foot[b]
  Mean house price[b]
  Vacancy rate[a]

- Housing stock characteristics (cont'd)
  Mean house age[a]
  Percentage of families with house payments over $3,000[a]

- Public service quality and cost
  Assessed valuation of community[c]
  Local public expenditures per capita[c]
  County public expenditures per capita[c]
  School expenditures per capita[c]

- Ethnic composition
  Percentage of households white[a]
  Percentage of households black[a]
  Percentage of households Asian[a]
  Percentage of households Hispanic[a]
  Percentage of nonwhite school enrollment[a]

- Physical characteristics
  Acres of vacant land available for development[d]
  Percentage of land developed[d]

- Recent growth experience
  Population change 1970–75[e]
  Percentage change in units 1970–75[e]

---

[a]State of California, Department of Finance, 1975 Special Census.

[b]Based on the author's analysis of Society of Real Estate Appraisers data tapes for single-family transactions occurring in 1975.

[c]U.S. Bureau of the Census, Census of Local Governments, 1977.

[d]Based on author's analysis of the Association of Bay Area Government's *Local Policy Survey*, 1975.

[e]Calculations based on State and U.S. Census data.

After collecting and organizing the data, we identified twenty-nine variables to use in the analysis. A listing of these variables and their means and standard deviations is presented in table B-2.

Various methods are available for identifying common attributes of communities. Most multivariate analyses have relied on factor analytic techniques: factor analysis, q-analysis, cluster analysis. Cluster analysis was chosen because it does not assume orthogonality between dimen-

TABLE B-2

MEANS AND STANDARD DEVIATIONS OF THE TWENTY-NINE
VARIABLES USED FOR COMMUNITY TYPING

Variable	Name	Mean	Standard Deviation
1.	% of families with income over $15,000	38.7	21.0
2.	% of households owning homes	58.7	17.6
3.	Median age of population	30.7	6.9
4.	% of persons over 65 years old	9.3	7.2
5.	% of persons under 18 years old	30.6	6.0
6.	Average persons per household	2.8	0.4
7.	Population	41,548	80,561
8.	Number of employed residents	1,863	2,673
9.	Employment in basic industry	705	1,459
10.	Employment in local-serving sector	984	1,754
11.	Workforce size	(deleted due to missing values)	
12.	Mean house size (sq. ft.)	1,537	301
13.	Mean house price (dollars)	71,845	26,812
14.	Vacancy rate	5.2	2.4
15.	Mean house age	19.6	9.5
16.	% of households with house payments over $3,000/year	15.5	13.6
17.	Assessed valuation, dollars per capita	3,547.04	1,365.20
18.	Public expenditures, dollars per capita	1,639	1,205
19.	County public expenditures, dollars per capita	1,969	850
20.	School expenditures, dollars per capita	1,277	368
21.	% of households white	82.2	14.6
22.	% of households black	3.4	7.6
23.	% of households Asian	2.3	1.8
24.	% of households Hispanic	6.0	6.7
25.	% of nonwhite school enrollment	20.6	13.6
26.	Acres of vacant developable land	2,017	2,605
27.	% of land developed	52.8	31.4
28.	% population change 1970–75	20.2	34.1
29.	% change in housing units	27.0	17.7

sions, and is therefore the least ad hoc.[3] It is also a simple procedure and easy to program for the computer. Cluster analysis is a two-step procedure. First, the number of variables is reduced to a set of dimensions that explain the pattern of variation exhibited by the original set. This is done by using a computer model known as "BC-TRY" to group collinear variables into clusters that are independent of one another. The computer program uses three statistical criteria for clustering variables: (1) that clusters be as "tight" (collinear) as possible, (2) as nearly independent of the others as possible, and (3) that together they account for as much general variability as possible.

Once the clusters of variables have been grouped, standardized cluster scores (means = 50, standard deviation = 10) are calculated, based on the underlying pattern of the variables. The cluster score is based on weighing each variable included in the cluster, developing a composite score, and then standardizing the score.[4]

The second step of cluster analysis is to calculate cluster scores for each observation (community). The pattern of how each community scores on each cluster serves as the empirical basis for grouping communities. Here the BC-TRY computer model uses an interactive process that reduces the euclidean distance between communities within groups and maximizes the distance between groups. This method finds a minimally sufficient set of types representing the whole configuration of communities, and sets aside any community whose cluster score pattern is unique and cannot be included in any type.[5]

Variation in scores of the twenty-nine variables for the sixty-one observations was reduced to five clusters. These five cluster dimensions, based on seventeen variables, explained 90 percent of the variation in the scores of the twenty-nine variables. Table B-3 presents the clusters, the variables making up each cluster, and the cumulative explained commonality.

Cluster 1, "Local Economic Base and Dominance," is composed of four variables: local employment (employment in economic activities that serve the local area), employed residents (the size of the employed work force), total population, and basic employment (employment in economic activities that sell or provide services to businesses or people located in other communities). These four variables tend to measure the economic structure of the community. Those communities with high cluster scores tend to have large employment bases (as opposed to "bedroom communities" that merely provide housing for commuters) and large populations. Examples of communities that score high on this cluster are Pittsburg, Oakland, San Jose, Richmond, and Santa Rosa. Examples of low-scoring

TABLE B-3

COMMUNITY CLUSTER DIMENSIONS

Cluster 1:	"Local Economic Base and Dominance"	
10	Local-serving employment	
8	Employed residents	
7	Population	
9	Basic employment	
	Cumulative explained commonality	.28
Cluster 2:	"Suburban Life Cycle"	
5	% of population under 18 years old	
−3	Median age of population (inverse)	
6	Average persons per household	
−5	% of populations over 65 years old (inverse)	
	Cumulative explained commonality	.51
Cluster 3:	"Housing Price and Quality"	
13	Mean house price (dollars)	
12	Mean house size (sq. ft.)	
16	% of households with house payments over $3,000 per year	
17	Assessed valuation	
	Cumulative explained commonality	.80
Cluster 4:	"Recent Growth Experience"	
29	% change in housing units 1970–75	
28	% change in population	
	Cumulative explained commonality	.85
Cluster 5:	"Ethnicity"	
25	% of nonwhite school enrollment	
24	% of households Hispanic	
23	% of households Asian	
	Cumulative explained commonality	.90

NOTE: Variables are listed in the order of inclusion.

communities are Brentwood, Clayton, Moraga, and Rio Vista. This first cluster accounts for 28 percent of the commonality.

Cluster 2, "Suburban Life Cycle," is marked by its emphasis on young age level, low median age, high rate of housing occupancy (large family size), and low percentage of residents over sixty-five years of age. A high score on this cluster reflects the life cycle characteristics of recently developed suburbs with a high proportion of young families. Examples of communities with these "young" characteristics are Clayton, Milpitas, Newark, Saratoga, and Rohnert Park. Examples of low-scoring "old" communities are El Cerrito, Hercules, and the resort/retirement communities of St. Helena, Sonoma, and Yountville. The first two clusters account for 51 percent of the variation in the community scores.

Cluster 3, "Housing Price and Quality," gauges the price and quality of each community's housing stock. It is comprised of four variables—mean housing price in 1975, mean housing size (in square feet) in 1975, percentage of households with annual housing payments over $3,000, and the total assessed value of property in the community. A high cluster score means that communities have high housing prices and quality, and high assessed property valuation. Examples of high scoring communities are Ross, Cupertino, and Saratoga; low scoring communities include San Pablo, Vallejo, and Newark. The first three clusters account for 80 percent of the commonality.

Cluster 4, "Recent Growth Experience," measures the extent of residential development in the community between 1970 and 1975. It is composed of two variables—the percentage of housing built since 1970 and the percentage of change in population since 1970. High scores indicate high growth during the period; low scores indicate stability. Examples of high growth areas are Morgan Hill, Livermore, Union City, Cotati, and Rohnert Park. Examples of stable community types are El Cerrito, San Pablo, Ross, and Palo Alto. Since this dimension is based on percentage of change, large communities will not show up even though the absolute change is substantial. The first four cluster dimensions account for 85 percent of the commonality.

Cluster 5, "Ethnicity," measures the percentage of minority groups represented in the community. It is based on three variables, percentage of nonwhite school enrollment, percentage of Hispanic households, and percentage of Asian families. Examples of high-ethnicity communities are Oakland, Gilroy, Richmond, Pittsburg, and San Jose. Examples of low-ethnicity communities are Clayton, Walnut Creek, Lafayette, Los Altos, and Sonoma. Together the five clusters account for 90 percent of the commonality.

O-TYPING COMMUNITIES

These five cluster dimensions were next used to group the sixty-one communities included in the data analysis. The grouping began by scoring each community on the basis of the five cluster dimensions. The program standardized the scores to means of 50 and standard deviations of 10. Using a routine that reduces the euclidean distance between communities within groups, and maximizes the distance between groups, the empirical procedure generated eleven groups containing fifty-seven communities accounting for 93.4 percent of the sample. These eleven O-types are discussed in order of their size. Table B-4 presents O-types standardized cluster scores, and table B-5 shows O-type membership.

O-type 1, "Moderate Income Suburban Communities with Above Average Recent Growth Experience," contains fourteen communities and accounts for 23 percent of the communities. This O-type is marked by above average scores on cluster 2, average scores on cluster 3, above-average scores on cluster 4, and low scores on cluster 5.

O-type 2, "High Income Suburbs," contains nine communities and accounts for 14.8 percent of the sample. This type is characterized by high scores on cluster 2, extremely high scores on cluster 3, and low scores on clusters 4 and 5.

O-type 3, "Low Income Stable Suburbs," contains seven communities and accounts for 11.5 percent of the sample. It is characterized by low scores on clusters 1, 3, and 4.

O-type 4, "Retirement and Mature Suburbs," contains six communi-

TABLE B-4

O-TYPE MEAN CLUSTER SCORES

	Clusters				
O-Type Description	1	2	3	4	5
1. Moderate income suburban communities with above-average recent growth experience	49.9	52.7	47.9	51.0	43.4
2. High-income suburbs	47.9	53.0	67.7	45.4	43.5
3. Low-income stable suburbs	46.1	50.0	39.7	44.2	48.4
4. Retirement and mature suburbs	46.4	28.4	45.5	51.0	43.6
5. Mature, economically developed communities	51.9	46.5	52.6	42.4	53.8
6. Lower-priced housing, ethnic suburbs	49.4	53.6	40.9	47.7	68.0
7. Stable ethnic suburbs	48.0	62.7	47.8	48.2	58.0
8. Extremely rapid-growth ethnic suburbs	46.5	59.8	48.0	73.3	67.1
9. Rapid-growth, white middle-income suburbs	48.2	54.7	44.3	78.2	45.0
10. Rapid-growth ethnic suburbs	46.2	57.2	48.9	61.6	56.3
11. Mature, stable suburbs	46.5	37.8	46.2	34.5	50.9

NOTE: Scores are standardized to a mean of 50.0 and a standard deviation of 10.0

ties and accounts for 9.8 percent of the sample. It is marked by low scores on clusters 1, 3, and 5, extremely low scores on cluster 2, and above-average scores on cluster 4.

O-type 5, "Mature Economically Developed Communities," contains six communities and accounts for 9.8 percent of the sample. O-type 5 can be characterized by high scores on clusters 1, 3, and 5, and low scores on clusters 2 and 4.

O-type 6, "Lower Price Housing Stock, Ethnic Suburbs," contains three communities and accounts for 4.9 percent of the sample. It can be characterized by low scores on clusters 3 and 4, and high scores on cluster 5.

TABLE B-5

O-TYPE MEMBERSHIP

O-Type 1		O-Type 2	
Antioch	San Rafael	Lafayette	Los Gatos
Clayton	Napa	Ross	Monte Sereno
Concord	Campbell	Cupertino	Saratoga
Martinez	Fremont	Los Altos	Benicia
Pinole	Vacaville	Los Altos Hills	
Pleasant Hill	Petaluma		
Novato	Santa Rosa		

O-Type 3		O-Type 4	
San Pablo[a]	Suisun	Walnut Creek[a]	Yountsville
Dixon	Cloverdale	Calistoga	Sebastopol
Fairfield	Healdsburg	St. Helena	Sonoma
Rio Vista			

O-Type 5		O-Type 6	O-Type 7
Richmond[a]	Palo Alto	Pittsburg	Pacifica
Milbrae	Santa Clara	Gilroy	Milpitas
Mountain View	Sunnyvale	Vallejo	Newark

O-Type 8	O-Type 9	O-Type 10	O-Type 11
Morgan Hill	Livermore	Brentwood	El Cerrito
Union City	Cotati	Pleasanton	Hercules
Rohnert Park			

[a]Towns removed from empirical O-types on the basis of informed judgment.

O-type 7, "Stable Ethnic Suburbs," also contains three communities. It is characterized by very high scores on clusters 2 and 5, and below-average scores on clusters 1, 3, and 4.

O-type 8, "Extremely Rapid-Growth, Ethnic Suburbs," also contains three communities. It is marked by very high scores on clusters 2, 4, and 5.

O-type 9, "Rapid Growth, White Middle-Income Suburbs," contains two communities and accounts for 3.3 percent of the sample. This O-type has high scores on clusters 2 and 4, and low scores on clusters 3 and 5.

O-type 10, "Rapid Growth Ethnic Suburbs," also contains two communities. It is similar to O-type 8 except for lower scores on clusters 4 and 5.

O-type 11, "Mature Stable Suburbs," also contains two communities. It is characterized by low scores on clusters 1, 2, 3, and 4.

The remaining four communities not grouped (Albany, Piedmont, Emeryville and Foster City) are viewed as being unique and not capable of being typed.

ANALYSIS OF O-TYPES

It is important to realize that the typing procedure did not contain data on community location or on the environmental aspects of particular communities. That knowledge had to be supplied by the informed judgment of the researchers, and several communities were eliminated from the groupings. Once the O-Types had been formed, we carefully assessed the pool of communities contained in each. First, we looked to see if the communities in each pool were located in the same general area. In some cases the O-Types contained communities that were mainly located in one portion of the region. For example, with the exception of Walnut Creek, O-type 4 consists of communities located in the North Bay county of Sonoma. This cluster of communities are retirement-oriented. Walnut Creek's removal improves the fit of the cluster dimensions for the remaining five communities. The removal of San Pablo from O-type 3 restricts the location of this group's communities to the North Bay counties of Sonoma and Solano. With the exception of Richmond, O-type 5 is composed of communities from the Santa Clara and San Mateo counties. O-type 2 is largely composed of communities located in Santa Clara County, the exceptions being Ross in Marin County, Benicia in Solano County, and Lafayette in Contra Costa County. The remaining O-types are composed of communities located throughout the region. The largest O-type, group 1, is composed of communities located in three distinct areas; seven of the fourteen communities are located in Alameda and Contra Costa Counties; six are located in the North Bay counties of Marin, Sonoma, Napa, and Solano, and one is located in Santa Clara County.

With the exceptions noted, we feel that the O-type procedure has generated reasonable clusters of similar communities. The next stage of the case selection process was to introduce communities for which 1975 Department of Finance data were not available.

The cluster analysis generated five factors that exhaust 90 percent of the variation in the original twenty-nine variables. Since these factors are based on seventeen variables, data only needed to be collected, and cluster scores determined, on these seventeen. But since data were not available on recent growth experience, cluster 4 could not be generated.

Data on twenty-three other communities were available from census documents. Analysis of the cluster score patterns identified three additional O-types. These are presented in table B-6.

O-type 12, "Suburban High Income," contains eleven communities located in San Mateo and Marin Counties. Similar to O-type 2, it exhibits low scores on cluster 1 (lower than the scores for O-type 2), average scores

TABLE B-6

O-TYPE MEMBERSHIP FOR TWENTY-THREE OTHER
COMMUNITIES

O-Type 12: "Suburban High Income"

Belmont	Belvedere-Tiburon
Hillsborough	Sausalito
San Carlos	Corte Madera
Woodside	Mill Valley
Atherton	Larkspur
Burlingame	

O-Type 13: "Mature, Economically Developed"

San Mateo	San Leandro	South San Francisco
Redwood City	Hayward	Castro Valley
Daly City	Alameda	San Bruno

O-Type 14: "Mature Moderate Income"

San Anselmo
Fairfax
Menlo Park

on cluster 2, and high scores on cluster 3 (although lower than O-type 2's score).

O-type 13, "Mature Economically Developed," consists of nine communities. This O-type is characterized by high scores on cluster 1, above-average scores on cluster 2, slightly below-average scores on cluster 3, and varied but above-average scores on cluster 5.

O-type 14, "Mature Moderate Income Suburban Area, " consists of three communities. It is characterized by low scores on clusters 1 and 2, and by slightly below-average scores on cluster 3.

The combination of the sixty-one communities enumerated by the State Department of Finance with the twenty-three additional communities brings the total coverage to eighty-four, representing 90 percent of the ninety-three Bay Area communities.

Those communities excluded range in size from San Francisco to Rodeo. Land use and environmental programs in these communities are either unique (in the case of San Francisco) or nonexistent. Exclusion of these communities is not felt to introduce any biases to the case study selection process.

The next step in the process of case study selection was the documentation of land use and environmental policies of Bay Area communities. From February to June 1979, telephone interviews of municipal and county planning offices were conducted. These interviews generated substantial information on the types of development pressures experienced by Bay Area communities and the planning and policy responses taken. This information proved useful for updating recent growth experiences beyond 1975. A matrix of community development policy and growth trends was prepared and used to identify "interesting" case study communities.

Criteria for pairing the list of eighty communities (the fifty-seven communities in the empirically determined O-types and the twenty-three in the manual O-types) were based primarily on the extent of development now occurring. Many of the communities were "built out," that is, they contained little developable land. Most of the communities were faced not with new development proposals but with proposals for redevelopment, conversion of housing units to apartments, or of apartments to condominiums. After reviewing current development trends, O-types 2, 5 11, 12, 13, and 14 were eliminated from the sampling frame. For similar reasons, several communities were eliminated from the remaining O-types. For example, Pleasant Hill and Pinole were eliminated from O-type 1 and Richmond, Millbrae, and Palo Alto were eliminated from O-type 5.

These eliminations reduced the O-types for case selection to numbers 1, 3, 4, 6, 7, 8, 9, and 10.

Examination of these remaining O-types led us to eliminate several because of their lack of geographic proximity and because their environmental and social character were not fully captured by the empirical analysis. As a consequence, O-types 6, 8, 9, and 10 were purged. The remaining O-types and their constituent communities are presented in table B-7.

O-type 4 was eliminated because of its peculiar retirement characteristics. The planning operations were minimal and the development problems confronted by these communities were not deemed to be particularly interesting or generalizable to the rest of the region. The possible pairing of Milpitas and Newark was considered, but the land use and environmental policies were not sufficiently different to generate interesting or robust findings. Healdsburg and Cloverdale were eliminated from O-type 3 because of their small size and limited information base. The remaining communities in O-type 3 were rejected due to the similarity of development policy.

This left us with O-type 1 as the pool for case selections. Various pairings of Concord with Antioch, Concord with Martinez, Fremont with Concord, Petaluma with Vacaville, Napa with Santa Rosa, Novato with San Rafael, Petaluma with Santa Rosa, and Clayton with Concord were considered. At this stage, we examined the original community scores on

TABLE B-7

O-TYPE MEMBERSHIP FOR CASE SELECTION

O-Type 1			O-Type 3
Antioch	Napa	Dixon	Suisun City
Clayton	Campbell	Fairfield	Cloverdale
Concord	Fremont	Rio Vista	Healdsburg
Martinez	Vacaville		
Novato	Petaluma		
San Rafael	Santa Rosa		

O-Type 4	O-Type 7
Calistoga	Pacifica
St. Helena	Milpitas
Yountsville	Newark
Sebastapol	
Sonoma	

the twenty-nine variables and local land use policy. After comparison of these possible pairings, discussions with knowledgeable planners, and visits to these communities, we decided that the pairings of Fremont with Concord, Napa with Santa Rosa, and Novato with San Rafael were best. Each pairing was considered in terms of its homogeneity of community characteristics and the differentiation of land use and environmental policies. We also felt that these three pairs covered the range of development experienced in the Bay Area and the types of policy responses. We would have liked to have included a pairing of the most wealthy communities, but the choices were not very interesting. The development pressures were too similar (e.g., pressures to fill in large lots), and most planning agencies in these exclusive communities followed similar policies.

Notes

CHAPTER 1

1. U.S. General Accounting Office, *Why Are New Housing Prices So High? How Are They Influenced by Government Regulation and Can Prices Be Reduced?* (Washington, 1978); U.S. Department of Housing and Urban Development, *Final Report of the Task Force on Housing Costs* (Washington, 1978).

2. Miles L. Colean, *American Housing: Problems and Prospects* (New York: Twentieth Century Fund, 1947); Leo Grebler, *Production of New Housing* (New York: Social Science Research Council, 1950); Sherman J. Maisel, *Housingbuilding in Transition* (Berkeley and Los Angeles: University of California Press, 1953); and Sherman J. Maisel, "Background Information on Costs of Land for Single Family Housing," in *Housing in California*, Governor's Advisory Commission on Housing Problems (Sacramento, April 1963).

3. National Commission on Urban Problems, *Building the American City*, to the Congress and the President of the United States (Washington, 1968); President's Committee on Urban Housing, *A Decent Home* (Washington, 1968).

4. Suburban Action Institute and the Potomac Institute are examples of groups attempting to get more low- and moderate-income housing built in the suburbs. See, for example, Herbert Franklin, *In-Zoning* (Washington, D.C.: Potomac Institute, 1972).

5. Natural Resources Defense Council, *Land Use Controls in the United States* (New York: Dial Press, 1977), p. 18.

6. American Society of Planning Officials, *Nongrowth as a Planning Alternative*, PAS Report no. 283 (Chicago, 1972).

7. International City Managers Association, "Managing the Environment at the Local Level," *Urban Data Service Report 2/74* (Washington, 1974).

8. State of California Office of Planning and Research, *Local Government Planning Survey: 1975* (Sacramento, 1976).

9. Leo Grebler and Frank H. Mittlebach, *The Inflation of Housing Prices* (Lexington, Mass.: Lexington Books, 1979).

10. David E. Dowall and Jesse Mingilton, *Effects of Environmental Regulations in Housing Costs*, CPL Bibliography no. 6 (Chicago: Council of Planning Librarians, 1979); Bernard J. Frieden, *The Environmental Protection Hustle* (Cambridge, Mass: MIT Press, 1978); Gary Hack and Greg Polk, "Housing Cost and Government Regulations: Is Regulatory Reform Justified by What We Know?" preliminary draft, Harvard-MIT Joint Center for Urban Studies and the Lincoln Institute for Land Policy, May 1981.

11. Ian McHarg, *Design with Nature* (New York: Natural Science Press, 1969).

12. U.S. Department of Agriculture, Soil Conservation Service, *National Agricultural Lands Study: Final Report* (Washington, 1981).

13. Eric Kelly, "Impact Zoning: Concept for Growth Management," *Colorado Municipalities* 51 (September/October 1975):142.

14. David E. Dowall, "Fiscal Impact Rationale for Growth Management," *Annals of Regional Science* 12 (July 1978):83–94.

15. F. Stuart Chapin, Jr., and Edward J. Kaiser, *Urban Land Use Planning*, 3rd ed. (Urbana: University of Illinois Press, 1979).

16. Rice Center, *Houston Initiatives* (Houston, 1982).

17. Peter Wolf, *Land In America: Its Value, Use and Control* (New York: Pantheon Books, 1981), pp. 140–82.

18. John S. Willson, Philip Tabas, and Marian Henneman, *Comprehensive Planning and the Environment: A Manual for Planners* (Cambridge, Mass.: Abt Books, 1979), pp. 139–49.

19. William D. Schulze, Ralph C. d'Avge, and David S. Brookshire, "Valuing Environmental Commodities: Some Recent Experiments," *Land Economics* 57 (May 1981): 151–72.

20. A. Myrick Freeman, III, *The Benefits of Environmental Improvements* (Baltimore: Johns Hopkins University Press, 1979).

CHAPTER 2

1. Association of Bay Area Governments, *Summary Report, Provisional Series 3 Projections* (Berkeley, 2 March 1977).

2. Stan Hoffman and Rune Carlson, *The "Compact Growth" Projection Alternative for the Air Quality Maintenance Plan*, PTEC Working Paper (Berkeley: Association of Bay Area Governments 19 July 1977).

3. Kingsley Davis and Eleanor Langlois, *Future Demographic Growth of the San Francisco Bay Area* (Berkeley: Institute of Governmental Studies 1963).

4. Ibid., p. 26–27.

5. Wurster was much concerned with the trends of sprawl in the Bay Area. See, for example, her "Housing and the Future of Cities in the San Francisco Bay Area," in *The San Francisco Bay Area: Its Problems and Future*, ed. Stanley Scott (Berkeley: Institute of Governmental Studies, 1966).

6. Alvin Toeffler, *Future Shock* (New York: Random House, 1970).

7. American Society of Planning Officials, *Urban Growth Management Systems*, P.A.S. Report nos. 309 and 310 (Chicago, n.d.).

8. International City Managers Association, "Managing the Environment at the Local Level."

9. State of California Office of Planning and Research, *Local Government Planning Survey* (Sacramento, 1976).

10. Richard F. Babcock, *The Zoning Game* (Madison: University of Wisconsin Press, 1966).

11. Steven H. Goldfarb, "Parochialism on the Bay: An Analysis of Land-Use Planning in the San Francisco Bay Area," *California Law Review* 55: 836–55.

12. Santa Clara County Industry and Housing Management Task Force, *Living Within Our Limits* (San Jose: County–San Jose Environmental Management Agency, November 1979).

CHAPTER 3

1. Williamson contracts guarantee owners of farmland low, agricultural-rate property taxes as long as the land remains in farming. The contracts run for ten years.

2. Napa County Planning Department, *Napa County General Plan*, Napa, 1975.

3. National Environmental Protection Act, 42 U.S.C. §4321, *et seq.*

4. Marin County Planning Department, *Marin Countywide Plan*, San Rafael, 1979.

5. For a discussion of ABAG's land supply data, see its *Local Policy Survey* (Berkeley, 1976).

CHAPTER 4

1. Association of Bay Area Governments, *Projections 1979* (Berkeley, 1980).

2. Telephone interview with Concord planners, May 1979.

3. Ibid.

4. City of Santa Rosa, *Santa Rosa General Plan*, 1962.

CHAPTER 5

1. Falling household size, rising energy costs, and the increased interest in home purchase by singles have stimulated the demand for smaller dwelling units.

2. Martin Mayer, *The Builders* (New York: Norton, 1978), p. 238.

3. Author's survey of developers, July 1979.

4. Telephone interviews with Napa real estate brokers, July 1979.

5. For a discussion of these effects and how to measure them, see David E. Dowall, "Effects of Land Use and Environmental Regulations on Housing Costs," *Policy Studies Journal* 8 (1979):277–88.

6. Telephone interviews with Napa real estate brokers, July 1979.

7. Bank of America Appraisal Department, "Subdivision Cost Trends," San Francisco, January 1980.

8. Lee Saylor, Inc., *Construction Cost Newsletter*, Concord, Calif., 1980.

9. Stephen R. Seidel, *Housing Costs and Government Regulations* (New Brunswick, N.J.: Center of Urban Policy Research, 1978).

10. The legislative intent of AB 884 is to have all local development approvals made within one year. Cities either reject all applications on the 363rd day, or require developers to sign a waiver exempting the city from complying with AB 884.

11. Rice Center, *The Delay Costs of Government Regulation in the Houston Housing Market* (Houston, 1978).

12. Interviews with Fremont developers, Summer 1979.

13. Association of Bay Area Governments, *Development Fees in the San Francisco Bay Area: A Survey* (Berkeley, 1980).

14. Stuart Gabriel, Leonard Katz, and Jennifer Wolch, *Local Land Use Regulation and Proposition 13: Some Findings from a Recent Survey*, Institute of Business and Economic Research, Working Paper no. 80–4 (Berkeley, 1979).

CHAPTER 6

1. Urban Land Institute and Gruen, Gruen and Associates, *Effects of Regulation on Housing Costs: Two Case Studies*, ULI Research Report no. 27 (Washington, 1977).

2. Ibid.

3. Santa Clara County Manufacturing Group, *Report on Estimates of Job Growth and Building Expansion of Sixty Santa Clara County Companies* (Sunnyvale, Calif., 11 July 1979).

4. Richard Cook, "Lot Prices and the Land Development Industry in Edmonton, Canada" (Master's Thesis, University of California, 1977).

5. Urban Land Institute and Gruen, Gruen and Associates, *Effects of Regulation*, p. 18.

6. Cook, "Lot Prices," p. 43.

7. Claude Gruen, "The Economics of Petaluma: Unconstitutional Regional Socio-Economic Impacts," in *The Management and Control of Growth*, ed. Randall W. Scott (Washington: Urban Land Institute, 1975), 2:173–86.

8. Field interviews held during July and August 1979.

9. Field interviews with Novato real estate brokers, Summer 1979.

CHAPTER 7

1. Joanna and Thomson Hirst, "Capital Facilities Planning as a Tool and a Case Study of Metropolitan Washington, D.C.," in Scott, *Management and Control of Growth*, 2:461–72.

2. National Commission on Urban Problems, *Building the American City* (Washington, D.C., 1968), p. 7.

3. Ibid., p. 17.

4. This term is taken from Babcock, *Zoning Game.*

5. A. Allan Schmid, *Converting Land from Rural to Urban Uses* (Baltimore: Johns Hopkins University Press, 1968), p. 8.

6. President's Committee on Urban Housing, *A Decent Home*, p. 140.

7. Ibid., p. 141.

8. Ibid., p. 140.

9. David E. Dowall, "An Examination of Population Growth Managing Communities," *Policy Studies Journal* 9 (1980):414–27.

10. *Land Trends*, 1 (August 1981):2.

11. U.S. Department of Housing and Urban Development, *Final Report of the Task Force on Housing Costs* (Washington, May 1978), p. 17.

12. Seidel, *Housing Costs and Government Regulations.*

13. Ibid., p. 168.

14. Thomas Muller and Franklin J. James, *Environmental Impact Evaluation and Housing Costs* (Washington, D.C.: Urban Institute, 1975).

15. Jim Hoben and J. Thomas Black, "Residential Land Prices: Variations Between Metropolitan Areas" (unpublished manuscript, 1982).

16. Norman Williams, Jr., and Thomas Norman, "Exclusionary Land Use Controls: The Case of North-Eastern New Jersey," in *Land Use Controls: Present Problems and Future Reform*, ed. David Listokin (New Brunswick, N.J.: Center for Urban Policy Research, 1974), p. 105.

17. For a description of the Ramapo program, see Israel Stollman, "Ramapo: An Editorial and Ordinance as Amended," in Scott *Management and Control of Growth*, 2:5–13.

18. Gruen, "Economics of Petaluma," pp. 173–186.

19. Economic Consultants Organization, Inc., *Residential Analysis for Westchester County, New York* (New York, 1970), p. vii.

20. See Hirst, "Capital Facilities Planning," p. 462.

21. Ibid., p. 463.

22. Gruen, "Economics of Petaluma," pp. 173–86.

23. Metropolitan Area Planning Council, *The Real Estate of the Region*, interim draft report, Boston, n.d.

24. Ibid., p. 25.

25. Gary Sands, *Land-Office Business* (Lexington, Mass.: D.C. Heath, 1982), pp. 63–78.

26. Rice Center, *Houston Initiatives*, p. 1.

27. Ibid, p. 16.

28. Ibid, pp. 70–89.

29. Barton A. Smith and Robert Ohsfeldt, "Housing-Price Inflation in Houston, 1970 to 1976," *Housing Policy for the 1980s*, ed. Roger Montgomery and Dale Rodgers Marshall (Lexington, Mass.: D.C. Heath, 1980).

30. Rice Center, *Multi-Family Housing in Clear Lake City* (Houston, July 1981).

31. See, for example, Morton Lustig and Janet Rothenberg Pack, "A Standard for Resi-

dential Zoning Based upon the Location of Jobs," *Journal of the American Institute of Planners* 40 (September 1974):333–45.

32. Gruen, Gruen and Associates and the Urban Land Institute, *Planning and Housing Prices in Tucson* (San Francisco, 1977).

33. W. Ed Whitelaw, "Measuring the Effects of Public Policies on the Price of Urban Land," in *Urban Land Markets: Price Indices, Supply Measures, and Public Policy Effects*, ed. J. Thomas Black and James E. Hoben, ULI Research Report no. 30 (Washington: Urban Land Institute, 1980), pp. 185–97.

CHAPTER 8

1. Interview with Francine Hardaway, a member of the mayor's Housing Task Force, on 30 June 1982 in Phoenix.

2. Lester Thurow, *The Zero Sum Society* (New York: Basic Books, 1980).

3. See discussion in chapter 7.

4. Constance Perin, *Everything in Its Place* (Princeton, N.J.: Princeton University Press, 1974).

5. See chapter 7.

6. Steve Weitz, "Affordable Housing: How Local Regulatory Reform Can Help," draft paper for the Office of Policy Development and Research, U.S. Department of Housing and Urban Development, Washington, April 1982.

7. Ibid.

8. Discussion with Rick Counts, Planning Director of Phoenix, 7 May 1982, in Dallas, Texas.

9. Weitz, "Affordable Housing."

APPENDIX B

1. Dowall and Mingilton, *Effects of Environmental Regulations.*

2. See, for example, Richard J. Sutton et al., "American City Types: Toward a More Systematic Urban Study," *Urban Affairs Quarterly* 9 (March 1974): 369–401; R. H. T. Smith, "Method and Purpose of Functional Town Classification," *Annals of the American Association of Geographers* 55 (1967): 539–48; and Mahlon R. Straszheim, *An Econometric Analysis of the Urban Housing Market* (New York: National Bureau of Economic Research, 1975).

3. R. C. Tryon and D. E. Bailey, *Cluster Analysis* (New York: McGraw-Hill, 1970).

4. Ibid, chaps. 5 and 6.

5. Ibid, chap. 8.

Index

Designer   Randall Goodall
Compositor   Innovative Media, Inc.
Printer   Thomson-Shore, Inc.
Binder   John H. Dekker & Sons
Text: 10/13 Sabon
Display: Sabon, Garamond Old Style